IMPROVING THE SOCIAL SECURITY DISABILITY DECISION PROCESS

Committee on Improving the Disability Decision Process: SSA's Listing of Impairments and Agency Access to Medical Expertise
Board on Military and Veterans Health

John D. Stobo, Michael McGeary, and David K. Barnes, Editors

INSTITUTE OF MEDICINE
OF THE NATIONAL ACADEMIES

THE NATIONAL ACADEMIES PRESS
Washington, D.C.
www.nap.edu

THE NATIONAL ACADEMIES PRESS 500 Fifth Street, N.W. Washington, DC 20001

NOTICE: The project that is the subject of this report was approved by the Governing Board of the National Research Council, whose members are drawn from the councils of the National Academy of Sciences, the National Academy of Engineering, and the Institute of Medicine. The members of the committee responsible for the report were chosen for their special competences and with regard for appropriate balance.

This study was supported by Contract No. 08820000 between the National Academy of Sciences and the Social Security Administration. Any opinions, findings, conclusions, or recommendations expressed in this publication are those of the author(s) and do not necessarily reflect the view of the organizations or agencies that provided support for this project.

International Standard Book Number-13: 978-0-309-10381-7
International Standard Book Number-10: 0-309-10381-9

Additional copies of this report are available from the National Academies Press, 500 Fifth Street, N.W., Lockbox 285, Washington, DC 20055; (800) 624-6242 or (202) 334-3313 (in the Washington metropolitan area); Internet, http://www.nap.edu.

For more information about the Institute of Medicine, visit the IOM home page at: **www.iom.edu.**

Printed in the United States of America.

The serpent has been a symbol of long life, healing, and knowledge among almost all cultures and religions since the beginning of recorded history. The serpent adopted as a logotype by the Institute of Medicine is a relief carving from ancient Greece, now held by the Staatliche Museen in Berlin.

Suggested citation: IOM (Institute of Medicine). 2007. *Improving the Social Security disability decision process.* Washington, DC: The National Academies Press.

"Knowing is not enough; we must apply.
Willing is not enough; we must do."
—Goethe

INSTITUTE OF MEDICINE
OF THE NATIONAL ACADEMIES

Advising the Nation. Improving Health.

THE NATIONAL ACADEMIES

Advisers to the Nation on Science, Engineering, and Medicine

The **National Academy of Sciences** is a private, nonprofit, self-perpetuating society of distinguished scholars engaged in scientific and engineering research, dedicated to the furtherance of science and technology and to their use for the general welfare. Upon the authority of the charter granted to it by the Congress in 1863, the Academy has a mandate that requires it to advise the federal government on scientific and technical matters. Dr. Ralph J. Cicerone is president of the National Academy of Sciences.

The **National Academy of Engineering** was established in 1964, under the charter of the National Academy of Sciences, as a parallel organization of outstanding engineers. It is autonomous in its administration and in the selection of its members, sharing with the National Academy of Sciences the responsibility for advising the federal government. The National Academy of Engineering also sponsors engineering programs aimed at meeting national needs, encourages education and research, and recognizes the superior achievements of engineers. Dr. Wm. A. Wulf is president of the National Academy of Engineering.

The **Institute of Medicine** was established in 1970 by the National Academy of Sciences to secure the services of eminent members of appropriate professions in the examination of policy matters pertaining to the health of the public. The Institute acts under the responsibility given to the National Academy of Sciences by its congressional charter to be an adviser to the federal government and, upon its own initiative, to identify issues of medical care, research, and education. Dr. Harvey V. Fineberg is president of the Institute of Medicine.

The **National Research Council** was organized by the National Academy of Sciences in 1916 to associate the broad community of science and technology with the Academy's purposes of furthering knowledge and advising the federal government. Functioning in accordance with general policies determined by the Academy, the Council has become the principal operating agency of both the National Academy of Sciences and the National Academy of Engineering in providing services to the government, the public, and the scientific and engineering communities. The Council is administered jointly by both Academies and the Institute of Medicine. Dr. Ralph J. Cicerone and Dr. Wm. A. Wulf are chair and vice chair, respectively, of the National Research Council.

www.national-academies.org

COMMITTEE ON IMPROVING THE DISABILITY DECISION PROCESS: SSA's LISTING OF IMPAIRMENTS AND AGENCY ACCESS TO MEDICAL EXPERTISE

JOHN D. STOBO (*Chair*), President, University of Texas Medical Branch at Galveston, University of Texas

FRANK S. BLOCH (*Vice Chair*), Professor of Law, Vanderbilt University Law School, Nashville, Tennessee

GUNNAR B. J. ANDERSSON, Professor and Chairman, Department of Orthopedic Surgery, Rush University Medicine Center

RICHARD V. BURKHAUSER, Sarah Gibson Blanding Professor of Policy Analysis, Department of Policy Analysis and Management, Cornell University

DIANA D. CARDENAS, Professor and Chair, Department of Rehabilitation Medicine, University of Miami Miller School of Medicine

SHEILA T. FITZGERALD, Associate Professor, Division of Occupational Health, Bloomberg School of Public Health and School of Nursing, Johns Hopkins University

ARTHUR GARSON, Jr., Dean, School of Medicine, Vice President, University of Virginia

KRISTOFER J. HAGGLUND, Associate Dean and Professor of Health Psychology, School of Health Professions, University of Missouri, Columbia

ALLEN W. HEINEMANN, Professor, Department of Physical Medicine and Rehabilitation, Feinberg School of Medicine, Northwestern University

RONALD LEOPOLD, National Medical Director and Vice President, MetLife, Alpharetta, Georgia

LARRY G. MASSANARI, Former Acting Commissioner, Social Security Administration, Exton, Pennsylvania

STEPHEN G. PAUKER, Professor, Department of Medicine, Tufts University School of Medicine; and Associate Physician-in-Chief, Vice Chairman for Clinical Affairs, Department of Medicine, Tufts-New England Medical Center

LINDA A. RANDOLPH, President and CEO, Developing Families Center, Inc., Washington, DC

BRIAN M. SCHULMAN, Private Practice in Occupational Psychiatry, Bethesda, Maryland

PETER W. THOMAS, Principal, Powers Pyles Sutter & Verville, PC, Washington, DC

CRAIG A. VELOZO, Associate Professor and Associate Chair, Department of Occupational Therapy, College of Public Health and Health Professions, University of Florida; Research Health Scientist, Rehabilitation Outcomes Research Center, North Florida/South Georgia Veterans Health System

Project Staff

MICHAEL McGEARY, Study Director
MORGAN A. FORD, Program Officer
SUSAN R. McCUTCHEN, Research Associate
REINE Y. HOMAWOO, Senior Program Assistant
RICK ERDTMANN, Director, Medical Follow-up Agency
PAMELA RAMEY-McCRAY, Administrative Assistant
ANDREA COHEN, Financial Associate
DAVID K. BARNES, Consultant
PETER M. SLAVIN, Editor

Reviewers

This report has been reviewed in draft form by individuals chosen for their diverse perspectives and technical expertise, in accordance with procedures approved by the National Research Council's Report Review Committee. The purpose of this independent review is to provide candid and critical comments that will assist the institution in making its published report as sound as possible and to ensure that the report meets institutional standards for objectivity, evidence, and responsiveness to the study charge. The review comments and draft manuscript remain confidential to protect the integrity of the deliberative process. We wish to thank the following individuals for their review of this report:

Barbara de Lateur, Johns Hopkins School of Medicine, Johns Hopkins Bloomberg School of Public Health and Johns Hopkins Bayview Medical Center
Robert E. Drake, Psychiatric Research Center, Dartmouth Medical School
Susan L. Garber, Department of Physical Medicine and Rehabilitation, Baylor College of Medicine
Katie Maslow, Initiative on Alzheimer's and Managed Care and Quality Care Advocacy, Alzeimer's Association Public Policy Division
Michael Msall, Department of Pediatrics, University of Chicago
Susan A. Randolph, Occupational Health Nursing Program, University of North Carolina at Chapel Hill
Virginia Reno, National Academy of Social Insurance

Although the reviewers listed above have provided many constructive comments and suggestions, they were not asked to endorse the conclusions or recommendations, nor did they see the final draft of the report before its release. The review of this report was overseen by **Joseph P. Newhouse,** Department of Healthcare Policy, Harvard University, and **M. Donald Whorton**, WorkCare, Inc., Alameda, California. Appointed by the National Research Council and Institute of Medicine, respectively, they were responsible for making certain that an independent examination of this report was carried out in accordance with institutional procedures and that all review comments were carefully considered. Responsibility for the final content of this report rests entirely with the authoring committee and the institution.

Preface

I would like to thank the committee members (see Appendix A), staff, consultants, and others who contributed to this report by providing their views of and information about the Social Security disability determination process. It was a very interesting and important endeavor that we hope will be of service to the Social Security Administration (SSA) and to those individuals with disabilities who are unable to engage in substantial work activities and need public support.

SSA asked the committee to address 10 tasks (see Appendix B). It further asked the committee to address three of the tasks on an urgent basis and report its findings and recommendations in an interim report. The committee began its work by addressing the three tasks, which concern the professional training and qualifications of medical personnel involved in the disability decision process. The interim report was issued in December 2005. It is reproduced in its entirety in Appendix C.

The committee has reviewed and affirmed the 13 recommendations in the interim report, except for the same revision in two recommendations. In Recommendations 1-2 and 1-7, the committee recommended that SSA require board certification of physicians and psychologists who serve as medical consultants for the state disability determination services agencies and medical experts who appear at appeals hearings held by administrative law judges. We noted in the interim report that, "board certification is rapidly becoming the standard credential for the practice of medicine or psychology." The committee realizes that almost all physicians become board certified, but board certification is not yet routine for psychologists. Implementing a board certification requirement for psychologists in the near term could seriously limit SSA's ability to obtain enough qualified experts in psychology. The committee has, therefore, modified its position. We recommend that SSA continue the current requirements for psychologists participating as medical consultants or medical experts but establish a long-term goal requiring that psychologists be board certified.

The body of the present report contains our findings and recommendations concerning the remaining tasks that SSA asked us to address. These seven tasks concerned the Listing of Impairments, a screening tool that SSA developed to expedite the approval of claims from obviously disabled individuals who have a high probability of being approved for benefits if they went through the full disability determination process. The Listings, as they are called, are not only useful for SSA as an administrative tool to reduce the time and resources needed for the disability determination process, they are also of great benefit for individuals with disabilities in having their claims decided more quickly. This report treats the Listings as a diagnostic test with properties such as sensitivity, specificity, and predictive values. The report recommends ways to improve the performance of the Listings as a quick screen to identify truly disabled applicants for Social Security disability benefits. It also discusses what can be expected from using the Listings and ways to keep the Listings up to date in the face of advances in medical practice and assistive technologies, demographic trends, and economic trends affecting the workplace.

During the second phase of the study, the committee was greatly helped by presentations at several meetings from SSA's Office of Disability Programs (ODP), which maintains and oversees the Listings and provides guidance on how to apply them. The committee would like to thank (in alphabetical order) Dr. Bernard Arseneau, medical officer, ODP; Dr. Ethan Balk, Agency for Healthcare Research and Quality Evidence-Based Practice Center, Tufts-New England Medical Center; Donna Sue Bongardt, Office of the Deputy Commissioner for Disability and Income Security Programs, SSA; Dale Cox, Office of Medical and Vocational Expertise, SSA; Robin Doyle, Office of Medical Policy, ODP; Dr. Terrence Dunlop, medical officer, ODP; Katherine Edwards, Disability Evaluation Services, University of Massachusetts Medical School; Barry Eigen, executive program policy officer, ODP; Dr. Christine Hartel, National Research Council (NRC); Dr. Monte Hetland, medical officer, ODP; Kristin Johnson, Disability Evaluation Services, University of Massachusetts Medical School; Jim Julian, director, Office of Medical Policy, ODP; Robin Kaplan, Office of the General Counsel, SSA; Barbara Kocher, Information Technology support staff, SSA; Cathy Lively, team leader, ODP; Patricia Owens, Consultation in Health and Disability Programs, Minisink, Pennsylvania; Dr. Marquita Rand, medical officer, ODP; Nancy Schoenberg, ODP; Dr. Frank Schuster, medical officer, ODP; Joshua Silverman, Office of Regulations, SSA; Glenn

Sklar, Associate Commissioner for Disability Programs; Dr. Charles Sweet, Disability Evaluation Services, University of Massachusetts Medical School; and Dr. Susan Van Hemel, NRC.

The names of the many people who assisted the committee and staff in preparing the interim report are listed in Appendix C.

We would also like to express our appreciation to Jo Anne B. Barnhart, then-Commissioner of Social Security, and Martin H. Gerry, then-Deputy Commissioner for Disability and Income Security Programs, who met with the committee at its October 2005 meeting to outline their goals for improving the disability decision-making process.

The committee also requested and was provided with a great deal of data on the disability determination process, which were analyzed by staff and are used throughout this report. Staff would like to thank those at SSA's Office of Disability Policy who helped provide the data—Nancy Schoenberg, the project officer for the study; Susan David; and Bob L. Appleton—and those who helped fact-check the descriptive parts of the report—Barry Eigen, Joe Herendeen, Nancy Schoenberg, and Glenn Sklar.

The committee also wants to acknowledge the expert support of the Institute of Medicine staff and consultants: Michael McGeary, David K. Barnes, Rick Erdtmann, Morgan A. Ford, Susan R. McCutchen, Reine Y. Homawoo, Andrea Cohen, Pamela Ramey-McCray, and Peter M. Slavin.

John D. Stobo, M.D.
Chair

Contents

Tables, Figures, and Boxes

TABLES

FIGURES

BOX

Abbreviations and Acronyms

AAJ	administrative appeals judge
AC	Appeals Council
ACS	American Community Survey
ADA	Americans with Disabilities Act
ADLs	activities of daily living
ALJ	administrative law judge
ANPRM	Advance Notice of Public Rulemaking
APA	Administrative Procedures Act
BRFSS	Behavioral Risk Factor Surveillance Survey
CWB	Civilian War Benefit
DDS	Disability Determination Service
DES	Disability Evaluation Study (renamed National Study of Health and Activity)
DRB	Decision Review Board
DRI	Disability Research Institute
DSI	Disability Service Improvement
DSM	*Diagnostic and Statistical Manual of Mental Disorders*
FACA	Federal Advisory Committee Act
FR	*Federal Register*
FRO	federal reviewing official

GAO	Government Accountability Office
GDP	gross domestic product
IADLs	instrumental activities of daily living
ICD	International Classification of Diseases
ICF	International Classification of Functioning, Disability and Health
ICIDH	International Classification of Impairment, Disability and Handicap
IOM	Institute of Medicine
IQ	intelligence quotient
Listings	Listing of Impairments
MAC	Medical Advisory Committee
MC	medical consultant
ME	medical expert
MET	metabolic equivalents of task
MVES	medical and vocational expert system
MVEU	medical and vocational expert unit
NASI	National Academy of Social Insurance
NCDDD	National Council of Disability Determination Directors
NCMRR	National Center for Medical Rehabilitation Research
NHANES	National Health and Nutrition Examination Survey
NHIS	National Health Interview Survey
NPRM	Notice of Public Rulemaking
NRC	National Research Council
ODISP	Office of Disability and Income Security Programs
ODP	Office of Disability Programs
OHA	Office of Hearings and Appeals
OMP	Office of Medical Policy
OQA	Office of Quality Assurance
POMS	Program Operations Manual System
PSID	Panel Study of Income Dynamics
QA	quality assurance
QDD	quick disability determination
SGA	substantial gainful employment
SIPP	Survey of Income and Program Participation

SSA	Social Security Administration
SSAB	Social Security Advisory Board
SSDI	Social Security Disability Insurance
SSI	Supplemental Security Income
SSR	Social Security Ruling
TERI	terminal illness
VA	Department of Veterans Affairs
VBA	Veterans Benefits Administration
WHO	World Health Organization

Summary

The Social Security Administration (SSA) asked the Institute of Medicine (IOM) to study its medical procedures and criteria for determining disability and to make recommendations for improving the timeliness and accuracy of its disability decisions. SSA asked the IOM to help in two broad areas, broken down into 10 specific tasks (see Appendix B).

First, SSA asked IOM to recommend ways to improve the use of medical expertise in the disability determination process, including how medical expertise can best be provided to support case adjudication by the 54 Disability Determination Services (the state agencies that make the initial disability determinations for SSA, called DDSs) and in appeals hearings held by SSA at 144 hearings offices around the country, as well as advice on the organization and qualifications of supporting medical experts.

At SSA's request, IOM addressed tasks related to medical expertise in an Interim Report in December 2005 (Tasks 8-10 in Appendix B). The Interim Report, with its recommendations, appears in Appendix C.

The committee has reviewed and affirmed the findings and 13 recommendations in the Interim Report, except for the requirement in two of the recommendations that psychologists be board certified. In Recommendation 1-2 of the Interim Report, the committee recommended that SSA require board certification of psychologists working for the state DDSs as medical consultants within five years. In Recommendation 1-7, the committee recommended that psychologists called on by administrative law judges to participate in hearings as medical experts also be board certified. The committee realizes that, although board certification has become the norm for physicians, relatively few psychologists are board certified. The committee therefore modified its recommendation to recommend instead that SSA continue the current requirements for psychologists participating as medical consultants or medical experts and establish a long-term goal requiring that psychologists be board certified.

Second, SSA asked IOM to recommend improvements in its Listing of Impairments (the Listings), which are used to screen applicants for quick approval of disability benefits. Specifically, SSA asked IOM to reexamine the conceptual basis of the Listings, consider alternative conceptual models, improve consistency in their application by program decision makers, and recommend a system for keeping the Listings current over time.

The body of this report contains the committee's findings and recommendations concerning the Listings (Tasks 1-7 in Appendix B).

CONCEPTUAL MODELS OF DISABILITY

When the Social Security Disability Insurance program was originally conceived and implemented, persons with disabilities were considered to be handicapped by their disease or impairment. Conceptually, disability was based on a medical model, in which disability is caused by a disease, injury, or other severe impairment for which the remedy, if any, is medical treatment.

Subsequently, the concept of disability has changed in recognition that disability, as distinct from impairment, is not just inherent in the individual and his or her medical condition but is the result of the interaction between the person with impairments and features of the socioeconomic environment in which the person lives, such as the presence or lack of accessible transportation and of practical workplace accommodations. Yet the antiquated medical model of disability continues to be reflected in the definition of disability in the Social Security Act.

SSA'S DEFINITION OF DISABILITY

Under the Social Security Act, an individual is considered to be "disabled" for Social Security purposes if he or she is unable "to engage in any substantial gainful activity by reason of any medically determinable physical or mental impairment which can be expected to result in death or which has lasted or can be expected to last for a continuous period of not less than 12 months."[1] Further, "[a]n individual shall be determined to be under a disability only if his physical or mental impairment or impairments are of such severity that he is not only unable to do his previous work but cannot, considering his age, education, and work experience, engage

[1]Social Security Act, Title II, § 223(d)(2)(A), and Title 16, § 1614(a)(3)(B).

in any other kind of substantial gainful work which exists in the national economy. . . ."

This definition of disability is complex, and it has medical, functional, and vocational components. A complete and comprehensive assessment of all aspects of the definition would require a detailed clinical evaluation of the underlying medical cause(s) for the impairment; analysis of the expected duration of the impairment (prognosis); a comprehensive assessment of the work-related functional limitations attributable to the impairment, as well as the individual's remaining functional capacity; a detailed vocational analysis of the individual's work history and acquired work skills, educational background, and age; and a thorough analysis of the individual's current vocational prospects. However, SSA does not have the resources to perform such an extensive assessment for every one of the 2.6 million disability applicants who will come through its doors in 2007.

THE DISABILITY DECISION-MAKING PROCESS

To apply the statutory definition in a way that allows it to manage its caseload, SSA uses a five-step sequential evaluation process when deciding whether an individual is disabled. Only the last step of the process requires a complete, comprehensive assessment of all aspects of the definition of disability. Each of the four steps that precede it is, to some degree, intended to enable SSA to reach a faster decision by looking only at selected aspects of the case. The first, second, and fourth steps identify cases that will be denied without performing a complete assessment of all aspects of the case. The third step identifies cases that will be allowed without a complete assessment.

THE LISTINGS

The third step of the five-step sequential evaluation relies on the Listings to identify cases that will be allowed. The Listings describe impairments that SSA considers severe enough to prevent an individual from doing "any gainful activity."[2] The "any gainful activity" standard is a stricter standard, i.e., a higher degree of impairment severity, than the "any substantial gainful activity" standard in the statutory definition of Social Security disability.

The Listings serve as a screening tool to expedite the identification of individuals who clearly meet the definition of disability in the Social Security Act. Quick identification of obvious cases deserving benefits permits

[2]20 CFR 404.1525 and 416.925.

SSA to avoid a time-consuming and resource-intensive inquiry into all of the facts of every case. Using the Listings as an administrative expedient, SSA is able to process more cases more quickly and cost-effectively than it would without the Listings. In addition to providing efficiency, the Listings are also intended to ensure that there is a medical basis for the disability and that all applicants receive equal treatment, as well as to ensure adjudicative consistency.

The Listings are organized by 14 major body systems (e.g., musculoskeletal impairments, respiratory impairments, neurological impairments). Altogether, there are more than 100 listed impairments.

For each body system, the Listings begin with a narrative introduction that defines key concepts used in that body system. The introduction also identifies specific medical findings that may be required to show the existence of an impairment listed in that section. This introduction is followed by the "Category of Impairments" section, which includes the specific criteria (medical signs, symptoms, and laboratory findings) that describe the required level of severity for each impairment listed in that body system. Although a few listings (e.g., certain cancers and amyotrophic lateral sclerosis) are evaluated based on diagnosis alone, most require a diagnosis in conjunction with some sort of assessment of impairment severity, either by the presence of specific clinical findings or by some sort of assessment of functional outcomes.

If the evidence in a case establishes the presence of all the criteria required by one of the impairment listings, then the individual "meets" (i.e., matches) that specific listing. However, even if the evidence does not show that an individual meets the exact requirements of a particular listing, the individual can still be found disabled at step 3 of the sequence if his or her impairment is equal in severity to the requirements of a listing, referred to as "medical equivalence."

By identifying a portion of the allowance cases early in the process, the Listings reduce case-processing time. Reduction of case-processing time is one of SSA's key goals for improved customer service, and concerns with claim-processing time also have been an important factor in a recent major SSA initiative to revise the disability program's administrative review process.

However, SSA is concerned that the Listings may not be as effective a screening tool as they were in the past. In the early days of the disability program, the Listings accounted for more than 90 percent of the initial allowances (SSAB, 2003:7). As recently as the early 1980s, they were the basis for 70 to 80 percent the initial allowances, and they accounted for less than 60 percent of allowances in 2000 (SSAB, 2001:5). According to more recent data supplied to the committee by SSA, the Listings accounted for only 52 percent of the initial allowances in 2004.

With more than 2.6 million applications filed annually, approximately 40 percent (1 million) of which are allowed initially, a 1-percentage-point increase of allowances made at step 3 of the initial decision process represents approximately 10,000 fewer cases that must go through the remainder of the decision-making process.

FINDINGS AND RECOMMENDATIONS

Value and Utility of the Current Listings

The committee believes that using the Listings as an administrative screening tool to identify and quickly allow obviously disabled applicants provides significant value and utility to a variety of different constituencies, including claimants, DDSs and SSA, and the general public. The committee could find no compelling reason for SSA to abandon the Listings process. However, the fact that the Listings have value and utility as a decision-making tool does not mean that they cannot and should not be improved.

One important improvement would be to address the validity of the Listings as a measure of work disability. The degrees of medical severity described in the Listings should be strongly correlated with not working. However, such a correlation has never been clearly established for most conditions in the Listings, and little work has been done to establish the extent to which the Listings are a valid measure of work disability. SSA began an effort to validate the Listings in 2001. However, this initial work was not continued. The committee believes that there are ways to evaluate the validity of the Listings, even in the absence of an objective "gold standard" for what constitutes disability for SSA purposes.

RECOMMENDATION 1. SSA should continue to use the current Listings as a screening test in its disability decision process, but should increase their value and utility by closely examining and monitoring their performance, conducting research to evaluate and improve their effectiveness in expediting awards in obvious cases, and making timely changes in response to these evaluations.

Conceptual Models for Organizing the Listings

The Listings are based on a medical model, which is not ideal, given what is known about the factors causing disability. However, a better model does not exist at this time. The bases for the Listings are anatomic, diagnostic, and functional, the mix of which varies from listing to listing and body system to body system. As medical treatments and assistive technologies advance, the anatomic and diagnostic bases for the Listings will become less and less useful as markers of disability. Therefore, the committee believes that SSA should begin now to look for better methods of determining disability for Social Security benefits.

One alternative to a body-system-based list of diagnoses and impairments would be to develop and apply a generic functional evaluation that does not attempt to assess the severity of impairment but goes directly to the functional capacities of claimants to engage in substantial gainful activity. However, the opinion of the committee is that a generic functional screening tool equal to the complexity of disability does not exist at this time.

A potential model for a functionally based screening tool is the current process that SSA uses to identify children applying for SSI whose impairments are "functionally equal" to the Listings. This process, in effect, establishes a universal "functional" listing that applies regardless of the nature of the child's impairment. A similar approach could be developed for adults, although it would most likely be a substantial undertaking for SSA to develop and validate appropriate functional criteria for adults. Another alternative would be to use SSA's own program data to identify the characteristics of claims that are highly likely to be allowed and use them as a screen.

RECOMMENDATION 2. SSA should continue to monitor advances in assessing disability, and it should support the development of promising alternative approaches to evaluating eligibility for Social Security disability benefits. SSA also should systematically compare the new quick disability determination process with the Listings and with the final determinations of disability.

Revising the Listings to Be More Consistent and Up to Date

Currently, SSA considers several factors in deciding whether to revise, add, or delete a listing, such as medical advances, experiences of its adjudicators, and input from the public as well as legislative or judicial actions that affect listings. SSA makes use of in-house medical experts, outside experts, and other agency personnel, but it does not make full use of its extensive program data in the Listings revision process. These data could be used to assess aspects of the performance of the current Listings, and to identify circumstances in which a new listing might be appropriate or a current listing is no longer needed. SSA could, for example, identify impairments that are frequently found to be disabling at the last step of SSA's sequential evaluation process, but for which no listings currently exist. Impairments that are frequently found to be equal in severity to a listing but are seldom found to meet a listing also suggest the possibility of new listings. A sudden decline in an allowance rate might signal an advance in medical treatment that has reduced the disabling effects of a listed impairment, which in turn might prompt revision or elimination of the listing.

Feedback

One way to help improve the consistency of decision making is to provide better feedback to adjudicators about the decisions they make and that other adjudicators are making. SSA does not systematically analyze its own programmatic data or provide feedback to adjudicators on aggregate results of their decision making.

RECOMMENDATION 3. SSA should develop a management information system that combines a balanced quality assurance process to promote consistency and reliability of individual allowances and denials and a program of analysis of aggregate patterns to evaluate consistency and reliability of the Listings. SSA should also develop feedback processes to inform adjudicators and program managers of decision results, including those found by subsequent adjudicators to meet or equal the Listings.

External Input Affecting the Listings

No matter how reliable and valid the Listings may be at any given moment, they are constantly affected by external trends that sooner or later make them obsolete. These include changes in disease patterns, advances in scientific knowledge and medical practice, advances in assistive technologies, and changes in the workplace affecting workers in terms of job requirements and potential sources of injury. The Office of Medical Policy, the staff component within SSA that is responsible for maintaining the Listings, is small and does not have experts in all the major specialties (although it can draw on the advice of specialists in the federal DDS), so its ability to supply all the necessary medical expertise to the Listing revision process is limited.

RECOMMENDATION 4. SSA should ensure that its Office of Medical Policy has the expertise relevant to the full range of listed impairments and has the resources to stay knowledgeable concerning new developments in medicine and rehabilitation, for example, by conducting systematic literature reviews on a periodic basis.

Use of Medical Advisory Committees

Historically, SSA has used a variety of different advisory committees, advisory councils, and similar groups as a source of expert advice and recommendations on addressing difficult issues. SSA formed an external medical advisory committee in 1955 to create the original Listings. More informal medical advisory groups were used into the 1980s and were part of the efforts to incorporate consideration of pain in the listings, revise cardiac listings, and revise and expand the mental listings. The use of medical advisory groups was stopped when the Federal Advisory Committee Act (FACA) was implemented. However, SSA's disability programs would benefit from external advice of clinical and other experts on disability determination criteria and procedures, and the involvement of external advisory groups would also serve to increase the understanding and acceptance of SSA disability determination requirements in the medical community.

RECOMMENDATION 5. SSA should reestablish a medical advisory committee under the Federal Advisory Committee Act to advise the commissioner on when scientifically based regulations, especially the Listings, should be revised to keep them up to date. Ad hoc advisory committees should be established under the auspices of the medical advisory committee to advise on the revision or addition of specific listings or body systems. The medical advisory committee should be multidisciplinary and include representation from all appropriate constituencies.

Responding to Advances in Medical Practice and Technology

Medicine evolves in ways that may result in the need to revise a listing, but it also makes more incremental advances that affect the way particular listings are applied. In such cases, the standard of severity in the listing does not change, but the method of evaluating it may. One way SSA has tried to make the Listings adapt better to these kinds of changes is to make them more generic. This approach is helpful and should be pursued.

Another way to respond to continuing improvements in methods of treating and evaluating impairments is to use agency rulings (Social Security Rulings, or SSRs) to provide adjudicators with up-to-date methods of obtaining and evaluating evidence and up-to-date guidance in applying the Listings. The committee believes that these efforts, in conjunction with the establishment of a medical advisory committee, can help SSA keep the Listings up to date, while maintaining the important protections embodied in the Administrative Procedures Act.

RECOMMENDATION 6. SSA should continue to develop procedures for expediting development of new regulations and fully involving the public and external experts in the regulatory process governed by the Administrative Procedures Act. Agency rulings, which are published in the *Federal Register* and made available on SSA's website, should continue to be used to explain and clarify the substantive rules developed in the full regulatory process.

Adaptability of the Listings

Some individuals may not meet a listing because they do not have access to treatment and the listing states that specific clinical or laboratory findings must exist or persist despite the treatment in order for the listing to be met. Variable access to quality health care services is unfortunate but beyond the capacity of SSA to remedy. Ideally, individuals applying for disability benefits would be evaluated and receive the medical, vocational rehabilitation, and employment services that would enable them to resume working gainfully. Instead, in the current system, many individuals with remediable work limitations are not eligible for medical care or vocational rehabilitation until after they have completed the process of qualifying for cash disability benefits. This requirement obviously disadvantages people without adequate health care coverage, but any unfairness is the result of the social and political system that created these inequities, not the Listings.

RECOMMENDATION 7. The committee recommends against attempting to consider variable access to health care at the Listings step in determining disability. It is not strictly a medical issue that can be incorporated easily in Listings criteria. Although medical evaluation is involved in gauging the severity and functional impacts of an untreated condition, the circumstances limiting access to health care and assistive technology should be considered separately.

Evaluating Multiple Impairments

Finding a combination of impairments equal in severity to a listed impairment justifies an allowance at step 3. Evaluating equivalence to a listing requires a medical assessment of whether the findings related to an individual's impairments are "at least of equal medical significance to those of a listed impairment." In practice, determining whether multiple impairments combine to equal listing-level severity medically is very difficult and quite subjective. Given the complexity and subjectivity of this process, and the absence of any scientific analysis of the process, it is a matter of conjecture whether adjudicators' judgments on equivalence for combinations of impairments are valid or reliable. The committee believes that, unless SSA is able to establish scientifically the value of adjudicator judgments on equivalence in cases involving combinations of impairments, the prudent and most practical way of deciding such cases is to assess the net functional impact that the impairments have.

RECOMMENDATION 8. Generally, SSA should not try to determine the medical equivalency of multiple impairments to the Listings at step 3. Such cases should be analyzed functionally. However, research may determine that some common comorbidities, each of a certain degree of severity or more, are typically allowed after going through steps 4 and 5, and these sets of conditions could be incorporated in the Listings to expedite decisions.

Integrating Functional Assessment in the Listings

In general, the Listings consider functioning in one of two distinct ways—at the body system/organ level (e.g., "cardiac dysfunction") and at the person level (e.g., "inability to ambulate effectively on a sustained basis for any reason"), which calls for an assessment of the disabling functional consequences of a disorder. Some adjudicators say that the Listings have evolved from supposedly objective, measurable clinical criteria (including organ/body system-level functioning), which can be easily and quickly applied, to more subjective, ill-defined, person-level, functional criteria, which are difficult and time consuming to apply. The earlier listings criteria were no doubt more clinical, shorter, and easier to apply, but there is no evidence that these earlier versions of the Listings were more accurate as a screening tool than more recent versions.

Recently, SSA has begun to incorporate function into the Listings in a systematic way. However, the committee is not aware of a generic functional assessment tool that has been empirically validated for all types of impairments, and functional evaluation in the Listings is not systematically based on research on such tools.

RECOMMENDATION 9. SSA should undertake a comprehensive assessment of the performance of both medical and functional listings, and should consider function at the Listings step when it can be shown to correlate with inability to perform substantial gainful activity (SGA). SSA should both monitor and sponsor current research regarding the extent to which medical and functional criteria are highly correlated with limitations on performance of SGA.

Research to Support the Listings

The committee believes that SSA's research programs should include research on the Listings to improve their evidence base and experiments to evaluate alternative listing criteria and procedures. The development of the Listings, like any regulation potentially affecting large numbers of people, is a major undertaking that takes time. Through the use of experimentation and pilot projects, new listings should be tested before they are finally adopted.

RECOMMENDATION 10. SSA, with input from the medical advisory committee, should develop a program of research to support the disability decision process, including the Listings. The research program should include experiments that test revised listings before they are adopted.

The Listing of Impairments is a screening test whose effectiveness and utility is measured by its sensitivity, specificity, predictive values, and other criteria. These in turn depend on knowledge of the validity of the test, which calls for a gold standard for comparison, and of the prevalence of listing-level disorders in the population. Therefore, SSA should also support research on the prevalence of common disorders that meet the Listings. This might be done by supplementing existing surveys, such as the National Health and Nutrition Examination Survey or the Behavioral Risk Factor Surveillance Survey.

RECOMMENDATION 11. SSA, in conjunction with other agencies that assist persons with disabilities, should conduct a periodic, nationally representative sample survey of the population to determine the distribution and extent of severe impairments that might meet the Listings. This might be done by supplementing existing surveys. The results would be useful for program planning and for evaluating the effectiveness of the Listings and other aspects of the disability decision process.

REFERENCES

SSAB (Social Security Advisory Board). 2001. *Charting the future of Social Security's disability programs: The need for fundamental change.* Washington, DC: SSAB. Available: www.ssab.gov/Publications/Disability/disabilitywhitepap.pdf (accessed November 17, 2005).

SSAB. 2003. *The Social Security definition of disability.* Washington, DC: SSAB. Available: www.ssab.gov/documents/SocialSecurityDefinitionofDisability_002.pdf (accessed November 17, 2005).

1

Introduction

The Social Security Administration (SSA) pays Social Security Disability Insurance (SSDI) benefits to disabled workers, who are insured against disability under Title II of the Social Security Act, and their dependents, as well as to certain disabled adult children of disabled, retired, or deceased workers and widows and widowers of deceased workers.[1] It also pays Supplemental Security Income (SSI) benefits to disabled adults and children who have limited income and resources under Title XVI of the Social Security Act. Some receive benefits from both programs.

SSDI and SSI are key components of the nation's social support system, providing vital social insurance and public assistance to individuals with disabilities. The majority of adult recipients of SSDI and SSI have disabling chronic mental disorders (30 percent), musculoskeletal impairments (19 percent), mental retardation (13 percent), or disorders of the nervous system and sense organs (9 percent) as their primary impairment (SSA, 2006g: Table 67). In December 2005, the average monthly payment under SSDI was $896 ($10,752 a year). The average age of disabled workers receiving SSDI is 52 (SSA, 2006g:Tables 5, 19). On average, SSDI payments replace 44 percent of the earnings of a disabled worker age 45 with medium earnings (SSA, 2006e:10).[2] In December 2004, most SSI beneficiaries under

[1]Technically, disabled workers, their dependents, and disabled adult children receive benefits from the SSDI trust fund. Widows and widowers and disabled adult children of retired or deceased workers are paid from the Social Security trust fund.

[2]In fiscal year (FY) 2006, SSDI replaced 59 percent of the earnings of the average disabled worker with low earnings (defined as $16,110 annually) and 82 percent of the earnings of the average disabled worker with low earnings and a dependent (SSA, 2006e:10).

age 18 (66 percent) had mental retardation or other mental disorders. The portion of SSI adults ages 18-64 with mental retardation or other mental disorders was 57 percent (SSA, 2005:Table 26). The average SSI benefit for disabled and blind adults 18-64 in December 2005 was $456 a month ($5,467 a year), and for children under age 18 the average benefit was $523 a month ($6,274 a year) (SSA, 2006f:Table 7).

These programs are large and costly, and they are growing. In 2004, SSA awarded SSDI benefits to more than 1.3 million disabled workers and their dependents, disabled adult children, and disabled widows and widowers (SSA, 2006h:Table 31). It awarded SSI benefits to almost 750,000 disabled adults and children (SSA, 2005:Table 47). As of December 2004, SSA was paying disability-based benefits to almost 9.8 million people ages 18-64. Of these, 5.8 million received benefits under the Social Security program only, 2.9 million received benefits under SSI only, and 1.2 million received both (SSA, 2006h:Table 59). In addition, nearly 1 million disabled children were receiving SSI benefits (SSA, 2006h:Table 3).

In 2007, as in 2006, SSA expects to process 2.6 million initial disability claims under these two programs (SSA, 2006a:7), using its network of more than 1,300 field offices and teleservice centers. It relies on 54 state Disability Determination Services agencies (DDSs), with more than 1,600 staff, as well as a federal DDS to make initial disability decisions and handle the first level of appeals, called "reconsiderations." SSA also expected to process almost 580,000 appeals hearings in 2007 (SSA, 2006a:7), using a network of 144 hearing offices and 10 regional hearing offices and relying on about 1,100 administrative law judges (ALJs) to decide appeals.

From 1990 to 2003, expenditures for cash benefits under the Social Security disability program rose 93 percent in real terms. For the SSI disability program, the increase was nearly 90 percent. For both programs, 2004 benefit payments exceeded $100 billion. As a percentage of gross domestic product, benefit payments under these programs rose from 1.26 percent in 1990 to 1.98 percent in 2001 (SSA, 2006b:Chart 17).

SSA expects the number of SSDI beneficiaries to increase by about 26 percent between 2005 and 2015 (SSA, 2006c:Table V.C5).[3] The number of blind or disabled SSI beneficiaries is expected to increase by 16 percent (SSA, 2006d:Tables IV.B6, IV.B1).

Although the program is expanding, it can be quite complicated and lengthy for individuals who apply for benefits (the process is described in detail in Chapter 4). It takes DDSs, the state agencies that make the initial determination of disability for SSA and handle the first level of appeal, three

[3]This is the intermediate estimate of the Board of Trustees of the Federal Old-Age and Survivors Insurance and Disability Insurance Trust Fund. The low and high estimates are 10 percent and 45 percent, respectively.

months on average to process an application and make an initial determination of eligibility (88 days in FY 2006, compared with 106 days in FY 2001).[4] In FY 2002, 38.5 percent of the initial decisions were allowances. If a denied applicant asks the DDS for reconsideration, the process averages another three months and, in FY 2002, increased the cumulative allowance rate to about 42 percent. The next level of appeal is a hearing before an ALJ, which averages more than a year to complete (483 days in FY 2006, compared with 447 days in FY 2001). In FY 2002, ALJs allowed about 60 percent of the cases they heard. If the applicant is denied after a hearing and appeals to the Appeals Council, and more than 100,000 applicants did in FY 2002, the process averages another six to eight months (203 days in FY 2006, compared with 447 days in FY 2001). About 14,000 applicants appeal to federal district court, which takes another 600 days to settle. The chance of an allowance from the Appeals Council or federal court is about 3 percent and 6 percent, respectively. The overall allowance rate in FY 2002 was about 57 percent.

The majority of those who appeal are eventually awarded benefits, mostly at the ALJ hearing level. As a result, although most applicants who are awarded benefits receive them through a favorable initial decision after an average of three months, a substantial share—about 24 percent—receives benefits one or more years later, after appealing.

Historically, SSA has used a Listing of Impairments to expedite decision making. The Listings (as they are called) are a set of approximately 100 medical conditions with criteria of severity set so high that anyone who meets them, or has a condition that equals them in severity, is presumed to be disabled and allowed benefits. SSA does not subject applicants who meet or equal the Listings to the more time-consuming and expensive process of considering vocational factors and the interaction between the person's limitations and the physical and mental demands of jobs they might seek. In the early years of SSDI, 80 to 90 percent of awards were based on meeting or equaling the Listings. The percentage of awards based on the Listings has steadily declined and accounted for about 50 percent of initial awards to adults in 2004.

SSA'S REQUEST TO IOM

SSA has undertaken a number of initiatives to decide disability claims more quickly and more accurately, goals that are difficult to maximize simultaneously. SSA asked the Institute of Medicine (IOM) to help in two broad areas, broken down into 10 specific tasks (see Appendix B).

---

[4]All statistics in this paragraph on processing times during FY 2001 and FY 2006 are from SSA (2006e).

First, SSA asked IOM to recommend improvements in the medical criteria it uses to screen applicants for disability benefits, which are the basis of the Listing of Impairments, so that the Listings are as sensitive as is practically possible in identifying individuals who would be highly likely to be approved for benefits if they went through the full individualized disability determination process. Specifically, SSA asked IOM to reexamine the conceptual basis of the Listings, consider alternative conceptual models, improve the consistency in their application by program decision makers, and recommend a system for keeping the Listings up to date over time. This request was broken down into seven specific tasks (Tasks 1-7 in Appendix B).

Second, SSA asked IOM to recommend ways to improve the use of medical expertise in the disability determination process, including how medical expertise can best be provided to support case adjudication at the state DDSs and in SSA's Office of Hearings and Appeals, as well as advice on the organization and qualifications of supporting medical experts (Tasks 8-10 in Appendix B).

The committee addressed SSA's request with respect to its use of medical expertise in the disability determination process in an Interim Report issued on December 21, 2005 (reproduced in Appendix C). The body of this report addresses the committee's deliberations, findings, and recommendations with respect to Tasks 1 through 7.

REFERENCES

SSA (Social Security Administration). 2005. *SSI annual statistical report, 2004.* Released September 2005. Available: www.ssa.gov/policy/docs/statcomps/ssi_asr/2004/ssi_asr04.pdf (accessed May 22, 2006).

SSA. 2006a. *Performance plan for fiscal year 2007 and revised final performance plan for fiscal year 2006.* Available: www.ssa.gov/performance/2007/16%20Page%20APP%20-%20Final%20%20(2-16-06).pdf (accessed May 22, 2006).

SSA. 2006b. *Trends in the Social Security and Supplemental Security Income Disability programs.* SSA Publication 13-11831. Released August 2006. Available: www.ssa.gov/policy/docs/chartbooks/disability_trends/trends.pdf (accessed September 28, 2006).

SSA. 2006c. *2006 Annual report of the Board of Trustees of the Federal Old-Age and Survivors Insurance and Disability Insurance Trust Fund.* Updated May 1, 2006. Available: www.ssa.gov/OACT/TR/TR06/tr06.pdf (accessed October 19, 2006).

SSA. 2006d. *2006 Annual report of the Supplemental Security Income Program.* Released May 24, 2006. Available: www.ssa.gov/OACT/SSIR/SSI06/ssi2006.pdf (accessed October 19, 2006).

SSA. 2006e. *SSA's Performance and accountability report for fiscal year 2006.* Available: www.ssa.gov/finance/2006/FY06_PAR.pdf (accessed December 4, 2006).

SSA. 2006f. *SSI monthly statistics, September 2006.* Released October 2006. Available: www.ssa.gov/policy/docs/statcomps/ssi_monthly/2006-09/table07.html (accessed December 4, 2006).

SSA. 2006g. *Annual statistical report on the Social Security Disability Insurance Program, 2005*. Released September 2006. Available: www.ssa.gov/policy/docs/statcomps/di_asr/2005/index.html (accessed December 4, 2006).

SSA. 2006h. *Annual statistical report on the Social Security Disability Insurance Program, 2004*. Released March 2006. Available: www.ssa.gov/policy/docs/statcomps/di_asr/2004/index.html (accessed December 4, 2006).

2

Evolving Concepts of Disability

In 1955, when the Listing of Impairments was originally conceived and implemented, persons with disabilities were considered to be handicapped by their disease or impairment. Conceptually, disability was based on a medical model, in which disability is caused by a disease, injury, or other severe impairment for which the remedy, if any, is medical treatment. The Listings were accordingly based on body systems and severity of impairment. The nine examples of Listing-level impairments that the Social Security Administration (SSA) originally provided to guide decision making included the loss of vision, hearing, or speech; loss of use of two limbs; progressive diseases such as diabetes, multiple sclerosis, and heart and lung conditions that have resulted in major loss of physical function; terminal cancers; and neurological or mental impairments requiring institutionalization or constant supervision.[1]

Subsequently, the concept of disability has changed in recognition that disability, as distinct from impairment, is not just inherent in the individual and his or her medical condition but is the result of the interaction between the person with impairments and features of the socioeconomic environment in which the person lives, such as the presence or lack or acces-

[1]These examples were first published by the director of the disability program in the *Social Security Bulletin* in 1957 (Hess, 1957:15). They were made part of SSA's regulations in 1957 (22 FR 4362) and were the only examples of Listings until 1961, when additional conditions and factors were published, although without specific criteria for meeting the Listings (26 FR 5572).

sible transportation and practical workplace accommodations. Under this concept, two people with the same impairment might have quite different degrees of work disability. For example, a person with an injury that permanently limits use of an arm, who is 55 years old, has limited education, and has a work history of manual labor, would be very disabled, while a person with the same impairment with a law degree may not be disabled at all. Similarly, two people with impairments of quite different severity might be equally disabled from working.

Several commonly used models of disability exist today, but all distinguish in some way between impairment, functional capacity, and disability (IOM, 1991; Nagi, 1976; WHO, 1980). More recent conceptualizations of these models have added external barriers to participation as factors in disability (IOM, 1997; NCMRR, 1993; WHO, 2001). These conceptual models were developed largely to help rehabilitation researchers understand the factors that disable people and to develop and evaluate interventions that reduce disability. They have also been stimulated by and useful in dealing with environmental barriers whose elimination would reduce the disability of impaired persons. Although these disability models were not developed for SSA's disability programs, which provide cash assistance to individuals whose impairments prevent them from engaging more than minimally in gainful activity, it is useful to distinguish among impairment, function, and disability when analyzing the basis for the Listings.

Some of these models of disability are described next in this chapter, followed by a discussion of how the SSA process for determining disability matches with current concepts of factors contributing to disability, especially the role of the Listings criteria in the process.

CONCEPTUAL MODELS OF DISABILITY

This section presents the conceptual evolution of disability in terms of a series of models that have been proposed since the advent of the Social Security Disability Insurance (SSDI) program. They are:

- Nagi's Disability Model
- World Health Organization's (WHO's) International Classification of Impairment, Disability, and Handicap (ICIDH)
- National Center for Medical Rehabilitation Research (NCMRR) Model
- Verbrugge and Jette's Model of the Disablement Process
- Institute of Medicine's (IOM's) Enabling-Disabling Model
- WHO's International Classification of Functioning, Disability and Health (ICF)

Nagi's Disability Model

In the 1960s and 1970s, Saad Z. Nagi developed an influential model of disability based on his research on rehabilitation outcomes (Nagi, 1964, 1965, 1976, 1987). Nagi differentiated among concepts of pathology, impairment, functional limitations, and disability, making them separate components of his model (Table 2-1). By using the term "disability" instead of "handicap," he avoided giving the concept a negative connotation; that is, he did not suggest an absolute limitation, one that failed to take into account circumstances outside the control of the person with a given health condition. Nagi considered disability to result from the interaction of a person with a health condition with his or her environment, which includes family support, employer accommodations, and physical and sociocultural barriers. Nagi also acknowledged other factors affecting disability, including the person's own characteristics and definition of the situation. He noted that not all impairments or functional limitations result in disability; two individuals with similar pathologies, impairments, and functional ca-

TABLE 2-1 Comparison of Components of Models of Disablement

	Components of the Model				
Model	Cells/Tissue	Organ	Person	Society	External Barriers
Nagi, 1969	Pathology	Impairment	Functional limitation	Disability	
IOM Modification of Nagi Model, 1991	Pathology	Impairment	Functional limitation	Disability	Social and physical environment
ICIDH (WHO, 1980)	Disease	Impairment	Disability	Handicap	
NCMRR, 1993	Patho-physiology	Impairment	Functional limitation	Disability	
Vergrugge-Jette, 1994	Pathology	Impairments	Functional limitations	Disability	
IOM, 1997	Pathology	Impairment	Functional limitation	Disabililty	
ICF (WHO, 2001)	Body functions and structures		Activity	Participation	Personal and environmental factors

SOURCE: Adapted in part from Butler et al., 1999.

pacities might have different patterns of disability, while similar patterns of disability might result from different kinds of health conditions.

Nagi provided an update of his model as an appendix to the 1991 report of the IOM, *Disability in America*. In it, he noted that certain disfiguring or stigmatizing impairments could result in disability without causing functional limitations at the organism level (Nagi, 1991:315).

The IOM report added several dimensions to the Nagi model. First, it proposed three interacting risk factors—biological, environmental (social and physical), and lifestyle/behavioral—that affect each element of the disabling process: pathology, impairment, functional limitation, and disability. Second, it added impact on quality of life as a part of the disabling process (IOM, 1991:84-91). In effect, it added another component to Nagi's model—features of the social and physical setting affecting an individual's degree of disability that could be targeted for change (Table 2-1).

The IOM report helped bring Nagi's conceptual model of disability to a wider audience and helped stimulate research on the environmental aspects of the disablement process. Nagi's concepts strongly influenced other models of disability, including those of the WHO and the NCMRR (both described below) and were adopted by rehabilitation organizations, such as the American Physical Therapy Association.

WHO's International Classification of Impairment, Disability, and Handicap (ICIDH)

WHO developed the ICIDH to complement the International Classification of Diseases (ICD) (WHO, 1980). The ICD classifies diseases, disorders, and other health conditions by diagnosis and is used to identify acute illnesses and injuries that can be cured or prevented. The ICD is not, however, well suited to classifying and tracking chronic or progressive disorders (Whiteneck, 2006:51). Therefore, WHO developed the ICIDH to classify the kinds and levels of function and disability associated with health conditions (Jette, 2006:730).

The ICIDH made conceptual distinctions, based on Nagi, among impairment, functional limitations (which, however, WHO called "disability"), and disability (called "handicap" by WHO), which allowed recognition that disability is based not just on the attributes of the individual (the medical model) but also on the interaction between the person and society (the biopsychosocial model) (Table 2-1). On the negative side, the ICIDH used the word "handicap" to label the result of the interaction between the person and the social setting. This label seemed to perpetuate the idea that the problem is more the inability of the person to fit into usual social roles rather than restrictions imposed by environmental barriers and social attitudes, which could be modified to enable an impaired person to participate in work and other normal activities. The model was also still medically based (i.e., diseases, injuries, or other disorders result in impairment, which cause functional limitations, which, in turn, reduce the person's ability to participate in society). This did not recognize the complexity of the disablement process, especially the role of contextual factors, or the fact that the correlations between degree of impairment, extent of functional limitation, and level of disability are low.

National Center for Medical Rehabilitation Research Model

NCMRR (1993) built on the Nagi model by including the impairment, functional limitation, and disability domains corresponding to the organ, person, and societal levels, but NCMRR added another level or "dimension," called "societal limitation" (Table 2-1). In the NCMRR model, societal limitations are barriers to full participation in society that result from attitudes, architectural barriers, and social policies. The NCMRR model pulled external barriers out of the environmental domain for special emphasis, highlighting the fact that these barriers could be reduced or eliminated by public policy.

Verbrugge and Jette's Model of the Disablement Process

Verbrugge and Jette elaborated on Nagi's model in "an attempt to attain a full sociomedical framework of disablement, which they defined as the impact that chronic and acute conditions have on functioning of specific body systems and on people's abilities to act in necessary, usual, expected, and personally desired ways in their society" (Jette, 2006:729). Altman (2001) notes that Verbrugge and Jette focused on task orientation, while Nagi focused more on role orientation toward limitation.

As already noted, Verbrugge and Jette accepted the elements of Nagi's model: active pathology, impairment, functional limitation, and disability (Table 2-1). They operationalized the Nagi model by identifying various types of necessary, usual, expected, and/or personally desired roles and activities under Nagi's concept of disability that should be tracked and measured. These included (Verbrugge and Jette, 1994):

- Basic activities of daily living—including behaviors such as basic personal care
- Instrumental activities of daily living—including activities such as preparing meals, doing housework, managing finances, using the telephone, and shopping

- Paid and unpaid role activities—including occupation, parenting, grandparenting, and student roles
- Social activities—including attending church and other group activities, and socializing with friends and relatives
- Leisure activities—including sport and physical recreation, reading, distinct trips, and so on

In addition Verbrugge and Jette (1994) tried to make the model more dynamic by identifying factors that affect what they called the "disablement process." They posited three sets of variables that affected the "pathway" to disablement of a given individual. These were:

Risk Factors. Risk factors are "predisposing phenomena that are present prior to the onset of the disabling event that can affect the presence or severity of the disablement process. Examples include sociodemographic background, lifestyle, and biologic factors."

Intra-individual Factors. Intra-individual factors "operate within a person, such as lifestyle and behavioral changes, psychosocial attributes and coping skills, and activity accommodations made by the individual following onset of a disabling condition."

Extra-individual Factors. Extra-individual factors are in the external "physical as well as the social context in which the disablement process occurs. Environmental factors relate to the social as well as the physical environmental factors that bear on the disablement process. These can include medical and rehabilitation services, medications and other therapeutic regimens (e.g., exercise or physical activity), external supports available in the person's social network, and the physical environment."

Verbrugge and Jette stimulated research into the impact of risk factors, intra-individual factors, and extra-individual factors on impairment, functional limitation, and disability and how they influence the disablement process. Jette (2006) cites a number of examples of this research: Lawrence and Jette (1996), Jette et al. (1998), Guralnik et al. (1994, 1995), Gill et al. (1995), and Ostir et al. (1998).

IOM's Enabling-Disabling Model (1997)

In 1997, an IOM committee issued a report, *Enabling America: Assessing the Role of Rehabilitation Science and Engineering*, which responded to a congressional request for an assessment of rehabilitation research and technology development efforts. The report extended the 1991 IOM model by making "clear reference to the importance of the environment in causing, preventing, and reducing disability" (IOM, 1997:1).

The committee explicitly adopted the elements of Nagi's disability model (but called them "components of the disabling process" in the report)—i.e., pathology, impairment, functional limitation, and disability—with disability defined as "a limitation in performing certain roles and tasks that society expects of an individual" (Table 2-1). The IOM report focused on the "enabling process," by which it meant efforts to reduce disability. Enabling could be accomplished by either restoring function in the individual (i.e., traditional rehabilitation) or expanding access to the environment, or both. The report also introduced the notion of secondary conditions as "any additional physical or mental health condition that occurs as a result of having a primary disabling condition" and that "quite often increase the severity of an individual's disability and are also highly preventable" (IOM, 1997:3-5).

According to the report, "the committee enhanced the 1991 IOM model to show more clearly how biological, environmental (physical and social), and lifestyle/behavioral factors are involved in reversing the disabling process, i.e., rehabilitation, or the enabling process. The enhancements include bidirectional arrows between the various states of the enabling–disabling process to indicate that the disabling process (described in the 1991 IOM model) can be reversed with proper interventions (i.e., the enabling process)" (IOM, 1997:6).

The graphic representation of the new IOM model did not include a box for "disability," in an effort "to help clarify the fact that disability is not inherent in the individual, but rather is a product of the interaction of the individual with the environment" (IOM, 1997:8). The report proceeded to recommend research and engineering needs and opportunities by domain: pathology and impairment research, functional limitation research, and disability research. Disability research would be "explicitly focused on the effects of the environment in producing or reducing disability" (IOM, 1997:12).

In the report, the committee noted that the 1991 IOM model had some shortcomings. First, disability was depicted in the 1991 model as a linear process, which was fine for the 1991 report's focus on ways to prevent disability but did not allow for reversal of disability through rehabilitation. Second, the earlier model gave a "limited characterization of the environment and the interaction of the individual with the environment." Third, the 1991 model provided a limited "representation of societal limitations" (IOM, 1997:67).

WHO's International Classification of Functioning, Disability and Health (ICF)

ICF resulted from a substantial revision of the 1980 ICIDH. ICF is based on the premise, supported by studies, that diagnosis alone does not predict service needs, length of hospitalization, level of care, or functional outcomes (WHO, 2001). In addition, the presence of a disease or disorder is not an accurate predictor of receipt of disability benefits, work performance, return-to-work potential, or likelihood of social interaction.

In the ICF, disability and functioning are seen as outcomes of interactions between health conditions and contextual factors. Contextual factors include external environmental factors, such as social attitudes, architectural characteristics, and the legal system, and internal personal factors, such as sex, age, coping styles, social background, education, profession, and other factors that influence how disability is experienced by an individual (WHO, 2001:214).

ICF is a rather complicated classification system, because its elements are interactive. Its domains include (Table 2-1):

Impairments in Body Functions and Structures

- "Body functions are the physiological functions of body systems (including psychological functions)."
- "Body structures are anatomical parts of the body such as organs, limbs and their components."
- "Impairments are problems in body function or structure such as a significant deviation or loss."

Limitations on Activities and Limitations on Participation

- "Activity is the execution of a task or action by an individual."
- "Participation is involvement in a life situation."
- "Activity limitations are difficulties an individual may have in executing activities."
- "Participation restrictions are problems an individual may experience in involvement in life situations."

Environmental Factors. "Environmental factors make up the physical, social and attitudinal environment in which people live and conduct their lives."

Although the ICF model is comprehensive, it is complex and difficult to operationalize. This and other shortcomings of the ICF are discussed in Whiteneck (2006). The main problem is distinguishing between activity limitations and participation limitations, which have shared activities in the model.

SUMMARY

During the past 50 years, researchers in rehabilitation have developed conceptual models of disability that have evolved in accord with a general consensus that it is useful to distinguish impairments, functional limitations, and disabilities, and to conceive of disability as an outcome of the interaction between specific individuals with health conditions and the environments in which they find themselves. Work disability, for example, results from the interaction of individuals' impairments, functional limitations resulting from the impairments, assistive technologies to which they may have access, and attitudinal and other personal characteristics (such as age, education, skills, and work history) with the physical and mental requirements of potential jobs, accessibility of transportation, attitudes of family members and coworkers, and willingness of an employer to make accommodations.

CONCEPTUAL BASIS OF THE LISTINGS

Disability in the SSDI and Supplemental Security Income (SSI) programs is legally defined as a "medically determinable physical or mental impairment" that prevents an individual from engaging in "substantial gainful activity" and is expected to last (or has lasted) at least 12 months or to result in death. Because children are not expected to engage in substantial gainful activity, childhood disability under SSI is defined as a physical or mental condition or combination of conditions that causes "marked and severe functional limitations" and is expected to last (or has lasted) at least 12 months or to result in death. It has elements of the medical model, because from the beginning, Congress has wanted to limit the program by requiring that the reason for work limitations be identified as medical (Stone, 1984). SSA thus requires a medical diagnosis and medical evidence (e.g., tests or examinations) that supports or is consistent with the claimant's work disability (or with marked and severe functional limitations if a child).

In terms of contemporary concepts of disability, the Social Security definition corresponds to a participation restriction, namely, severe or complete difficulty in engaging in remunerative employment. Applicants for Social Security benefits who do not meet or equal the Listings are given a residual functional capacity (RFC) evaluation, based on information provided by treating sources, other medical sources (e.g., nurse-practitioners, physicians' assistants, audiologists, and physical and occupational therapists), and nonmedical sources (e.g., teachers, counselors, social workers, spouses, parents, friends, neighbors, and clergy). The RFC includes both activity limitations, such as activities of daily living, and participation restrictions, such as work history. It takes into account nonmedical factors, such as age, education, training, and work experience, and also variable access to health care and assistive technology that, if available, might reduce disability. It cannot, however, take into account all the factors in disability, for example, accessibility to potential work sites or willingness of employers to make accommodations.

But determining whether someone meets the SSA disability standard by taking all these factors into account is complex and time consuming. Accordingly, SSA developed the Listings as a screening tool to identify obviously disabled applicants without having to go through the full evaluation process.

The criteria in the Listings, however, are generally not measures of disability. Listings criteria are mostly measures of the severity of impairment and degree of functional limitations on organs or body systems (e.g., treadmill tests, pulmonary function test, range of motion of joints, and IQ tests). Conceptually, most criteria in the Listings are based on evaluation of body functions and structures, and some are based on activity limitations, such as activities of daily living. The criteria are based on the assumption that, for the conditions in the Listings, there is a strong correlation between the presence of a severe impairment or functional limitation and inability to work. For example, a person is considered disabled by SSA if they are not working and have chronic diminished pulmonary function, documented by having specified values on a one-second forced expiratory volume or forced vital capacity test (Listing 3.02). Applicants with heart conditions meet the Listings and receive benefits if they have a left ventricular ejection fraction of 30 percent or less and are unable to perform on an exercise test at a workload equivalent of 5 metabolic equivalents of task or less without exhibiting certain signs or symptoms, such as electrocardiogram abnormalities or chest pain (Listing 4.02). Some listings are based on a diagnosis alone, such as amyotrophic lateral sclerosis (Listing 11.00) and malignancies that are inoperable or unresectable or that are progressive and unresponsive to treatment (e.g., Listing 13.09, metastatic melanoma). The mental and childhood listings, however, include results of testing, where they are appropriate (e.g., IQ tests in the mental retardation listing), but they also consider factors in the disability domain, such as social and employment limitations.[2]

Some of the Listings have an evidence basis and others are based on expert consensus. The report addresses the importance of research on the relationships among impairment, functional capacity, and work disability as a basis for evidence-based Listings in Chapter 7. Meanwhile, it is important to keep in mind that the Listings essentially correspond to the impairment and to some degree what is called activity limitations domains and, with some exceptions, do not consider factors in the disability domain. The concept is that the listings in the Listings of Impairments constitute a screening

---

[2]An IQ of 59 or less alone meets a listing (Listing 12.05B for adults or Listing 11.205C for children).

test based on severity criteria that are so high that claimants who meet or equal them can be presumed unable to work. In other words, judged by the gold standard of SSA disability, the Listings are expected to have high specificity (that is, a low false-positive rate). Of course, an imperfect test required to have high specificity will, by nature, have limited sensitivity (e.g., it will miss identifying true positives). The only way to avoid such inherent tradeoffs is to improve the test, that is, enhance its ability to separate SSA-disabled from SSA-non-disabled claimants, or choose a better test.

REFERENCES

Altman, B.M. 2001. Disability definitions, models, classification schemes, and applications. In *Handbook of disability studies,* edited by G. Albrecht, K.D. Seelman, and M. Bury. Thousand Oaks, CA: Sage Publications. Pp. 97-122.

Butler, C., H. Chambers, M. Goldstein, S. Harris, J. Leach, S. Campbell, R. Adams, and J. Darrahet. 1999. Making sense of research in developmental disabilities: A conceptual framework for reviewing treatment outcomes. *Developmental Medicine and Child Neurology*, 41(1):55-59.

Gill, T.M., C.S. Williams, and M.E. Tinetti. 1995. Assessing risk for the onset of functional dependence among older adults: The role of physical performance. *Journal of the American Geriatric Society,* 43:603-609.

Guralnik, J.M., E.M. Simonsick, L. Ferrucci, et al. 1994. A short physical performance battery assessing lower extremity function: Association with self-reported disability and prediction of mortality and nursing home admission. *Journal of Gerontology*, 49:M85-M94.

Guralnik, J.M., L. Ferruci, E.M. Simonsick, et al. 1995. Lower-extremity function in persons over the age of 70 years as a predictor of subsequent disability. *New England Journal of Medicine*, 232:556-561.

Hess, A.E. 1957. Old-age, survivors, and disability insurance: Early problems and operations of the disability provisions. *Social Security Bulletin*, 12:11-21.

IOM (Institute of Medicine). 1991. *Disability in America: Toward a national agenda for prevention,* edited by A.M. Pope and A.R. Tarlov. Washington, DC: National Academy Press.

IOM. 1997. *Enabling America: Assessing the role of rehabilitation science and engineering.* Edited by E. Brandt and A.M. Pope. Washington, DC: National Academy Press.

Jette, A.M. 2006. Toward a common language for function, disability, and health. *Physical Therapy*, 86(5):726-734.

Jette, A.M., S.F. Assmann, D. Rooks, B.A. Harris, and S. Crawford. 1998. Interrelationships among disablement concepts. *The Journals of Gerontology Series A: Biological Sciences and Medical Sciences*, 53A:M395-M404.

Lawrence, R.H., and A.M. Jette. 1996. Disentangling the disablement process. *The Journals of Gerontology Series B: Psychological Sciences and Social Sciences,* 51:S173-S182.

Nagi, S. 1964. A study in the evaluation of disability and rehabilitation potential: Concepts, methods, and procedures. *American Journal of Public Health*, 54:1568-1579.

Nagi, S. 1965. Some conceptual issues in disability and rehabilitation. In *Sociology and rehabilitation,* edited by M.B. Sussman. Washington, DC: American Sociological Association. Pp. 100-113.

Nagi, S.Z. 1969. *Disability and rehabilitation: Legal, clinical, and self-concepts and measurements.* Columbus: Ohio State University Press.

Nagi, S.Z. 1976. An epidemiology of disability among adults in the United States. *Milbank Memorial Fund Quarterly*, 54:439-467.

Nagi, S.Z. 1987. The concept and measurement of disability. In *Disabled Policies and Government Programs,* edited by E.D. Berkowitz. New York: Praeger.

Nagi, S.Z. 1991. Disability concepts revised: Implication for prevention. In *Disability in America: Toward a national agenda for prevention,* edited by A.M. Pope and A.R. Tarlov. Washington, DC: National Academy Press. Pp. 309-327.

NCMRR (National Center for Medical Rehabilitation Research). 1993. *Research plan for the National Center for Medical Rehabilitation Research, National Institute of Child and Human Development, NIH, DHHS.* Washington, DC: U.S. Government Printing Office.

Ostir, G.V., K.S. Markides, S.A. Black, and J.S. Goodwin. 1998. Lower body functioning as a predictor of subsequent disability among older Mexican Americans. *The Journals of Gerontology Series A: Biological Sciences and Medical Sciences*, 53:M491-M495.

Stone, D.A. 1984. *The disabled state*. Philadelphia, PA: Temple University Press.

Verbrugge, L.M., and A.M. Jette. 1994. The disablement process. *Social Science & Medicine*, 38(1):1-14.

Whiteneck, G. 2006. Conceptual models of disability: Past, present, and future. In *Workshop on disability in America: A new look,* edited by M. Field, A.M. Jette, and L. Martin. Washington, DC: The National Academies Press. Pp. 50-66.

WHO (World Health Organization). 1980. *International classification of impairments, disabilities, and handicaps*. Geneva: WHO.

WHO. 2001. *International classification of functioning, disability and health*: *ICF*. Geneva: WHO.

3

Individuals with Disabilities

The purpose of the Social Security Disability Insurance (SSDI) and Supplementary Security Income (SSI) programs is to provide cash assistance to individuals who, because of physical or mental impairment, are unable to engage in "substantial gainful activity." This is currently defined by the Social Security Administration (SSA) as earning no more than $900 a month ($1,500 for blind individuals). The purpose of the Listing of Impairments (the Listings) is to provide a standardized test or tool to quickly "screen in" claimants whose medical condition is of such a severity that few, if any, individuals having that condition could be expected to engage in substantial gainful activity. Assessing the effectiveness of the Listings as a quick screening tool requires information about who is screened in, especially those who should not be, and who is not screened in, especially those who should be. This chapter summarizes what is known about individuals in the population with impairments and functional limitations that make it very difficult or impossible for them to work and what is known about the characteristics of the SSDI and SSI applicant pools and of those who are awarded benefits and those who are denied.

INFORMATION FROM SURVEYS ON INDIVIDUALS WITH DISABILITIES

From time to time, SSA has conducted surveys to obtain information on individuals with disabilities, those who do and do not apply to Social Security for disability benefits, and on what happens to those who are denied. In addition, a number of national population surveys include questions about disability.

Social Security Surveys

SSA has sponsored three major surveys to provide information useful for understanding and projecting enrollment trends in the disability programs (Hu et al., 1997). They were the:

- 1966 Social Security Survey of the Disabled
- 1972/1974 Survey of Disabled and Nondisabled Adults
- 1978 Survey of Disability and Work

The surveys were used in a number of analyses of disability enrollment patterns, but they are dated. Program enrollment increased significantly and unexpectedly in the late 1980s to early 1990s. Studies of this growth identified a number of factors that might have caused it, primarily socioeconomic and demographic trends, court decisions, and changes in program eligibility (IOM and NRC, 2002:Chapter 2). Lack of information about the pool of potential applicants and the factors influencing their decision whether or not to apply for benefits made it impossible to understand or predict program dynamics. Accordingly, SSA began to develop another national sample survey in the 1990s, the Disability Evaluation Study (DES). The DES, later renamed the National Study of Health and Activity, was to collect more detailed information from respondents about health conditions and limitations affecting ability to work, and this self-reported information was to be supplemented by medical examinations of respondents. SSA fielded a pilot in 2000 and a revised pilot in fiscal year (FY) 2002. SSA found that the need to conduct in-person screening to achieve an adequate response rate and to increase the sample size to make the results representative would have doubled the original estimate of costs. SSA decided to discontinue the effort in FY 2003, because "although extensive testing of the National Study of Health and Activity developed a workable methodology, . . . the benefits of the survey would not justify the substantial projected costs" (SSA, 2002:141).

National Surveys

Several ongoing national surveys include questions about impairments, functional limitations, employment limitations, and other disability-related topics. None provide information on the number and characteristics of individuals who are prevented from earning more than a minimal amount by engaging in productive work because of identifiable chronic physical or mental impairments that would meet the Social Security definition of disability. Little is known about individuals who meet SSA's disability criteria in every respect except that they are engaged in substantial gainful activity despite their medical condition. The surveys rely on self-report and so at best can only estimate the number of people who say they are unable to work because of a disability. Most of the surveys simply ask the respondent to report any limitation on their ability to work and, in some cases, the nature of the limitation and its cause. Mostly, however, surveys separate questions about work limitations from those about functional limitations, such as activities of daily living (ADLs) and instrumental activities of daily living (IADLs), and about actual employment at the time of the survey and during the previous year.

The main surveys with information about disability are the:

- Survey of Income and Program Participation (SIPP)
- National Health Interview Survey
- American Community Survey (ACS)
- Panel Study of Income Dynamics (PSID)
- Decennial Census

Each of these surveys and their findings are described below. Table 3-1 summarizes recent results from the surveys. The surveys estimate that indi-

TABLE 3-1 Number and Prevalence of Individuals Ages 25-61 with and without Disabilities and Number and Percentage of Those Employed, by Disability Category and by Survey

	2003 American Community Survey			
	Total Population		Employed	
Disability Category	Number	Percent	Number	Percent
All	143,796,355	100.0	107,425,071	74.7
With any disability	17,146,845	11.9	6,738,710	39.3
With a sensory disability	3,944,398	2.7	1,968,255	49.9
With a physical disability	10,819,521	7.5	3,656,998	33.8
With a mental disability	5,745,569	4.0	1,620,250	28.2
With a self-care disability	2,925,715	2.0	535,406	18.3
With a go-outside-home disability	4,227,427	2.9	756,709	17.9
With an employment disability	9,854,223	6.9	1,862,448	18.9
With no disability	126,649,510	88.1	100,686,360	79.5
	1994-1995 National Health Interview Survey-Disability Supplement			
	Total Population		Employed	
Disability Category	Number	Percent	Number	Percent
All	128,104,461	100.0	100,914,424	78.8
With any disability	21,457,049	16.7	11,543,892	53.8
With a sensory disability	5,400,346	4.2	3,477,823	64.4
With a physical disability	4,660,568	3.6	1,868,888	40.1

TABLE 3-1 Continued

With a mental disability	5,402,293	4.2	2,387,814	44.2
With a self-care disability	1,534,615	1.2	329,942	21.5
With a go-outside-home disability	1,613,015	1.3	277,439	17.2
With an employment disability	14,903,532	11.6	6,334,001	42.5
With no disability	106,647,412	83.3	89,370,531	83.8
	2002 Survey of Income and Program Participation			
	Total Population		Employed	
Disability Category	Number	Percent	Number	Percent
All	142,520,000	100.0	108,518,780	76.1
With any disability	26,620,000	18.7	13,017,180	48.9
With a sensory disability	6,490,202	4.6	3,472,258	53.5
With a physical disability	18,790,000	13.2	8,718,560	46.4
With a mental disability	4,394,330	3.1	1,625,902	37.0
With a self-care disability	3,362,523	2.4	766,655	22.8
With a go-outside-home disability	4,931,252	3.5	1,001,044	20.3
With an employment disability	14,420,000	10.1	3,994,340	27.7
With no disability	115,900,000	81.3	95,501,600	82.4
	2003 Panel Study of Income Dynamics			
	Total Population		Employed	
Disability Category	Number	Percent	Number	Percent
All	143,132,000	100.0	115,235,114	80.5
With any disability	30,566,000	21.4	19,103,750	62.5
With a sensory disability	na	na	na	na
With a physical disability	na	na	na	na
With a mental disability	13,897,000	9.7	8,574,449	61.7
With a self-care disability	9,395,000	6.6	4,237,145	45.1
With a go-outside-home disability	12,375,000	8.6	5,927,625	47.9
With an employment disability	19,304,000	13.5	10,018,776	51.9
With no disability	112,566,000	78.6	96,131,364	85.4
	Decennial Census 2000			
	Total Population		Employed	
Disability Category	Number	Percent	Number	Percent
All	138,500,000	100.0	103,955,780	75.1
With any disability	14,006,000	10.1	5,854,508	41.8
With a sensory disability	3,346,000	2.4	1,743,266	52.1
With a physical disability	9,448,000	6.8	3,363,488	35.6
With a mental disability	5,218,000	3.8	1,575,836	30.2
With a self-care disability	2,628,000	1.9	570,276	21.7
With a go-outside-home disability	na	na	na	na
With an employment disability	na	na	na	na
With no disability	124,494,000	89.9	98,101,272	78.8

NOTE: The percentage of those with specific disabilities adds up to more than the percentage of those with any disability, because some people report having more than one disability.
SOURCE: Burkhauser et al., 2006:Tables 11, 13.

viduals ages 25-61 with disabilities constitute between 12 and 21 percent of the total population in that age group. These estimates are due to different survey procedures, definitions of disability, and time periods. Generally, the more questions that a survey has about disability, the higher the estimates of population and prevalence (PSID is an exception) (Weathers, 2005:28).

The percentage of individuals reporting limitations on employment due to a disability ranges from 7 percent in the 2003 ACS to 14 percent in the PSID. According to ACS, which has the strictest definition of work disability, 19 percent of those who reported a work limitation were employed at the time of the survey (9 percent reported full-time employment during the preceding year). Those reporting functional limitations, such as the inability to perform one or more ADLs or IADLs, worked less than those reporting impairments, whether mental, physical, or sensory, according to all the surveys. Between 18 and 20 percent of those with IADLs were employed at the time of the survey. For those with ADLs, the employment rate was between 18 and 23 percent. Among those reporting an impairment, those with a mental impairment were least likely to be employed (between 28 and 37 percent), the physically impaired somewhat more likely (between 34 and 46 percent), and the sensory impaired most likely (between 50 and 59 percent).

Survey of Income and Program Participation

According to the most recent report on disability based on SIPP, "In 2002, 18.1 percent of the 282.8 million people in the civilian noninstitutionalized population reported having a disability. Among the 51.2 million people with a disability, 32.5 million (11.5 percent of all people) had a severe disability."[1] Approximately 10.7 million people 6 years old and older (4.1 percent of this age group) needed assistance with one or more ADLs or IADLs (U.S. Census Bureau, 2006).

The rates of nonsevere disability, severe disability, and needing personal assistance were higher for women than men overall, although the relation-

[1]The Census Bureau report is based on responses to questions about the ability to perform various activities in the fifth wave of the SIPP (U.S. Census Bureau, 2006). The respondent was classified as having a nonsevere disability if he or she had difficulty performing one or more functional activities (seeing, hearing, speaking, lifting/carrying, using stairs, walking, or grasping small objects), one or more ADLs, or one or more IADLs, or if he or she had certain conditions, such as a learning disability or some other type of mental or emotional condition. They were classified as having a severe disability if they were unable to perform one of more of the functional activities, ADLs, or IADLs; used a wheelchair, cane, crutches, or walker; or had one or more specified conditions, such as mental retardation or Alzheimer's disease; or had any other mental or emotional conditions that seriously interfered with everyday activities; or had a condition that limited the ability to work around the house or made it difficult to remain employed.

ship was reversed in age groups under 25 years. The disability rate also went up with age. The rate of severe disability was 3.4 percent for those under 15 years old, 12.6 percent for those ages 45-54, and 19.3 percent for those ages 55-64. The rate of disability also varied by race and ethnic group. The rate of severe disability was 7.2 percent among Asians and Pacific Islanders, 8.8 percent among Hispanics, 11.8 percent among non-Hispanic whites, and 14.0 percent among non-Hispanic blacks. The rates of need for personal assistance in these groups were 2.5, 2.9, 3.9, and 4.7 percent, respectively.

Persons with disabilities were more likely to be in poverty. Among 25-64-year-olds, 11 percent of those with nonsevere disability and 26 percent of those with severe disability were poor, compared with 8 percent of those who reported not having any disability. About 77 percent of those ages 25-64 with severe disability had an annual income under $20,000, and 38 percent were in households with an annual income less than $20,000, compared with 39 and 12 percent, respectively, of nondisabled persons in that age group. Individuals 25 to 64 years old with severe disability were much more likely than nondisabled individuals to receive some form of public assistance (53 percent compared with 7 percent). This included Social Security and SSI. Approximately 29 percent of those in the severe disability group were receiving Social Security benefits and 21 percent were receiving SSI, compared with less than 3 percent and 0.3 percent of the nondisabled.[2]

Among individuals 21 to 64 years old, 88 percent of those without a disability were employed at some point during the preceding year, compared with 82 percent of those with nonsevere disability and 43 percent of those with severe disability. The median annual earnings of those with a severe disability were barely half those of people without a disability ($12,800 compared with $25,000).

Among people in the labor force during the preceding year, 53 percent of the nondisabled worked full-time all year, compared with 13 percent of the severely disabled. About 12 percent of the nondisabled were unemployed all year, compared with 58 percent of the severely disabled.

Employment and annual earnings varied by type of disability in terms of functional domains (communication, physical, and mental), limited ability to perform ADLs or IADLs (or both), and specific diagnoses. Of individuals 21-64 years old with a disability in one functional domain, 61 percent were employed for at least part of the preceding year, with median annual earnings of $18,300, compared with median annual earnings of $25,046 among those without disability. About 52 percent of those with disability in two

---

[2]This age bracket includes those 62-64 years of age who have taken their Old-Age and Survivors Insurance benefits early as well as those receiving SSDI benefits and/or SSI payments.

domains were employed, with median annual earnings of $15,364. About 32 percent of those with disability in all three domains were employed, with median earnings of $8,520. About 29 percent with an ADL limitation requiring personal assistance were employed at some point during the year, with median annual earnings of $9,902. The percent employed varied according to which ADL was limited from 17 percent (difficulty eating—required personal assistance) to 41 percent (difficulty dressing—did not need personal assistance). About 31 percent with an IADL limitation requiring personal assistance were employed, with median earnings of $8,953. Like ADLs, the percentage employed varied somewhat according to which IADL was limited. About 47 percent of those with a mental disability were employed during the year, with median annual earnings of $13,771.

Survey respondents who reported an activity limitation or being in fair or poor health were asked about the cause or causes. The largest group (consisting of 8.1 million individuals) were those with back or spine problems, of which 61 percent were employed during the preceding year, with $17,825 in median annual earnings. The next largest group (5.6 million) reported arthritis or rheumatism as a cause of activity limitation or of fair or poor health, of which 58 percent were employed, with median annual earnings of $18,000. The group with the lowest employment rate were those with mental or emotional problems. About 29 percent of the 1.7 million in this group were employed, with median annual earnings of $8,383.[3]

Researchers have used a data set of individuals who reported applying for SSDI and/or SSI in the 1990 SIPP and were matched with SSA administrative records to obtain detailed information on their interactions with the disability decision process and decisions at each step. The matched sample consists of adults who applied for SSDI or SSI disability benefits and whose claims were decided by DDSs during calendar years 1986 through 1993 at the initial or reconsideration level. Lahiri et al. (1995) and Hu et al. (1997) compiled the data set and used it to model the sequential decision process that the DDSs use to determine disability. They identified several health and activity limitation variables that increased the likelihood of meeting or equaling the Listings, which is decided at step 3 of the five-step decision process. These were having three or more severe limitations in their ability to perform ADLs, two or more IADL limitations, a mental disability, and no history of work. Individuals limited in working due to musculoskeletal impairments, however, were more likely to be moved on to the later steps of the decision process, where vocational factors are considered in conjunction with medical factors. The model predicted an overall allowance rate for the

[3]Other groups reporting employment rates under 30 percent were those with paralysis and stroke, but their numbers were too small for a reliable estimate. The 90 percent confidence intervals were 14.4 and 10.4, respectively.

sample of applicants of 38.9 percent, which was 1.5 percentage points less than the actual allowance rate of 39.5 percent. Dwyer et al. (2001) used the model parameters from Hu et al. (1997), after making some adjustments in procedures involving the sample selection cutoff method and sample restrictions, to predict eligibility among the population of individuals not currently receiving benefits. They estimated that "4.4 million people, or 2.9 percent of the nonbeneficiary population aged 18-64, would meet SSA's medical criteria for disability" (Dwyer et al., 2001:27). Of these, 3 million had average earnings less than the substantial gainful activity amount ($500 a month at that time). They predicted that, when a recession occurs, some of the 1.4 million who were medically eligible but had earnings larger than $500 a month would be likely to lose their jobs and apply for disability benefits.

American Community Survey

In the 2003-2005 ACS, respondents 5 years old or older were asked six disability questions. People ages 16-64 were classified as having a disability if they reported at least one of the following six conditions:

- **Sensory Impairment.** Question 15a asked respondents to mark yes or no as to whether they had any of the following long-lasting conditions: "Blindness, deafness, severe vision or hearing impairment."
- **Physical Disability.** Question 15b asked if they had a long-lasting "condition that substantially limits one or more basic physical activities such as walking, climbing stairs, reaching, lifting, or carrying."
- **Mental Disability.** Question 16a asked if they had a physical, mental, or emotional condition lasting six months or more that made "learning, remembering, or concentrating"difficult.
- **Self-care Disability.** Question 16b asked if they had a physical, mental, or emotional condition lasting six months or more that made "dressing, bathing, or getting around inside the home" difficult.
- **Going-Outside-Home Disability.** Question 17a asked those 16 years old and older if they had a physical or mental condition that made it difficult to "go outside the home alone to shop or visit a doctor's office."
- **Employment Disability.** Question 17b asked if they had a physical, mental, or emotional condition lasting six months or more that made "working at a job or business" difficult.

According to the 2005 ACS, 12 percent of the population 16-64 years old reported a disability (Table 3-1). About 3 percent reported having a sensory disability, 7 percent a physical disability, 5 percent a mental disability, 2 percent a self-care disability, 3 percent a go-outside-home disability, and

6.8 percent an employment disability, using the ACS definitions. Overall, women were slightly more likely to report disabilities than men (12.2 percent compared with 12.0 percent).

About 38 percent of 16-64 year-olds who reported any disability were employed at the time of the survey, compared with 74 percent of the same age group without disabilities. The employment percentages ranged from about 17 percent among those with employment or go-outside-home disabilities to about 30 percent among those with a mental or physical disability to 47 percent with a sensory disability. Approximately 49 percent worked at some time during the year, compared with 85 percent of the nondisabled population.

SOCIAL SECURITY DISABILITY APPLICANTS

In calendar year (CY) 2005, slightly more than 2.1 million workers applied for SSDI benefits, compared with 1.3 million in 1995. The increase reflects in part an increase in the number of workers insured for disability and in part a higher incidence of claims (from 10.6 per 1,000 covered workers in 1995 to 14.6 per 1,000 covered workers in 2005).[4]

In CY 2005, almost 1.5 million adults ages 18-64 applied for SSI disability benefits, as did approximately 0.4 million children. In 1995, the numbers of SSI applications for adults and children were 1.3 million and 0.5 million, respectively.[5]

The total of 4 million applications for SSDI and SSI benefits in 2005 represented approximately 3 million individuals, because more than a quarter of the adults who applied filed for both SSDI and SSI benefits.

The four populations of applicants—SSDI-only adults, concurrent SSDI/SSI adults, SSI-only adults, and SSI children—differ in terms of disabilities claimed (Figure 3-1). In 2004, musculoskeletal disorders were the dominant diagnoses among adult applicants, especially those with a substantial work history (SSDI-only adults). Mental disorders were prominent among SSI children and second in frequency among adults without enough work history to qualify for Social Security benefits (i.e., SSI-only adults).

SSA expects the aging of the baby-boom generation to increase the rate of applications for musculoskeletal disability disorders in the coming years (Zayatz, 2005).

---

[4]Internet table: "Disabled Workers: Applications for Disability Benefits & Benefit Awards." Available: www.ssa.gov/OACT/STATS/table6c7.html (accessed October 4, 2006).

[5]Table V.C1, "Disabled Adult Claims," and V.C2, "Disabled Child Claims," in 2006 *Annual Report of the SSI Program*. Available: www.ssa.gov/OACT/SSIR/SSI06/AllowanceDate.html (accessed October 4, 2006).

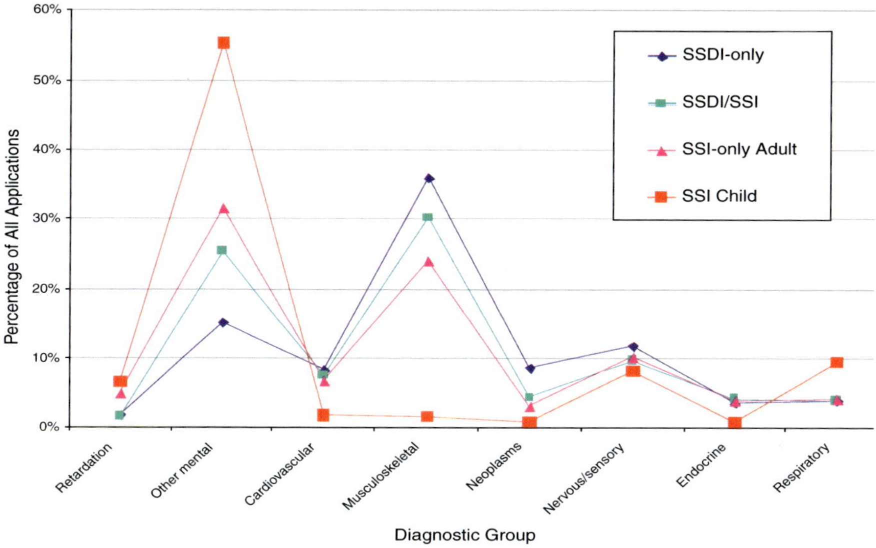

FIGURE 3-1 Distribution of applications for Social Security disability benefits among program and selected diagnostic groups, 2004 (percentage of all applications).
SOURCE: Appendix Table 3-1.

Recent Social Security Disability Awardees

In 2004, the state Disability Determination Services (DDSs) made more than 2.3 million initial decisions on claims, allowing benefits in 944,000 cases (41 percent) and denying 1,385,000 (59 percent). The allowance rate varied by program segment, however. It was highest for SSDI-only applicants, at 48 percent, and lowest for concurrent SSDI/SSI applicants, at 30 percent (Table 3-2).

The mix of impairments among beneficiaries allowed benefits at the initial decision differed somewhat from the mix among applicants (Figure 3-2). Although 36 percent of SSDI-only applicants claimed a musculoskeletal problem, only 24 percent of those allowed initially had a musculoskeletal problem. Similarly, 30 percent of the concurrent SSDI/SSI claims were musculoskeletal, but only 16 percent of the allowances were. The percentage of SSI child claims based on mental problems was also lower among awards than applications—52 percent compared with 55 percent—and the percentage of awards based on respiratory disorders among children (primarily asthma) was also lower among awards than applications—2 percent compared with 9 percent. The largest percentage of SSDI/SSI claims

TABLE 3-2 Initial Allowance Rate for Claims by Program Segment, 2004

Program Segment	Number of Decisions	Number of Allowances	Percentage of Claims Allowed
SSDI-only claims	741,471	356,696	48.1
Concurrent SSDI/SSI claims	725,011	219,198	30.2
SSI-only adult claims	466,182	187,603	40.2
SSI child claims	395,714	180,045	45.5
All SSDI and SSI claims	2,328,378	943,542	40.5

NOTE: SSDI applicants and beneficiaries are mostly workers but also include disabled adult children of workers and disabled widows and widowers of deceased workers.
SOURCE: Table provided by SSA/ODISP/ODP/ODPIS, November 2005.

was musculoskeletal, but the largest percentage of awards was for mental disorders.

Mental disorders other than retardation are the largest basis for both awards and claims in SSI child and SSI-only adult cases.

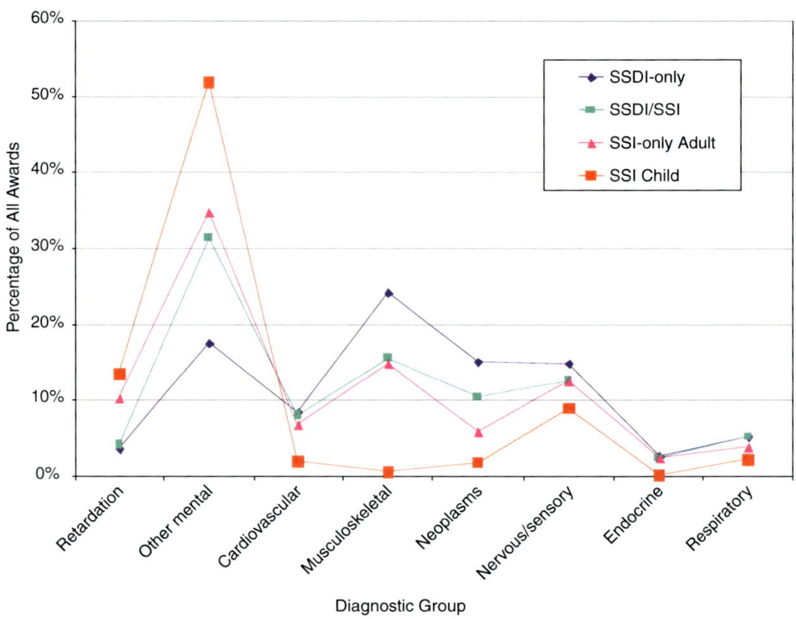

FIGURE 3-2 Distribution of initial awards of Social Security disability benefits among program and selected diagnostic groups, 2004 (percentage of all awards).
SOURCE: Appendix Table 3-2.

Impairment Trends Among Awardees

SSA reports annual statistics on disabled worker awards by diagnostic group since 1961 (Figure 3-3).[6] The series is not exactly comparable to the data reported above, because it combines SSDI-only and concurrent SSDI/SSI awards and does not break out retardation from other mental disorders until 1995. The figure shows a substantial shift in the mix of impairments among SSA disabled worker beneficiaries over time, as the number of annual awards increased by 170 percent. The changing mix of diagnostic groups reflects in part changes in program eligibility and take-up rates, in part the aging of the insured worker population, and in part advances in medical knowledge and treatments, especially in reducing heart attacks and stroke. Cardiovascular claims have dropped from more than 30 percent of awards in the early 1970s to barely 10 percent currently. This reflected a decrease in incidence from approximately 2.0 allowances per 1,000 insured workers from 1973 to 1977 to less than 0.6 since 1997. The percentage of awards for mental disabilities, meanwhile, increased from about 10 percent in the 1960s and 1970s to about 25 percent in the 1990s (the incidence per 1,000 insured workers increased from 0.5 to between 1.0 and 1.3). The share of musculoskeletal claims increased from between 15 and 20 percent during the 1970s and 1980s to about 25 percent in the 1990s (the incidence per 1,000 workers was about 0.6 in 1981 and 1.4 in 2003).

Among SSI adults, awards for mental disability have increased from 22 to 32 percent of all awards since 1985 (Figure 3-4). Musculoskeletal cases have experienced a similar relative increase but at a lower level: from 7 to 16 percent of all awards. The percentage of infectious disease cases increased from near 0 to more than 4 between 1985 and 1990, then declined after 1995, probably due to the advent and increased prevalence of HIV infection and AIDS and the subsequent development of effective therapies.

The annual number of awards in SSI child cases increased by 285 percent from 1985 to 2003. Although the number of annual awards increased in all the diagnostic categories in Figure 3-5, the awards for mental disabilities other than retardation increased so much relative to the other categories that they accounted for more than half the awards in 2003, compared with less than 10 percent in 1985.

SSA's Office of the Actuary anticipates that the aging of the baby boomers will result in a growing proportion of awards based on arthritic, back, and bone disorders in the adult groups. The actuaries also expect to see a temporary increase in annual SSDI awards for mental disability continue for several years because of an effort beginning in 2001 to identify SSI ben-

[6]Disabled widows and widowers and disabled adult children of workers are not included in this data series.

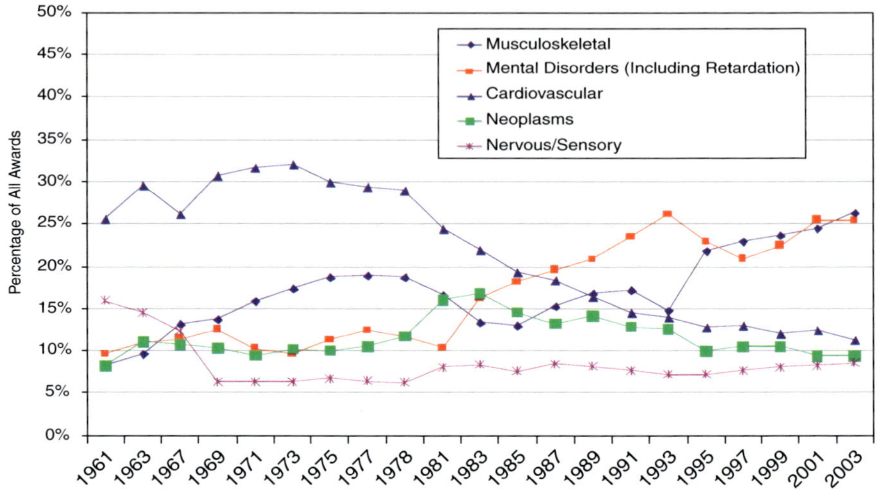

FIGURE 3-3 Distribution of annual disabled worker (DI) awards among selected diagnostic groups, 1961-2003 (percentage of all awards).
NOTE: The table includes SSDI-only and SSDI/SSI concurrent awards. SSA reported the distribution of awards among diagnostic groups on the basis of initial awards until 1995, when it began to report the distribution among awards made at all stages of the decision process, including the various appeals levels. Because the rate of successful appeals is relatively high for musculoskeletal cases, the percentage of awards based on musculoskeletal disability jumped and depressed the percentage of awards for mental disabilities.
SOURCE: Appendix Table 3-3.

eficiaries whose SSDI eligibility has not been recognized (Zayatz, 2005). In the latest annual report on the SSI program, SSA predicts that the number of SSI beneficiaries will continue to grow, largely due to growth in the U.S. population, but this projection is based on historical disability incidence rates by age and sex, not on any analysis of how factors that affected those rates might be changing (SSA, 2006).

Denied Applicants

Little is known about applicants who are not allowed, although it would be useful in assessing the Listings to know about the rate of false negatives (i.e., applicants who actually meet the requirements but are turned down). Information about subsequent employment and earnings would also be helpful in assessing the validity of the Listings. It might become evident

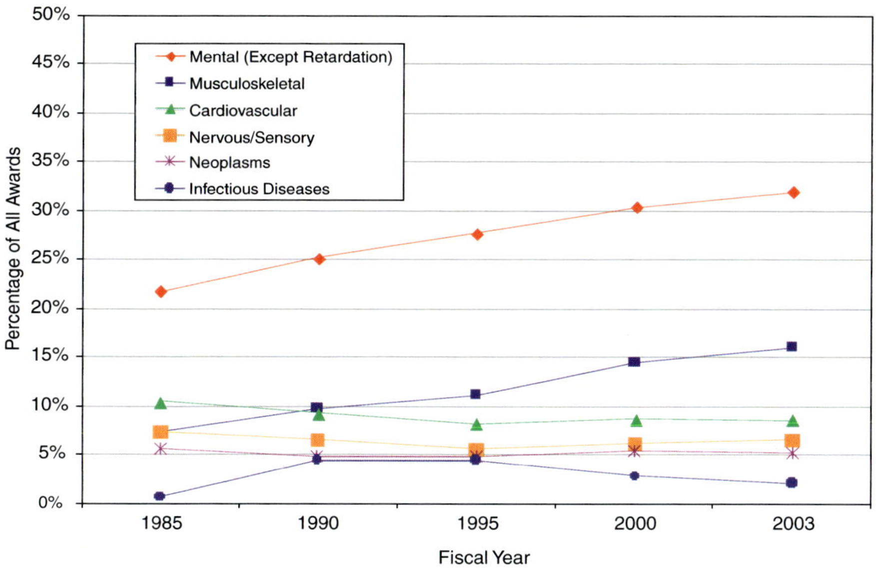

FIGURE 3-4 Distribution of annual SSI adult awards among selected diagnostic groups, 1985-2003 (percentage of all awards).
SOURCE: Appendix Table 3-4.

that individuals with a certain type of condition and examination results are rarely, if ever, employed after being denied, which could indicate that the criteria in the Listings are not measuring what they are supposed to measure or the wrong tests are being used.

Denied applicants have been studied in the past, but recent studies are few. In 1976, Treitel used SSA administrative records to determine the subsequent fate of men denied benefits on medical-vocational grounds. By 1973, 14 percent had died (compared with 7 percent of the same-age general population); another 16 percent had reached retirement age, and 40 percent had not worked in the four years after denial. Less than half (47 percent) of those alive and of working age in 1972 had worked at some point during the year (based on Bound, 1989:490).

Treitel then studied applicants denied at the hearing level. He found that:

> Persons persisting in claims rarely returned to substantial employment. While many of those denied at hearings in 1970 had some form of earnings in the next 5 years, only about 10 percent had substantial earnings of

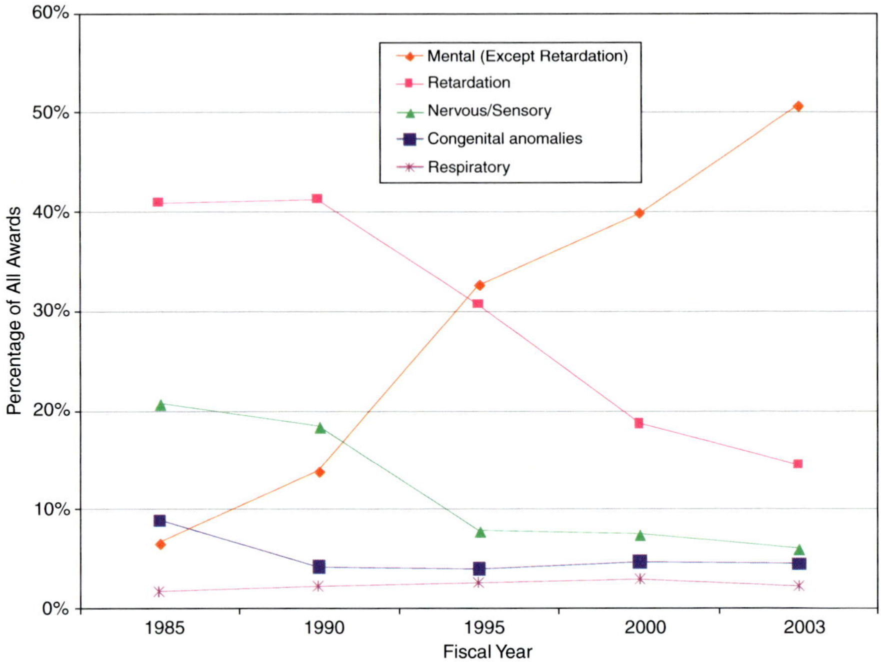

FIGURE 3-5 Distribution of annual SSI child awards among selected diagnostic groups, 1985-2003 (percentage of all awards).
SOURCE: Appendix Table 3-5.

> $3,600 or more 5 years later. Most claimants for benefits appear to remain out of the labor market whatever the decision on their disability insurance claim (Trietel, 1979).

Bound (1989) used data on denied applicants from the 1972/1974 Survey of Disabled and Nondisabled Adults and the 1978 Survey of Disability and Work matched with Social Security earnings records to compare applicants awarded benefits with those denied benefits. Bound found that 33 percent of the denied applicants were employed at the time of the 1972 survey and 29 percent at the time of the 1978 survey, compared with 92 and 87 percent, respectively, of the same-age general population. More did some work during the past year, 45 percent in 1972 and 40 percent in 1978, but their earnings were less than half of the same-age population overall—$4,000 compared with $9,000 in 1972 and $5,300 compared with $14,000 in 1978. About 51 percent of the denied applicants in 1972 reported having severe work limitations, compared with 93 percent of the beneficiaries and

12 percent of the general population. The comparable percentages in 1978 were 64, 97, and 14 percent. The percentages with specific health conditions were much higher than those reported by the general population and nearly as high as those who were awarded benefits.

Bound also cited a study of Nagi (1969) in which independent multidisciplinary clinical teams consisting of a physician, psychologist, occupational therapist, social worker, and vocational counselor evaluated the medical status and work capacity of a sample of SSDI applicants in person. The teams found 68 percent of those later allowed benefits and 36 percent of those denied benefits to be "not fit for work." The teams determined that another 25 percent of those allowed were only fit for work under "special conditions," "sheltered conditions," "at home only," or "part-time under normal conditions." Nearly a third of the denied applicants (31 percent) were similarly categorized, and another third (34 percent) were deemed fit for work under normal conditions (about half of them at their former job, the rest at other jobs).

More recently, Bound et al. (2003) used the same matched SIPP data set as Hu et al. (1997) and Dwyer et al. (2001) to track the change in earnings and income before and after the disability decision of both those allowed and those denied. The average monthly earnings of SSDI applicants were about 15 percent of what they were three years earlier. Three years later, applicants who were denied benefits earned about 35 percent of what they did six years before (the authors did not report how many were employed full-time, part-time, or not at all). The pattern was similar for those denied SSI benefits.

REFERENCES

Bound, J. 1989. The health and earnings of rejected disability insurance applicants. *American Economic Review*, 79(3):482-503.

Bound, J., R.V. Burkhauser, and A. Nichols. 2003. Tracking the household income of SSDI and SSI applicants. *Research in Labor Economics*, 21:113-158.

Burkhauser, R.V., R.R. Weathers II, and M. Schroeder. 2006. *A guide to disability statistics from the Panel Study of Income Dynamics*. Rehabilitation Research and Training Center on Disability Demographics and Statistics, Cornell University. Available: digitalcommons.ilr.cornell.edu/edicollect/1207/ (accessed October 4, 2006).

Dwyer, D., J. Hu, D.R. Vaughn, and B. Wixon. 2001. *Counting the disabled: Using survey self-reports to estimate medical eligibility for Social Security's disability programs*. ORES Working Paper #90. Office of Research, Evaluation, and Statistics, SSA. Available: www.ssa.gov/policy/docs/workingpapers/wp90.pdf (accessed October 4, 2006).

Hu, J., K. Lahiri, D.R. Vaughn, and B. Wixon. 1997. *A structural model of Social Security's disability determination process*. Working Paper No. 72. Office of Research, Evaluation, and Statistics, SSA.

IOM and NRC (Institute of Medicine and National Research Council). 2002. *The dynamics of disability: Measuring and monitoring disability for Social Security programs*, edited by G.S. Wunderlich, D.P. Rice, and N.L. Amado. Washington, DC: National Academy Press.

Lahiri, K., D.R. Vaughan, and B. Wixon. 1995. Modeling SSA's sequential disability determination process using matched SIPP data. *Social Security Bulletin*, 58(4):3-42.

Nagi, S.Z. 1969. *Disability and rehabilitation: Legal, clinical, and self-concepts and measurements*. Columbus, OH: Ohio State University Press.

SSA (Social Security Administration). 2002. *FY 2002 performance and accountability report.* Available: www.ssa.gov/finance/2002/fy02PAR.pdf (accessed October 18, 2006).

SSA. 2006. *2006 Annual report of the SSI program.* Available: www.ssa.gov/OACT/SSIR/SSI06/index.html (accessed October 5, 2006).

Treitel, R. 1979. Disability claimants who contest denials and win reversals through hearings. ORS Working Paper No. 2. Baltimore, MD: Office of Research and Statistics, SSA.

U.S. Census Bureau. 2006. *Americans with disabilities: 2002*. Current Population Report P70-107. Available: www.census.gov/prod/2006pubs/p70-107.pdf (accessed October 5, 2006).

Weathers II, R.R. 2005. A *guide to disability statistics from the American Community Survey.* Rehabilitation Research and Training Center on Disability Demographics and Statistics, Cornell University. Available: digitalcomons.ilr.cornell.edu/cgi/viewcontent.cgi?article=1123&context=edicollect (accessed October 4, 2006).

Zayatz, T.A. 2005. *Social Security Disability Insurance Program worker experience*. Actuarial Study No. 114, Office of the Actuary, SSA. Available: www.ssa.gov/OACT/NOTES/s2000s.html (accessed October 5, 2006).

4

SSA's Disability Programs

The subject of disability insurance was discussed and debated extensively from the very beginnings of Social Security, although in the end, the original 1935 Social Security Act did not contain a provision for the payment of disability benefits. Many people thought that the program should include wage replacement for individuals who became unable to work before age 65 due to disability. However, there was much debate about the potential costs of such a program and about the complexity of administering it. "There was concern about the dynamic nature of the disability program, and the administrative difficulty in making disability determinations, i.e., the subjectivity of determining whether a person was truly disabled or out of work for other reasons such as age, obsolete skills or experience, etc." (SSA, 1996:1).

Between 1935 and passage of the Disability Freeze in 1954 (followed shortly by the Disability Insurance program in 1956), the Social Security Board (which became the Social Security Administration [SSA] in 1946) and Congress worked extensively on the design of a disability benefit program. However, "the administrative problems of separating those truly unable to work from those merely out of work colored the debate over disability insurance and delayed its passage" (Berkowitz, 1987:41).

As the political debate about whether to establish a disability program continued, officials within SSA were working on the difficult problem of how to implement such a program if it eventually passed. They recognized the complexity of making disability determinations, and they knew that they had a great deal of preparatory work to do. As later recalled by one of the key figures in the development of the disability program:

> . . . as we approached the 1950s, it looked like disability insurance was coming—and we had to study how it would be administered. I found that there was little or no appreciation and no detailed work being done on how Social Security would go about administering various conceivable provisions (Hess, 1993:6, 7).

Early on, officials at the Social Security Board decided that the definition of disability for any disability benefit program had to be a strict one to be politically acceptable and financially feasible. They also recognized that the concept of disability was highly elastic and that determining disability was likely to be quite imprecise. They thought that too strict a definition might result in pressure to "swing in the opposite direction" (Berkowitz, 1987:44). The definition they chose, which became the model for the definition that was eventually adopted in the legislation establishing the disability freeze and disability insurance benefit programs many years later, was borrowed from the War Risk Insurance Act (administered by the Veterans Administration), which defined disability as:

> Any impairment of mind or body which continuously renders it impossible for the disabled person to follow any substantial gainful occupations, and which is founded on conditions which render it reasonably certain that the total disability will continue throughout the life of the disabled person (cited in Berkowitz, 1987:44).

The definition of disability eventually adopted in the Social Security Amendments of 1954 was:

> Inability to engage in any substantial gainful activity by reason of any medically determinable physical or mental impairment which can be expected to result in death or to be of long-continued and indefinite duration (cited in SSA, 1996:2).

The Social Security definition of disability has evolved over the last 50 years, especially in the 1960s. In 1965, the definition was changed, easing the strictness of the duration requirement. Impairments were no longer required to "be of long-continued and indefinite duration." Rather, the impairment only had to last or be expected to last for 12 months. In 1967, the law was again amended in response to a series of judicial decisions that placed an increasing burden on the SSA to establish the existence of jobs that denied applicants might reasonably obtain. The change in the definition was intended to emphasize its medical focus by providing that an individual would be found disabled "only if his physical or mental impairment or impairments are of such severity that he is not only unable to do his previous work but cannot, considering his age, education, and work experience, engage in any other kind of substantial gainful work which exists in the national economy, regardless of whether such work exists in the immediate area in which he lives, or whether a specific job vacancy exists for him, or whether he would be hired if he applied for work." In order to further emphasize the importance of medical factors, the 1967 law changed the definition to state that a physical or mental impairment is "an impairment that results from anatomical, physiological, or psychological abnormalities which are demonstrable by medically acceptable clinical and laboratory diagnostic techniques" (Kollmann, 2000; SSA, 1996).

Initially, Social Security Disability Insurance (SSDI) covered insured workers between 50 and 65 and dependent children 18 or over of deceased or retired workers who had become disabled before age 18. It was subsequently expanded to provide benefits to nondisabled dependents of workers. The Social Security Amendments of 1960 eliminated the minimum age requirement of 50, which increased the range of disability benefits to workers between 18 and 65. Supplemental Security Income (SSI), launched in 1974, provided benefits to disabled children through age 17 as well as adults 18-65.

INITIAL DISABILITY CLAIMS PROCESS

In order to apply this definition of disability in 2.6 million disability claims per year, SSA has established a fairly complex disability claim process. Generally, an individual claiming entitlement to disability benefits (referred to as the "claimant") files the initial application with one of SSA's 1,138 field offices or 35 teleservice centers distributed across the country, either in person, by telephone, by mail, or over the Internet.[1] Field office personnel gather information about:

- the nature of the claimant's disability and how it limits the ability to work
- the claimant's medical treatment sources, medications, and tests
- the claimant's work history, education, and training
- any other matters that relate to the alleged disability

The field office also gathers information about nondisability issues. Depending on the type of claim and the specific case circumstances, these might include the claimant's age, employment history, marital status, or financial resources. The field office then determines if the nondisability eligibility requirements are met (for example, whether the claimant is insured

[1]In fiscal year (FY) 2006, SSA had 1,318 field offices, including resident stations, 35 teleservice centers, and 144 hearing offices (SSA, 2006a:13).

for SSDI benefits). If so, the field office sends the case to a state Disability Determination Service (DDS) agency to determine whether the claimant is "disabled" according to SSA law.

With the exception of a single federal unit that is located in SSA's central office, all DDSs are state agencies fully funded by SSA. The 54 state and territorial DDSs are responsible for making the initial decision about whether an individual is disabled. Upon receiving a new claim from an SSA field office, a DDS obtains medical records from the claimant's own medical sources. If necessary, the DDS may also obtain additional medical evidence on a consultative basis from independent medical sources. Based on all the medical and other information, the DDS makes the initial disability decision and then returns the case to the field office. If the DDS finds the claimant to be disabled, the field office then completes the paperwork and initiates the benefit payments. If the DDS finds the claimant not disabled, the field office retains the file in case the claimant requests an appeal.

THE ADMINISTRATIVE REVIEW (APPEAL) PROCESS

A claimant who is dissatisfied with the initial disability determination may appeal the determination, making use of SSA's administrative review process, often referred to as the appeal process.[2] SSA's appeal process consists of four levels, which usually must be followed in order and within specific time limits. Generally, an individual who wishes to appeal the decision made at any level must make the appeal within 60 days of the decision or lose the right to further review.

The administrative review process is informal and nonadversarial. Claimants may present any information they believe to be relevant, and may be represented by someone, including (but not limited to) an attorney. The four levels of the administrative review process are:[3]

- Initial Determination—For disability decisions, the initial determination is generally made in a state DDS by a two-person adjudicative team

[2]SSA's administrative review process is described in the Code of Federal Regulations in title 20, part 404, subpart J, and title 20, part 416, subpart N (20 CFR §§ 404.900-999 and 416.1400-1499). See also, *The Appeals Process.* SSA Publication No. 05-10041, January 2006. Available: www.ssa.gov/pubs/10041.html (accessed October 5, 2006).

[3]SSA has been testing modifications to its disability determination procedures under the authority of 20 CFR §§ 404.906, 404.966, 416.1406, and 416.1066, and some of these tests involve changes to the appeal process. For example, certain states are testing a prototype process that eliminates the second step of the appeal process, the reconsideration step. In addition, SSA recently published new rules (71 FR 16424, March 31, 2006) describing a gradual roll out of several substantive changes to the current administrative review process. These changes, which are discussed later in this chapter, were implemented in the Boston region in August 2006.

consisting of a medical or psychological consultant and a lay disability examiner.

- Reconsideration—Reconsiderations of initial disability determinations are also processed by the state DDS, but by a different adjudicative team than the one that made the initial decision.
- Hearing—Hearings on disability cases are conducted by administrative law judges (ALJs), who are appointed by the associate commissioner for hearings and appeals. There are about 1,100 ALJs located in 144 hearings offices distributed around the country. The claimant may personally appear at the hearing and can bring witnesses. He or she may also submit new evidence and review the evidence used in the decision. The ALJ may also ask other witnesses to appear. For example, the ALJ may ask for testimony from a medical or vocational expert, and does so in about 12 and 46 percent of the hearings, respectively (SSA, 2005b). The ALJ makes the hearing decision based on the evidence and testimony presented.
- Appeals Council Review—A claimant may request review of an ALJ disability decision by SSA's Appeals Council. Administrative appeals judges (AAJs) on the appeals council will grant such a request for review only in specific circumstances. Otherwise, the ALJ's hearing decision becomes SSA's final administrative decision in the case.

After completing all steps of the administrative review process, if a claimant is still dissatisfied with SSA's final decision, he or she may ask for judicial review by filing a civil lawsuit in federal district court.

For every 100 disability claims decided in FY 2005, DDSs allowed about 36 at the initial decision step. Of the remaining 64, about 22 appealed for reconsideration. DDSs approved about 3 of the 22 reconsiderations and denied about 19, almost all of whom filed a second appeal requesting a hearing before an ALJ. ALJs approved about 12 and denied about 7, 3 of whom filed a third appeal requesting review by the appeals council. The appeals council approved 1 and denied 2 (see Figure 4-1).

THE DISABILITY DECISION-MAKING PROCESS

The process used for making a disability decision is the same, regardless of the level at which the decision is made in the administrative review process (initial, reconsideration, hearing, or appeals council review), and regardless of the specific personnel or components involved (a disability examiner/medical consultant team in a DDS, ALJ in a hearing office, or AAJ at the appeals council).

Under the Social Security Act, an individual is considered to be "disabled" for Social Security purposes if he or she is unable "to engage in

FIGURE 4-1 Percentages of allowances and denials at each stage of the claims process.
NOTE: Data based on decisions made during FY 2005, not on longitudinal tracking of a cohort of claims made in FY 2005.
SOURCE: Based on SSA data accessed April 20, 2007, at: www.ssa.gov/disability/disability_process_welcome_2005.htm.

any substantial gainful activity by reason of any medically determinable physical or mental impairment which can be expected to result in death or which has lasted or can be expected to last for a continuous period of not less than 12 months."[4] Further, "[a]n individual shall be determined to be under a disability only if his physical or mental impairment or impairments are of such severity that he is not only unable to do his previous work but cannot, considering his age, education, and work experience, engage in any other kind of substantial gainful work which exists in the national economy . . ."

This definition of disability is complex, and it has medical, functional, and vocational components. A complete and comprehensive assessment of all aspects of the definition would require a detailed clinical evaluation of the underlying medical cause(s) for the impairment; analysis of the expected duration of the impairment (prognosis); a comprehensive assessment of the work-related functional limitations attributable to the impairment as well as the individual's remaining functional capacity; a detailed vocational analysis of the individual's work history and acquired work skills, educational

[4]Social Security Act, Title II, § 223(d)(2)(A) and Title XVI, § 1614(a)(3)(B).

background, and age; and a thorough analysis of the individual's current vocational prospects. However, SSA does not have the resources to perform such an extensive assessment for each of the approximately 2.6 million disability applicants who will come through its doors each year.

To apply the statutory definition in a way that allows it to manage its caseload, SSA uses a five-step sequential evaluation process when deciding whether an individual is disabled. The five-step process is used by the DDS at the initial and reconsideration decision levels and in the quick disability determination process being piloted in Region 1. Only the last step of the process requires a complete, comprehensive assessment of all aspects of the definition of disability. Each of the four steps that precede it is, to some degree, intended to enable the DDS to reach a faster decision by looking only at selected aspects of the case. The first, second, and fourth steps identify cases that will be *denied* without performing a complete assessment of all aspects of the case. The third step identifies cases that will be *allowed* without a complete assessment (Figure 4-2).

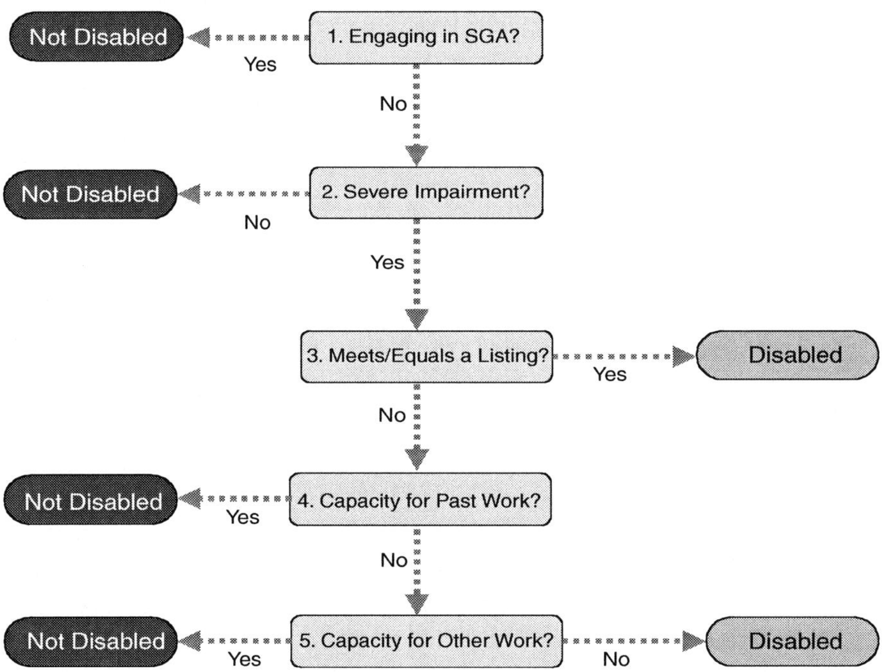

FIGURE 4-2 SSA's five-step sequential disability evaluation process.
SOURCE: 20 CFR §§ 404.1520 and 416.920.

The five-step sequential evaluation process is as follows:

Step 1. Is the individual working and engaging in "substantial gainful activity"?

- If so, the individual is not disabled. The claim is denied and there is no further evaluation.
- If not, no decision is made and the evaluation proceeds to step 2.

Step 2. Does the individual have an impairment or combination of impairments that significantly limits his or her physical or mental ability to do basic work activities?

- If not, the individual is not disabled. The claim is denied and there is no further evaluation.
- If so, no decision is made and the evaluation proceeds to step 3.

Step 3. Does the individual have an impairment(s) that meets or equals the severity of an impairment listed in the Listings (Appendix 1 of subpart P of part 404 of SSA's regulations)?

- If so, the individual is disabled. The claim is allowed and there is no further evaluation. If not, no decision is made and the evaluation proceeds to step 4.

Step 4. Considering the individual's residual functional capacity (RFC) and the physical and mental demands of the work he or she did in the past, does the individual's impairment(s) prevent him or her from doing past relevant work?

- If not, the individual is not disabled. The claim is denied and there is no further evaluation.
- If so, no decision is made and the evaluation proceeds to step 5.

Step 5. Considering the individual's RFC, age, education, and past work experience, is he or she able to do any other work?

- If so, the individual is not disabled. The claim is denied.
- If not, the individual is disabled. The claim is allowed.

The third step of the five-step sequential evaluation relies on the Listing of Impairments (the Listings) to identify cases that will be allowed. The Listings describe impairments that SSA considers severe enough to prevent an individual from doing "any gainful activity."[5] The "any gainful activity" standard is a stricter standard (i.e., a higher degree of impairment severity)

---

[5]20 CFR 404.1525 and 416.925.

than the "any substantial gainful activity" standard in the definition of disability.

DISABILITY DECISIONS OUTCOMES AND THE SEQUENTIAL EVALUATION PROCESS

In 2003 (the most recent year for which complete data for both programs are available), SSA made favorable medical decisions on 37 percent of the initial claims filed under either SSDI or SSDI/SSI concurrently and on 38 percent of the SSI-only claims. After the appeals process, in which additional allowances were made, the favorable medical decision rates were 53 and 46 percent for SSDI and SSI, respectively. However, because a substantial percentage of claims were pending, the allowance rates on appeal are probably understated and will rise as the remaining 2003 claims complete all appeals. In recent years, the eventual overall allowance rate has been more than 60 percent for SSDI cases and more than 50 percent for SSI cases (SSA, 2006b:Tables 53, 54; 2005a:Table 53, 54).

For the same year, SSA allowed benefits for SSDI and SSDI/SSI concurrent cases on the basis of the Listings in 44 percent of allowances and on the basis of medical/vocational factors in 42 percent of allowances. For adult SSI claims, 46 percent of the allowances were based on the Listings and 36 percent on the basis of medical/vocational factors. (The remaining allowances—14 percent of SSDI and 19 percent of adult SSI—were applications for which the disability was previously established or the basis for the determination unknown. The majority of "unknown" cases were allowed at or above the hearing level.)

SSA denied benefits for SSDI cases for insufficient impairment severity or duration in 17 percent of the denials, for capacity to do usual past work in 28 percent of denials, and for capacity to do other type of work in 31 percent of denials. For adult SSI cases, 12 percent of the denials were based on insufficient impairment severity or duration, 22 percent on ability to do past work, and 35 percent on ability to other work. (The remaining denials—24 percent of SSDI and 31 percent of adult SSI—were based on a variety of other causes, such as insufficient evidence, failure to cooperate, and cases at or above the hearing level in which the basis of the denial is unknown; SSA, 2006b:Tables 57, 58; 2005a:57, 58). See Figure 4-3.

The percentage of allowances based on meeting or equaling the Listings varied widely from condition to condition (Figure 4-4). Conditions in which allowances are based mostly on the Listings (i.e., on the left side of Figure 4-4) include malignancies, such as melanoma, pancreatic cancer, and lung cancer; ALS; Down syndrome; deafness; blindness; chronic renal failure; and spinal cord injury. Conditions in which about half the allowances are based on the Listings include Parkinson's disease; congenital

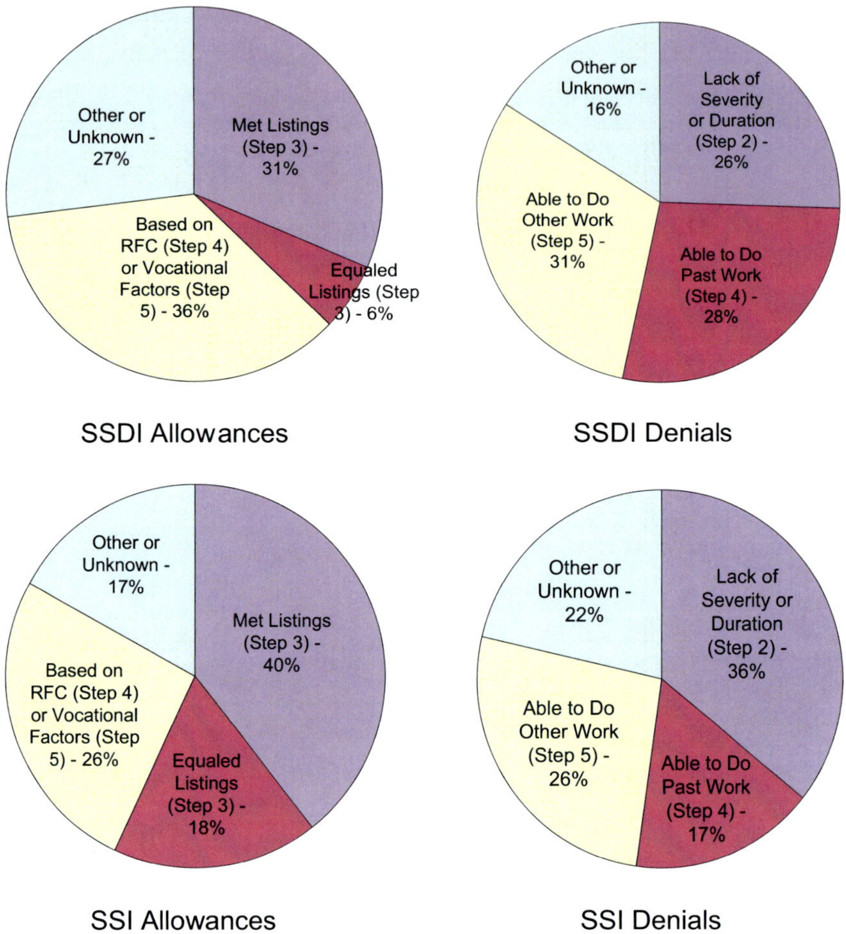

FIGURE 4-3 Bases for allowances and denials, by program segment, 2003.
NOTE: Totals may not equal 100 percent because of rounding.
SOURCE: SSA, 2005a:124-126, 2006b:131-132.

heart anomalies; and many of the mental disorders, such as organic mental, somatoform, personality, and anxiety-related disorders. Conditions on the right side of the figure, such as back and other musculoskeletal disorders, osteoarthritis, diabetes mellitus, and chronic ischemic heart disease are not usually allowed at the Listings step (6, 8, 13, and 18 percent of the time, respectively).

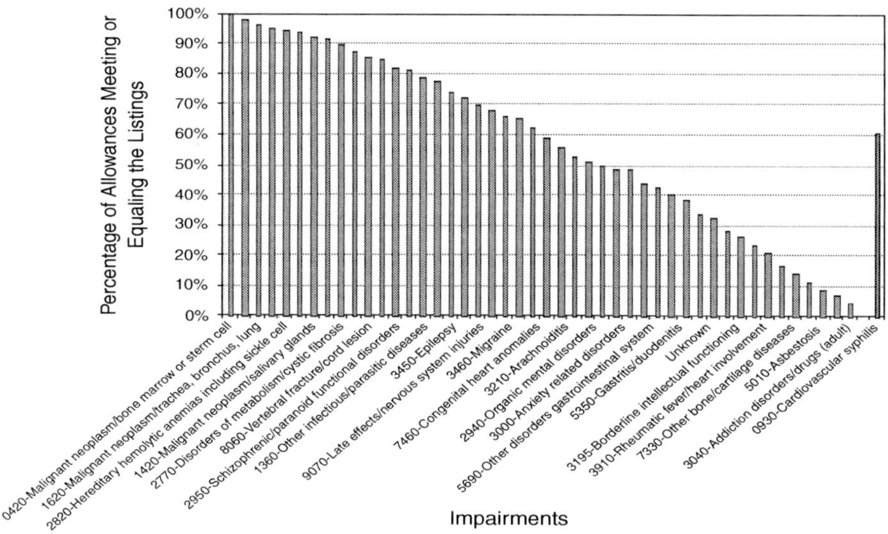

FIGURE 4-4 Percentage of allowances made on the basis of meeting or equaling the Listings, by selected impairment codes, 2004.
NOTE: The bar on the right denotes the median allowance rate, 61 percent.
SOURCE: Data provided by SSA.

PROBLEMS WITH THE DISABILITY DECISION PROCESS

Problems with SSA's current system for determining eligibility for disability benefits include:

- the length of time it takes to process a claim to completion
- the variability in decision outcomes among different state DDSs, among different Office of Hearings and Appeals (OHA) offices, and between DDSs and OHA
- the high rate at which decisions are reversed on appeal

In recent years, the Government Accountability Office (GAO) has conducted many reviews of SSA's disability programs. Because of SSA's management difficulties—particularly the long disability claim-processing times and inconsistencies in disability decisions across adjudication levels and locations—as well as similar problems experienced by other disability programs, such as those of the Department of Veterans Affairs, GAO added federal disability programs to its list of high-risk government programs in 2003. GAO concluded that concerns about claim-processing time and inconsistency in decisions "raise questions about the fairness, integrity, and cost of these programs" (GAO, 2006:3-4). In addition, the rate at which unfavorable disability decisions are reversed on appeal is higher than comparable reversal rates for other programs providing benefits to disabled persons. For example, at the Veterans Administration between 22 and 26 percent of initial decisions are reversed upon appeal (Lewin, 2001).

Claim-Processing Time

In FY 2006, it took an average of three months (88 days) for DDSs to process initial disability determinations. Processing time for reconsiderations averaged another three months. On average, it took more than a year (483 days) to process requests for hearings and about seven months (203 days) to process requests for appeals council review (SSA, 2005c:71-72). Although these processing times represent a small recent improvement, the process remains lengthy. In 2002, SSA completed an in-depth examination of disability claim-processing time in FY 2001. It found that, if an applicant went through every step of the SSA appeals process, it averaged 1,153 days for a claim to get through the appeals council level of review and receive a decision (SSA, 2002).[6] An update of the study for FY 2004 found that total time in this worst-case situation had been cut by 10 percent to 1,049 days. In actual practice, however, the majority of cases are decided at the initial level and only about 4 percent of initial claims make it all the way to the appeals council (SSA, 2004:17).

In addition to long claim-processing time, there has been an overall upward trend in disability claim filings since 1989 (SSAB, 2006:17) and a corresponding increase in case backlogs. At the DDS initial claim level, case backlogs that totaled less than 300,000 in the late 1980s were nearly 625,000 by 2004. At the ALJ hearing level, the increase has been even more dramatic—from less than 200,000 to more than 700,000 (SSAB, 2006:84-85). By the end of FY 2006, the initial backlog had fallen by 11 percent to 555,000 but the queue for ALJ hearings had grown by 13 percent to 715,000.

Variability in Decision Making

All DDSs throughout the country operate under the same federal procedures for making disability decisions for SSA, yet there is considerable variation among states in decision outcomes. In 2004, the percentage of initial claims allowed by individual state DDSs varied widely, from around 25 percent in low-allowance-rate states such as Tennessee and Mississippi

[6]Approximately 972 days were actual processing time. The other 181 days were the time claimants took to file appeals.

to more than 50 percent in high-allowance-rate states such as Hawaii, New Jersey, and New Hampshire. There is also wide variation in the bases for allowances. In 2003, initial claims were allowed based on meeting the Listings in less than 35 percent of the initial favorable decisions in New York, Vermont, and Minnesota. But the same basis was used for allowance in more than 55 percent of the initial favorable decisions in Illinois, South Dakota, Indiana, and Oklahoma. In North Dakota, the figure was almost 65 percent. States like Indiana and Washington found impairments equivalent to the Listings in only 2-3 percent of the allowances. In contrast, Vermont found impairments equivalent to the Listings in more than 21 percent of its allowances.

The percentage of allowances based on the Listings varies less across states in some conditions than in others. The percentage of allowances made for malignant neoplastic disease ranges between 85 and 98 percent across DDSs (Figure 4-5). The range is much wider for mental disorders. The percentage of allowances for mental disorders based on the Listings varies between 36 and 86 percent (Figure 4-6).

Variability in decision making is not limited to allowances. North Carolina denied claims because the claimant had no "severe" impairment in

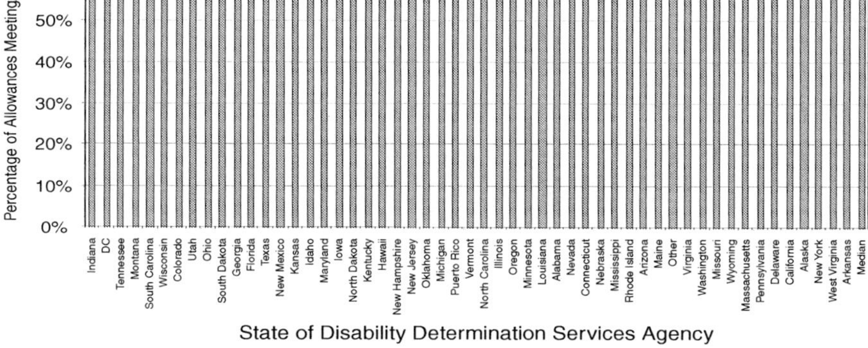

FIGURE 4-5 Percentages of allowances for malignant neoplasms meeting or equaling the Listings, 2004.
SOURCE: Data provided by SSA.

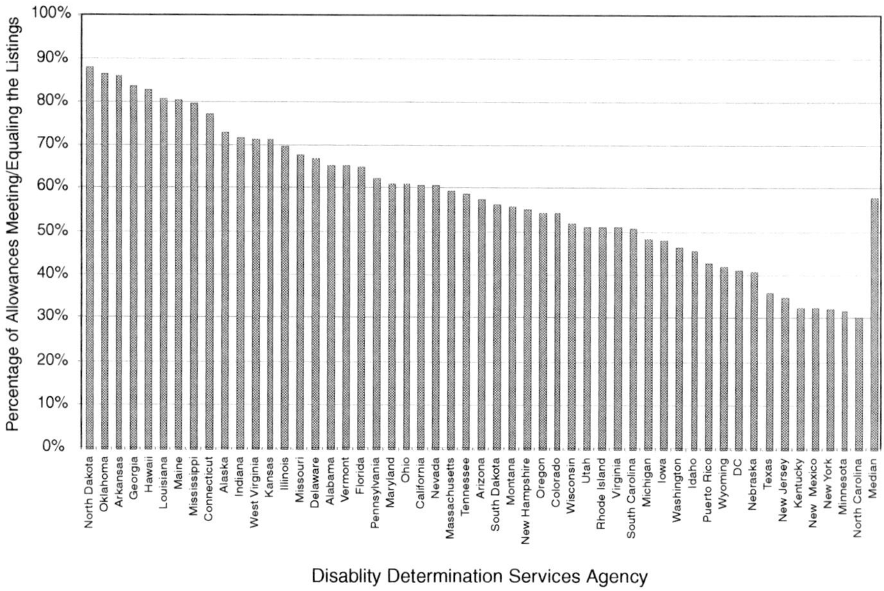

FIGURE 4-6 Percentages of allowances for mental disorders meeting or equaling the Listings, 2004.
SOURCE: Data provided by SSA.

about 5 percent of the initial denials, while Mississippi used the same basis for denial about 32 percent of the time (SSAB, 2006:61-63).

There are also significant state-to-state variations in procedures and administrative arrangements. In 2004, the Vermont DDSs obtained consultative examinations in less than 14 percent of its initial claims, but Tennessee, New York, and Indiana obtained them in more than 60 percent of their initial claims. DDSs "follow State established personnel policies with respect to salaries, benefits and educational requirements; and they do their own hiring, provide most of the training for adjudicators, and establish their own internal quality assurance procedures. Also, reimbursement rates for purchasing medical evidence and diagnostic tests vary from State to State" (SSAB, 2006:7).

ALJs, who decide disability appeals throughout the country, also operate under the same federal rules in making disability decisions. However, data about hearing decision outcomes on a state-by-state basis show considerable variation in outcomes. In 2004, ALJs in Alaska and Louisiana allowed approximately 50 percent of cases, while ALJs in New Hampshire and Connecticut allowed over 80 percent. In addition, there is wide variation in individual ALJ allowance rates (SSAB, 2006:74, 76).

A claimant cannot be awarded disability benefits unless there is a medical basis for his or her impairment. Therefore, SSA relies heavily on medical expertise for claims adjudication. However, not all DDSs or regional appeals offices have access to a full range of medical expertise. For example, according to data supplied to the committee by SSA, in 2004, 29 of 52 DDSs had no medical consultants specializing in cardiology, 28 had no neurologists, and 25 had no orthopedic surgeons or orthopedic specialists.[7] There is also variation in expertise available to provide expert testimony at ALJ hearings. In 2005, for instance, ALJs in the Atlanta region had access to expertise within 41 specialties while ALJs in the Denver region had access to 12.

In 2002, the average salary for a DDS examiner was $40,464, compared with $49,684 for examiners working for the Veterans Benefits Administration (VBA). The average DDS examiner salary was lower than the average VBA examiner salary in 47 states (GAO, 2004:21). A 2004 GAO study reports that two-thirds of interviewed DDS directors felt that noncompetitive pay was contributing to examiner turnover at their agency (GAO, 2004:20). In 2004, minimum salary levels for initial-level DDS examiners varied significantly among the states, with examiners in low-paying states such as Wyoming, North Dakota, and Tennessee making about half that of examiners in high-paying states such as Connecticut and New York (SSAB, 2006:70).

At the field office level, states do not have formal or systematic quality assurance procedures for evaluation of medical information collected on applications for disability. Occasionally, particularly in complex cases or cases being handled by new field office personnel, claims are reviewed by field office management (Lewin, 2001:25). At the DDS level, states are also not required to have internal quality assurance departments or formal quality assurance procedures in place. At minimum, most DDSs perform an end-of-line review of cases, often to measure disability examiner performance. Beyond that, however, there is wide variability in the quality assurance practices among states, and such activities often change in response to specific quality or workload issues (Lewin, 2001:25).

As summarized by the Social Security Advisory Board (SSAB, 2006:7-8):

> Over the years policy makers and administrators have identified many factors, in addition to the inherent subjectivity of the statutory definition of disability, that may affect the consistency of disability decision making. These include:

[7]The 50 states plus the District of Columbia and Puerto Rico.

- economic differences among the States;
- demographic differences among the States;
- differences in health status and access to care;
- State public policy actions (e.g., eliminating general assistance programs; requiring individuals to file for SSA's disability programs as a condition of eligibility for State benefits);
- differences in assessing the accuracy of State decision making among SSA's regional Offices of Quality Assurance;
- differences in quality assurance procedures applied to ALJs and State agencies;
- hearing office differences in administrative practices (e.g., variation in use of and training of vocational and medical experts at ALJ hearings);
- differences in the training given to ALJs and State adjudicators;
- differences in State agency training practices;
- the fact that most claimants are never seen by an adjudicator until they have an ALJ hearing;
- involvement of attorneys and other claimant representatives at the ALJ hearing;
- changes in the adjudicative climate (the "message" sent by SSA, the Congress, or others to those who adjudicate claims);
- rules that allow claimants to introduce new evidence and allegations at each stage of the appeals process;
- lack of clear and unified policy guidance from SSA;
- insufficient funding and staffing for the State agencies and for hearing offices; and
- SSA pressures on State agencies and on ALJs to meet productivity goals.

DISABILITY SERVICE IMPROVEMENT PLAN

In March 2006, SSA issued a final rule implementing a Disability Service Improvement plan. The plan, which SSA began to roll out in August 2006, is intended to "improve the accuracy, consistency, and fairness of [SSA's] disability determination process and to make the right decision as early in the process as possible" (71 FR 16423-16462). Major features of the plan include:

- creating quick disability determination (QDD) units within DDSs to identify individuals who are clearly disabled and to make a favorable determination within 20 days
- establishing a Medical and Vocational Expert System (MVES) to enhance the quality and availability of medical and vocational expertise available to adjudicators
- creating a new federal reviewing official (FRO) position to review DDS initial determinations at the claimant's request

- creating a new decision review board (DRB) to identify and correct errors in decisions and to identify issues that may impede consistent adjudication at all levels of the process

The plan preserves the claimant's right to request and be provided a *de novo* hearing conducted by an ALJ, but it closes the case record after the ALJ issues a decision. In addition, the plan eliminates the current appeals council review step.

Quick Disability Determination (QDD) Units

Under the plan, SSA will use a predictive model to screen incoming claims for cases that have a greater likelihood of allowance. Cases received in the state DDSs that are identified by the predictive model will be sent to the QDD unit within the DDS. The files will then be reviewed by a team consisting of a disability examiner and a medical expert. Although both members of the team will decide the case, the medical expert will verify that medical evidence is sufficient to establish that the claimant meets the standards to be established by SSA. If the evidence is insufficient to make a QDD decision, the case will be returned to the DDS.

Medical and Vocational Expert System (MVES)

The plan also calls for establishing a national network of medical, psychological, and vocational experts who meet qualification standards to be set by SSA. A medical and vocational expert unit (MVEU) will help adjudicators at all levels both find and arrange for expert assistance when needed. The MVEU will maintain a registry of medical, psychological, and vocational experts who meet SSA qualifications. Because SSA is currently transitioning to electronic medical records, adjudicators will be able to use experts from across the country, not just experts available within their region.

Federal Reviewing Officials (FROs)

Instead of the current reconsideration process (in which adjudicative teams within the DDSs reconsider the claims of applicants unsatisfied with their initial determinations), the plan calls for establishing a new FRO position to handle the first level of administrative review. FROs will be attorneys who review initial determinations at the request of claimants. Claimants will be able to submit new evidence at this stage, and the FROs will be able to request more evidence from a state DDS (including clarification of the initial determination), consult with medical experts, and request consultative examinations. FROs will affirm, reverse, or modify DDS decisions, but will not be able to remand cases to DDSs. After a case is developed, an FRO will affirm, deny, or modify the initial determination and notify both the applicant and, for quality assurance purposes, the state DDS of the decision. If an FRO disagrees with the DDS decision, or if new evidence is submitted, he or she will consult with an expert through the MVES.

Decision Review Board (DRB)

The appeals council and its review process will be abolished, and the DRB will be established, composed of experienced ALJs and AAJs appointed by the SSA commissioner. Claimants denied after an ALJ hearing will not be able to initiate appeals to the DRB. Rather, the DRB will select cases for review using a new sampling procedure to identify error-prone or complex ALJ decisions—both allowances and denials.

Claimants will receive notifications that their claims will be reviewed by the DRB along with the ALJ's decision letters. Claimants will be able to submit written statements to the board within 10 days explaining why they agree or disagree with the ALJ's decision. The DRB may affirm, modify, or reject an ALJ's decision, or it may remand a claim back to an ALJ for further review. To improve consistency in disability decision making, a copy of any DRB decision that is in disagreement with the ALJ hearing decision will be sent to the ALJ.

The DRB will have 90 days from the date the claimant was notified that his or case would be reviewed by the DRB to make a decision (this compares with the average time the appeals council takes to complete a case—242 days in FY 2004). If the DRB takes longer, the ALJ's decision will become the final decision, unless there is the possibility of a decision favorable to the claimant. Applicants whose claims are denied by the DRB will be able to seek judicial review. When a claimant disagrees with an ALJ's decision and the case is not selected to go to the DRB, the next level of appeal will be to federal district court.

The DRB will also serve several other functions, including review of claims rejected for hearings, handling cases remanded back to SSA from a federal court for further administrative review, and study of claims post-effectuation for understanding and improvement of the disability decision process.

REFERENCES

Berkowitz, E.D. 1987. *Disabled policy: America's programs for the handicapped.* New York: Cambridge University Press.

GAO (Government Accountability Office). 2004. *Strategic workforce planning needed to address human capital challenges facing the Disability Determination Services.* Washington, DC: GAO. Available: www.gao.gov/new.items/d04121.pdf (accessed April 12, 2006).

GAO. 2006. Statement of Robert E. Robertson, Director, Education, Workforce, and Income Security Issues. *Social Security Administration: Agency is positioning itself to implement its new disability determination process, but key facets are still in development.* Washington, DC: GAO. Available: www.gao.gov/new.items/d06779t.pdf (accessed September 28, 2006).

Hess, A. *Comments at the January 21, 1993 Disability Forum, the Disability Program: Its origins—our heritage. Its future—our challenge.* Available: www.ssa.gov/history/dibforum93.html (accessed November 3, 2005).

Kollmann, G. 2000. *Social Security: Summary of major changes in the cash benefits program.* CRS report RL30565. Washington, DC: Congressional Research Service. May 18, 2000. Available: www.ssa.gov/history/reports/crsleghist2.html (accessed October 6, 2006).

Lewin (The Lewin Group, Pugh Ettinger McCarthy Associations, and Cornell University). 2001. *Evaluation of SSA's disablity quality assurance (QA) processes and development of QA options that will support the long-term management of the disability program.* Final Report Prepared for the Social Security Administration. March 31, 2001. Available: www.lewin.com/NR/rdonlyres/ekhzi4f6bl2iwvway5ibsoerh7acjf6lpnwh3etwt6jd246bw5cdaymmastvdiojiljc7jt3cozp3nosoj56dr2k2zf/1325.pdf (accessed April 6, 2006).

SSA (Social Security Administration). 1996. *A history of the Social Security disability programs.* SSA staff paper produced in 1986. Available: www.ssa.gov/history/1986dibhistory.html (accessed November 3, 2005).

SSA. 2002. *Flow of cases through the disability process.* Available: www.ssa.gov/disability/disability_process_welcome.htm (accessed September 28, 2006).

SSA. 2004. *SSA's FY 2004 performance and accountability report.* Available: www.ssa.gov/finance/2004/Full_FY04_PAR.pdf (accessed April 28, 2006).

SSA. 2005a. *SSI annual statistical report, 2004.* Released September 2005. Available: www.ssa.gov/policy/docs/statcomps/ssi_asr/2004/index.html (accessed May 22, 2006).

SSA. 2005b. *Findings of the disability hearings quality review process.* SSA Pub. No. 30-013. Baltimore, MD: Office of Quality Assurance and Performance Assessment, SSA.

SSA. 2005c. *SSA's performance and accountability report for fiscal year 2005.* Available: www.ssa.gov/finance/2005/FY_05_PAR.pdf (accessed September 29, 2006).

SSA. 2006a. *SSA's performance and accountability report for fiscal year 2006.* Available: www.ssa.gov/finance/2006/FY06_PAR.pdf (accessed December 4, 2006).

SSA. 2006b. *Annual statistical report on the Social Security Disability Insurance Program, 2004.* SSA Publication 13-11826. Released March 2006. Available: www.ssa.gov/policy/docs/statcomps/di_asr/2004/index.html (accessed May 22, 2006).

SSAB (Social Security Advisory Board). 2006. *Disability decisionmaking: Data and materials.* Available: www.ssab.gov/documents/chartbook.pdf (accessed September 28, 2006).

5

The Listing of Impairments—Overview

The Listings serve as a screening tool at the initial decision stage to expedite the identification of individuals whose impairments clearly more than equal the level of severity that defines disability in the Social Security Act. Quick identification of obvious cases deserving benefits permits the Social Security Administration (SSA) to avoid a time-consuming and resource-intensive inquiry into all of the case facts. Using the Listings as an administrative expedient, SSA is able to process more cases more quickly and cost effectively than it would otherwise. As SSA explained in a February 10, 1994, final regulation, *Revised Medical Criteria for Determination of Disability, Cardiovascular System* (59 FR 6468):

> The listings are intended to be a screening device by which we can identify and allow claims filed by the most obviously disabled individuals; they are not an all-inclusive list of disabilities under which all individuals must be found disabled.

In addition to efficiency, the Listings are intended to ensure that there is a medical basis for the disability and that all applicants receive equal treatment. As noted by SSA in a more recent regulatory notice from November 2001, *Revised Medical Criteria for Determination of Disability, Musculoskeletal System and Related Criteria* (66 FR 58010):

> The Listings contain examples of some of the most frequently encountered impairments in the disability program. The criteria include specific symptoms, signs, and laboratory findings that are considered to characterize

> impairments severe enough to prevent a person from doing any gainful activity. . . . The Listings help to ensure that determinations and decisions regarding disability have a sound medical basis, that claimants receive equal treatment through the use of specific criteria, and that people who are disabled can be readily identified and awarded benefits if all other factors of entitlement or eligibility are met.

In addition to providing equal treatment for all applicants, the Listings were intended to ensure adjudicative consistency:

> In the fall of 1959, only 3 years after the program was enacted, the Ways and Means Subcommittee on the Administration of the Social Security Program (the Harrison Subcommittee) held a series of hearings that focused in part on variation in decision making among the States. During these hearings, the Social Security Administration's Deputy Commissioner, George Wyman, told the Subcommittee that the objective of achieving reasonable consistency represented "a real challenge." However, as explained by former Commissioner of Social Security Robert Ball, who at that time was Deputy Director of the Bureau of Old-Age and Survivors Insurance, the agency had developed a set of medical guidelines for use in adjudication. These guides were developed for the express purpose of achieving "as high degree of equity in the application of this law across the country as possible" (SSAB, 2006:2).

The Listings are organized by 14 major body systems (e.g., musculoskeletal impairments, respiratory impairments, neurological impairments). There are separate listings for adults (part A of the Listings) and children (part B of the Listings), although the adult criteria can be applied to children if the disease processes have a similar effect on adults and children. Altogether, there are more than 100 listed impairments.

For each body system, the Listings begin with a narrative introduction that defines key concepts used in that body system. The introduction also identifies specific medical findings that may be required to show the existence of an impairment listed in that section. Symptoms alone cannot be the basis for establishing the existence of an impairment. The introduction is followed by the "Category of Impairments" section, which includes the specific criteria (medical signs, symptoms, and laboratory findings) that describe the required level of severity for each impairment listed in that body system. Although a few listings (e.g., certain cancers, amyotrophic lateral sclerosis) are evaluated based on diagnosis alone, most require a diagnosis in conjunction with some sort of assessment of impairment severity, either by the presence of specific clinical findings or by some sort of assessment of functional outcomes.

If the evidence in a case establishes the presence of all the criteria required by one of the impairment listings, then the individual "meets" (i.e., matches) that specific listing. However, even if the evidence does not show that an individual meets the exact requirements of a particular listing, the individual can still be found disabled at step 3 of the sequence if his or her impairment is equal in severity to the requirements of a listing, referred to as "medical equivalence."

Medical equivalence to a listing is established if the medical findings are at least equal in severity and duration to the listed findings. SSA compares the signs, symptoms, and laboratory findings in the medical evidence with the listing criteria for the individual's impairment (or the listed impairment most like the individual's impairment). If the individual has a combination of impairments, all of the medical findings of the combined impairments are compared to the most closely related listed impairment. However, medical equivalence cannot be established merely because an individual has many impairments. Medical equivalence is evaluated based on not only the medical evidence, but also on consideration of a designated physician's medical judgment about equivalence (20 CFR §§ 404.1526 and 416.926; Social Security Ruling 86-8: Titles II and XVI: The Sequential Evaluation Process). See Box 5-1 for an illustration of how SSA applies the Listings.

ORIGINS AND DEVELOPMENT OF THE LISTINGS

SSA's first experience with implementation of a disability benefit program occurred well before the Disability Freeze program in 1954 or the Disability Insurance Benefits Program in 1956. It came with the Civilian War Benefit (CWB) program, which was established in the early 1940s by executive, rather than legislative, action. CWB provided for payment of disability and medical benefits to civilians injured in the war effort. The disability benefit covered permanent, temporary, total, and partial disabilities. The disability evaluation policies and procedures included a list of conditions that automatically qualified an individual for permanent total disability benefits:

> Under CWB, an applicant was presumptively entitled to permanent total disability benefits if he/she suffered any of the following conditions:
>
> 1. Loss of both feet, or permanent loss of use of both feet;
> 2. Loss of both hands, or permanent loss of use of both hands;
> 3. Loss of one hand and one foot, or permanent loss of use of one hand and one foot;
> 4. Permanent loss of vision; or
> 5. Any disability which requires the individual to be permanently bedridden.

Box 5-1 How SSA Uses the Listings

Listings Example—Peripheral Arterial Disease

If "Susan" applies for disability insurance benefits, alleging that she is unable to work due to the effects of peripheral arterial disease, SSA first determines whether she meets the nondisability requirements for entitlement (e.g., sufficient work credit for disability insurance coverage). Assuming that the nondisability requirements are met, SSA evaluates her disability status, using the five-step sequential evaluation process.

If she is not working at substantial gainful activity (step 1) and has an impairment that significantly limits her ability to perform basic work activities (step 2), SSA determines whether her impairment meets the requirements of the Listings.

Peripheral arterial disease is evaluated in the "cardiovascular" body system, in section 4.00 of the Listings. For peripheral arterial disease, listed in section 4.12, the specific requirements are:

4.12 Peripheral arterial disease, as determined by appropriate medically acceptable imaging (see 4.00A3d, 4.00G2, 4.00G5, and 4.00G6), causing intermittent claudication (see 4.00G1) and one of the following:

A. Resting ankle/brachial systolic blood pressure ratio of less than 0.50, OR
B. Decrease in systolic blood pressure at the ankle on exercise (see 4.00G7a and 4.00C16—4.00C17) of 50 percent or more of pre-exercise level and requiring 10 minutes or more to return to pre-exercise level, OR
C. Resting toe systolic pressure of less than 30 mm Hg (see 4.00G7c and 4.00G8), OR
D. Resting toe/brachial systolic blood pressure ratio of less than 0.40 (see 4.00G7c).

SSA compares Susan's medical records to these specific requirements. To meet these requirements, the medical records must first establish the existence of peripheral arterial disease, using "medically acceptable imaging." The listing shows, in the introductory text to the listing section, where the specific imaging requirements are to be found (in sections 4.00A3D, 4.00G2, 4.00G5, and 4.00G6). In addition, the impairment must cause "intermittent claudication." The listing also shows where in the introductory text that requirement is explained. Finally, the evidence must document one of four specific clinical findings (blood pressure readings) that indicate impairment severity, described in subsections A, B, C, and D.

If the medical records show that all these requirements are met, SSA determines that Susan is disabled without evaluating her work capacity, age, education, or work experience.

SOURCE: CFR chapter 20, part 404, subpart P, appendix 1, section 4.00.

The rating schedule for evaluating disability was organized according to six body systems (DeWitt, 1997):

- musculoskeletal
- organs of special sense
- the nose and throat
- scars and disfigurements
- neuropsychiatric disabilities
- dental and oral disabilities

Although the full extent to which these CWB provisions served as a model for later disability evaluation procedures is unclear, there is an obvious similarity between the CWB approach and the process that eventually became know as the Listings.

Later, as SSA staff worked on procedures to process large numbers of disability applications throughout the late 1940s, they fixed on a process that involved classifying applicants into eight groups according to disability severity. The most severely impaired were assigned to Group I, and the least severely affected placed in Group VIII. Later, the number of groups was reduced from eight to six, with each group including several examples of the kinds of impairments expected in the group. For Group I, total disability was considered automatic. The list of impairment examples (cited in Cowles, 2005:5-6) was:

- advanced pulmonary tuberculosis
- congestive heart failure
- aneurysm of aorta or branches
- myocardial infarction
- bronchiectasis
- colitis
- nephritis
- tuberculosis (kidneys)
- any cardiac lesion classified under Class IV (American Heart Association grouping)
- leukemia
- cerebral accident
- multiple sclerosis
- pellagra
- inoperable malignancies
- osteomyelitis of pelvis or vertebra
- tuberculosis of hip, spine, or larynx
- bronchial asthma

Shortly after the Disability Freeze program was established by the Social Security Amendments of 1954, SSA appointed a 15-member medical advisory committee, which "recommended the issuance of evaluation guides and standards setting forth medical criteria for the evaluation of specific impairments with the degree of severity prescribed for each. The panel also suggested that factors such as age, education, training and experience may be important in the evaluation of disability, even though the law [at that time] did not specifically require consideration of these factors" (SSA, 1996). These evaluation guides later came to be known as the "Listing of Impairments."

From the beginning, the guides were conceived as a way to quickly identify allowance cases without performing a comprehensive analysis of an individual's capacity to work:

> . . . we recognized that there were going to be a vast majority of the cases that might be pretty cut and dried on the medical evidence and where you didn't have to go into vocational issues. And we wanted to find a way to get people through the listings and get them on. The listings were not intended administratively to close the case and foreclose the consideration of capacity to work and substantial activity of one kind or another. But the listings were a scrape to get people in (Hess, 1993).

There was also an expectation that the Listings would apply in the vast majority of the cases, thus allowing the most efficient adjudication of large numbers of claims, as well as uniformity in adjudication:

> . . . we are faced with the need to adjudicate more cases in a short period of time than ever attempted by insurance companies or any other disability organization, including the Federal Government. The gross numbers, coupled with the operational complexities that arise when 48 States participate in the adjudicative process, demand a method which would assure reasonable uniformity in adjudication and which lends itself to a mass process. The proposed Guide lists impairments under medical diagnostic headings with a degree of severity for each that, if met, would allow a finding that an individual not actually working is unable to work. . . . While it is recognized that some people with the scheduled disability will engage in substantial gainful activity, the severity should be pitched at a level where experience shows us the majority cannot. These standards may then permit relatively quick decisions in 85 to 90 percent of all cases. If so, the Guide will be worthwhile, because it will have screened out the cases, one way or the other, where it is not necessary to go deeply into individualized adjudication, beyond the medical picture (SSA, 1955:6).

Nevertheless, these guides were still supposed to allow some leeway for the exercise of professional judgment. Listings were not to be applied mechanically, and decision makers were expected to exercise judgment and arrive at decisions only after considering all the facts in the case (Cowles, 2005). Thus, the Listings were originally illustrative, rather than determinative.

The first Listings were fairly brief. They were organized into 10 categories according to body system, similar to the Veterans Administration's 1945 Schedule for Rating Disabilities:

- musculoskeletal system
- special sense organs
- respiratory system
- cardiovascular system
- digestive system
- genito-urinary system
- hemic and lymphatic system
- skin
- endocrine system
- nervous system, including neurology and psychiatry

Each section began with a general introduction, followed by the specific Listing criteria, which focused more on the clinical criteria for diagnoses than functional consequences (Cowles, 2005:9).

This focus on "objective" clinical criteria reflected some of the same concerns that framed the debate during the 1940s about establishing a disability program in the first place, and it compelled adoption of a definition of disability that relied heavily on objective medical evidence. "A strict, medically based definition of disability was considered necessary to avoid payment of unnecessary claims, thus keeping down costs; with an emphasis on objective medical evidence, as opposed to subjective symptoms, it was thought that decision making would be easier and more accurate" (Bloch, 1992:91). As explained by the 1948 Advisory Council on Social Security:

> To qualify for benefits, a disabled person would have to be incapable of self-support for an indefinite period—permanently and totally disabled. He would have to be unable, by reason of a disability medically demonstrable by objective tests, to perform any substantially gainful activity. . . .
>
> Benefits should be paid to an insured individual who is permanently and totally disabled. A "permanent and total disability" for the purpose of this program should mean any disability which is medically demonstrable by objective tests, which prevents the worker from performing any substantially gainful activity, and which is likely to be of long-continued and indefinite duration. . . .

> The definition of "disability" used in a disability program will in large part determine the feasibility of administration and the costs of the program. The proposed definition is designed to establish a test of disability which will operate as a safeguard against unjustified claims. It is an administratively practicable test and it will facilitate the evaluation of permanent and total disabilities.
>
> The Council recommends that compensable disabilities be restricted to those which can be objectively determined by medical examination or tests. In this way, the problems involved in the adjudication of claims based on purely subjective symptoms can be avoided. Unless demonstrable by objective tests, such ailments as lumbago, rheumatism, and various nervous disorders would not be compensable. The danger of malingering which might be involved in connection with such claims would thereby be avoided (Advisory Council on Social Security, 1948:71, 74).

Although the medically based Listings were a logical outgrowth of the medically based definition of disability eventually established in the 1954 Amendments to the Social Security Act (which had its origin in the 1948 advisory council report), nothing in the law has ever required SSA to have these kinds of guides or Listings. They were developed by SSA as an administrative tool to increase the efficiency of case processing. As SSA noted in a November 2001 final regulation, *Revised Medical Criteria for Determination of Disability, Musculoskeletal System and Related Criteria* (responding to a public comment that claimed that SSA's proposed listing criteria were inconsistent with the Social Security Act, in 66 FR 58027):

> The [Social Security] Act does not, in fact, make any provision for the listings at all. The listings are an administrative convenience established by regulation to identify obviously disabled individuals.

EVOLUTION OF THE LISTINGS

For many years after they were first devised in 1955, the Listings did not appear anywhere in SSA's disability regulations or other public information. Policy makers were concerned that widespread knowledge of the specific disability criteria could compromise program integrity:

> . . . we didn't want to give those listings out to the public generally . . . we told the State agencies and we ourselves said these listings are not to be made public because they are the key to the bank. And doctors and litigators and others would know what the listings were. And it's easy to write up a medical report. I don't mean it's a fraudulent medical report that is slanted in terms of highlighting those manifestations (Hess, 1993).

Instead, the regulations included a brief list of examples of the kinds of impairments that might be considered disabling, while the actual Listings were only contained in the agency's internal operating instructions. Following passage of the Freedom of Information Act in 1966, SSA began making the Listings available to the public by publishing them in its regulations. The first such publication occurred on August 20, 1968 (33 FR 11749).

Between 1955 and 1967, when the Listings existed only in agency operating instructions, they were revised frequently, since they were "being developed based on operating experience" (Program Operations Manual System [POMS], section DI 34101.005). The last version of the Listings before their publication in the regulations (dated July 4, 1967) is still preserved in the SSA operating manual (POMS DI 34101.015). By 1967, the Listings had expanded considerably and evolved from a relatively short set of criteria that relied primarily on diagnoses and "disease specifications" to a much more elaborate set of standards that relied on specific observations, "highly-specific criteria involving signs, symptoms and laboratory findings," and functional outcomes (Cowles, 2005:9, 12, 13).

Another major development in the evolution of the Listings also occurred in 1968. The 1967 Amendments to the Social Security Act (Public Law [P.L.] 90-248) established a new disability benefit for widows and widowers age 50 and above. This benefit was based on a new, more restrictive definition of disability. To qualify, the widow or widower had to be unable to engage in any "gainful activity" (as compared with the standard for the existing disability program—inability to engage in *substantial* gainful activity). The new widows/widowers test was "based on the medical severity of the impairment and . . . not . . . on non-medical factors and work activity" (U.S. House of Representatives, 1974:118). The law required SSA to define this higher degree of severity by regulation, and SSA decided that the Listings represented the degree of severity contemplated in the law (SSA, 1968). Despite the fact that the widows/widowers disability standard was later revised to equal the degree of severity required for disability insurance benefits (in the 1990 Amendments to the Social Security Act, the Omnibus Budget Reconciliation Act of 1990 [P.L. 101-508]), "listing-level severity" has continued to represent a higher degree of severity than the statutory definition of disability (i.e., inability to engage in any gainful activity vs. inability to engage in any substantial gainful activity).

The first significant revision to the Listings after 1968 occurred in 1977, when SSA published a new set of listings criteria that would apply to children under the age of 18 who were applying for Supplemental Security Income benefits (42 FR 14705). In 1979, SSA issued a comprehensive update and revision of all the adult Listings (44 FR 18170).

In 1984, Congress directed SSA to revise its mental disorders listing criteria (Section 5(a) of P.L. 98-460, The Disability Benefits Reform Act of 1984). These revisions, which were published in the regulations on August 28, 1985 (50 FR 35038), marked the first time that SSA included an expiration date for any listing. The adult mental disorders listings were to expire three years from their effective date. As SSA explained in its *Federal Register* notice, ". . . [t]he dynamic nature of the diagnosis, evaluation and treatment of the mental disease process requires that the rules in this area be periodically revised and updated" (50 FR 35038).

Later that year, SSA updated listings for most of the remaining body systems and added expiration dates for all the other body systems. Although the law does not require SSA to periodically update the criteria in the Listings, SSA noted in its December 6, 1985, *Federal Register* notice (50 FR 50068):

> Medical advancements in disability evaluation and treatment and program experience require that these listings be periodically reviewed and updated. . . . We intend to carefully monitor these listings over the period prescribed for each body system to ensure that they continue to meet program purposes. When changes are found to be warranted, the listings for that body system will be updated in the Federal Register again. Therefore, during the periods ranging from 4 to 8 years after the date of publication of these final rules, the listings under each body system will cease to be effective on the specified dates unless extended or revised and promulgated again.

The 1985 updates (which took effect in January 1986) were the last comprehensive revision to the Listings. Since then, SSA has focused on updates that are more targeted—addressing a single body system or even individual listings. According to the Government Accountability Office (GAO), SSA's Listings update activities were curtailed in the mid-1990s due to staff shortages, competing priorities, and lack of adequate research (GAO, 2002:7).

One of the competing priorities in the mid-1990s was the agency's effort to fundamentally redesign the disability decision-making process through business process reengineering—an initiative that became known as "disability redesign." One component of the disability redesign was a project to develop a new approach to making disability decisions to replace the existing sequential evaluation process (SSA, 1994). However, by 1999, SSA had undertaken an internal reassessment of its disability initiatives and was no longer pursuing a new decision-making process. Rather, it had decided to focus on improving the current process and had resumed efforts to update the Listings (IOM and NRC, 2002).

Since that time, SSA has completed a number of revisions and updates to specific sections of the Listings, including:

- Revised Medical Criteria for Determination of Disability, Endocrine System and Related Criteria (64 FR 46122, August 24, 1999)
- Addition of Medical Criteria for Evaluating Down Syndrome in Adults (65 FR 31800, May 19, 2000)

• Revised Medical Criteria for Evaluating Mental Disorders and Traumatic Brain Injury (65 FR 50745, August 21, 2000)

• Supplemental Security Income; Determining Disability for a Child Under Age 18 (65 FR 54747, September 11, 2000) [included limited revisions to the childhood listings]

• Revised Medical Criteria for Determination of Disability, Musculoskeletal System and Related Criteria (66 FR 58009, November 19, 2001)

• Technical Revisions to Medical Criteria for Determinations of Disability (67 FR 20018, April 24, 2002)

• Revised Medical Criteria for Evaluating Amyotrophic Lateral Sclerosis (68 FR 51689, August 28, 2003)

• Revised Medical Criteria for Evaluating Skin Disorders (69 FR 32260, June 9, 2004)

• Revised Medical Criteria for Evaluating Hematological Disorders and Malignant Neoplastic Diseases (69 FR 67017, November 15, 2004)

• Revised Medical Criteria for Evaluating Genitourinary Impairments (70 FR 38582, July 5, 2005)

• Revised Medical Criteria for Evaluating Impairments That Affect Multiple Body Systems (70 FR 51252, August 30, 2005)

• Revised Medical Criteria for Evaluating Cardiovascular Impairments (71 FR 2311, January 13, 2006)

SSA has also initiated, but at the time of this report had not yet completed, several other Listings revisions, including:

• Revised Medical Criteria for Evaluating Growth Impairments (65 FR 37321, June 14, 2000 and 70 FR 53323, September 8, 2005)

• Revised Medical Criteria for Evaluating Impairments of the Digestive System (66 FR 57009, November 14, 2001, and 69 FR 64702, November 8, 2004)

• Revised Medical Criteria for Evaluating Mental Disorders (68 FR 12639, March 17, 2003)

• Revised Medical Criteria for Evaluating Immune System Disorders (68 FR 24896, May 9, 2003)

• Revised Medical Criteria for Evaluating Neurological Impairments (70 FR 19356, April 13, 2005)

• Revised Medical Criteria for Evaluating Respiratory System Disorders (70 FR 19358, April 13, 2005)

• Revised Medical Criteria for Evaluating Hearing Impairments and Disturbance of Labyrinthine-Vestibular Function (70 FR 19353, April 13, 2005)

• New Medical Criteria for Evaluating Language and Speech Disorders (70 FR 19351, April 13, 2005)

• Revised Medical Criteria for Evaluating Endocrine Disorders (70 FR 46792, August 11, 2005)

• Revised Medical Criteria for Evaluating Visual Disorders (70 FR 48342, August 17, 2005)

REFERENCES

Advisory Council on Social Security. 1948. *Recommendations for Social Security legislation. The reports of the Advisory Council on Social Security to the Senate Committee on Finance. Part 2, Permanent and total disability.* Available: www.ssa.gov/history/pdf/48advise6.pdf (accessed May 20, 2006).

Bloch, F.S. 1992. *Disability determination: The administrative process and the role of the medical professional.* West London, CT: Greenwood Press.

Cowles, A. 2005. *History of the disability listings.* Available: www.ssa.gov/history/DisabilityListings.html (accessed November 3, 2005).

DeWitt, L. 1997. *The Civilian War Benefits Program: SSA's first disability program.* Available: www.ssa.gov/history/civilwar.html (accessed November 3, 2005).

GAO (Government Accountability Office). 2002. Social Security Administration: Fully updating disability criteria has implications for program design. Testimony before the Subcommittee on Social Security, Committee on Ways and Means, House of Representatives. GAO-02-919T. July 11, 2002. Available: www.gao.gov/new.items/d02919t.pdf (accessed November 17, 2005).

Hess, A. 1993. Comments at the January 21, 1993 Disability Forum, The disability program: Its origins—our heritage. Its future—our challenge. Available: www.ssa.gov/history/dibforum93.html (accessed November 3, 2005).

IOM and NRC (Institute of Medicine and National Research Council). 2002. *The dynamics of disability: Measuring and monitoring disability for Social Security programs,* edited by G.S. Wunderlich, D.P. Rice, and N.L. Amado. Washington, DC: National Academy Press.

SSA (Social Security Administration). 1955. *Summary report: Medical Advisory Committee meeting, February 9-10, 1955.* Social Security Administration History Archives, Baltimore, MD.

SSA. 1968. SSA program circular on disability insurance. *Disability regulations—The listing of impairments.* May 6, 1968.

SSA. 1994. *Plan for a new disability claim process.* SSA Publication Number 01-005. Washington, DC: U.S. Government Printing Office.

SSA. 1996. *A history of the Social Security disability programs, January 1986.* Available: www.ssa.gov/history/1986dibhistory.html (accessed November 3, 2005).

SSAB (Social Security Advisory Board). 2006. *Disability decisionmaking: Data and materials.* Available: www.ssab.gov/documents/chartbook.pdf (accessed September 28, 2006).

U.S. House of Representatives, Committee on Ways and Means. 1974. *Committee staff report on the Disability Insurance Program.* Available: www.ssa.gov/history/pdf/dibreport.pdf (accessed November 3, 2005).

6

The Listing of Impairments—Issues

The Social Security Administration (SSA) has asked the committee to make recommendations on how to improve the Listings, specifically addressing:

1. The value and utility of the current Listings for all users (claimants, SSA, health care professionals, state offices, and officials involved in the adjudication process)
2. Conceptual models for organizing the Listings, beyond the current "body systems" model at 20 CFR, Part 404, Subpart P, Appendix I
3. Processes for determining when the Listings require revision and criteria upon which to add new listings or remove old ones
4. Feedback mechanisms to continuously assess and evaluate the Listings for the purpose of improving consistency in application by all adjudicators throughout the country
5. Adaptability of the Listings, including methods to account for variable access to health care services (including diagnostics and pharmaceuticals) in determining whether an individual's condition meets or equals the Listings
6. Methods to assess and quantify the effects of multiple impairments that may not individually cross the eligibility threshold (i.e., SSA's "equivalence" concept)
7. Advisability of and methods for integrating functional assessment into the Listings

In subsequent discussions with the committee, SSA made clear that its concerns focus on three major areas:

- The value and validity of the Listings as a screening tool
- Use of functional criteria in the Listings
- The process of updating and revising the Listings

THE LISTINGS AS A SCREENING TOOL

As discussed previously, the Listings are an administrative expedient. They are intended to make the decision-making process more expeditious and more efficient by identifying a portion of the allowance cases early in the process, without engaging in a time-consuming and resource-intensive inquiry into all of the issues that would otherwise be required.

Case-processing time is a major concern for SSA. The agency has made reduction of case-processing time one of its key goals for improved customer service, as reflected in the very first strategic objective in its Strategic Plan for FY 2006-FY 2011: "Make the Right Decision in the Disability Process as Early as Possible." As SSA explains in the Strategic Plan (SSA, 2006:8-9):

> In light of the significant growth in disability claims, the increased complexity of those claims, and the younger age of beneficiaries in recent years, the need to make substantial changes in the Agency's disability determination process has become urgent. The length of time it now takes to process these claims is unacceptable. It places a significant physical, financial, and emotional burden on applicants and their families. It also leads to recontacts, and rehandling, thus placing an enormous drain on Agency resources.
>
> According to the Agency's service delivery assessment of the disability process conducted in 2001, persons pursuing their disability claims through all levels of Agency appeal wait an average of 1,153 days for that final decision. . . .
>
> The most significant external factors affecting the Social Security Administration's ability to improve service to disability applicants are the dramatic growth of workloads and the increasing complexity of those workloads. Receipts will continue to rise as more baby boomers enter their disability-prone and then retirement years. With Disability Insurance rolls projected to grow 35 percent in the ten years ending 2012, the Social Security Administration cannot keep doing things the same way. Moreover, the type of impairments that have formed the basis for disability claims have changed over the years. The percentage of claims involving allegations of mental impairments has increased dramatically, particularly in the Supplemental Security Income program. Claims of disability involving mental impair-

> ments raise particular administrative resource issues because they involve complex psychological issues and the evidence for these claims may be difficult to develop. The percentage of disability claims decided on the basis of vocational considerations rather than more readily determinable medical factors have also been increasing steadily. Thus, in addition to the growth in the number of claims, there has been a corresponding increase in the volume of complex claims.

Concerns with claim-processing time have also been an important factor in a major SSA initiative to revise the administrative review process. First announced in testimony before the Subcommittee on Social Security of the House Committee on Ways and Means on September 25, 2003, the plan proposed to implement a new "quick decision step" at the very beginning of the initial claim process, which would sort cases based on the existence of various medical conditions, and promote early identification of individuals who are obviously disabled (Barnhart, 2003). These new procedures are explained more fully in final rules published in the *Federal Register* on March 31, 2006 (71 FR 16424).

In meetings with the committee, SSA staff discussed the agency's concerns about the declining utility of the Listings as a quick screening tool and the resulting increase in case-processing time and cost. They said that at one time the Listings were used to identify up to 80 percent of the allowance cases at the initial decision level. However, the Listings currently identify only about 50 percent of allowances (Sklar, 2005a). As a result of this decrease, fewer allowance cases are processed quickly, contributing to larger caseloads, longer average case-processing time, and higher case-processing costs.

Historically, SSA has based most allowances on meeting or equaling the criteria in the Listings. In the earliest days of the disability program, the Listings accounted for more than 90 percent of the initial allowances (SSAB, 2003:7). As recently as the early 1980s, they were the basis for 70 to 80 percent of the initial allowances. Since then, use of the Listings has declined steadily, accounting for less than 60 percent of allowances in 2000 (SSAB, 2001:5). According to more recent data supplied to the committee by SSA, reliance on the Listings as the basis for allowance at the initial level has continued to decline. In 2004, the Listings accounted for 52 percent of the initial allowances (Figure 6-1).

Validity is another major concern. SSA does not want to expedite the decision process by approving some cases with less scrutiny if the screen is not able to distinguish between claims that meet the SSA definition of disability and those that do not. Neither type of error would be acceptable: either granting benefits to individuals who are not actually disabled or denying benefits to those who are disabled.

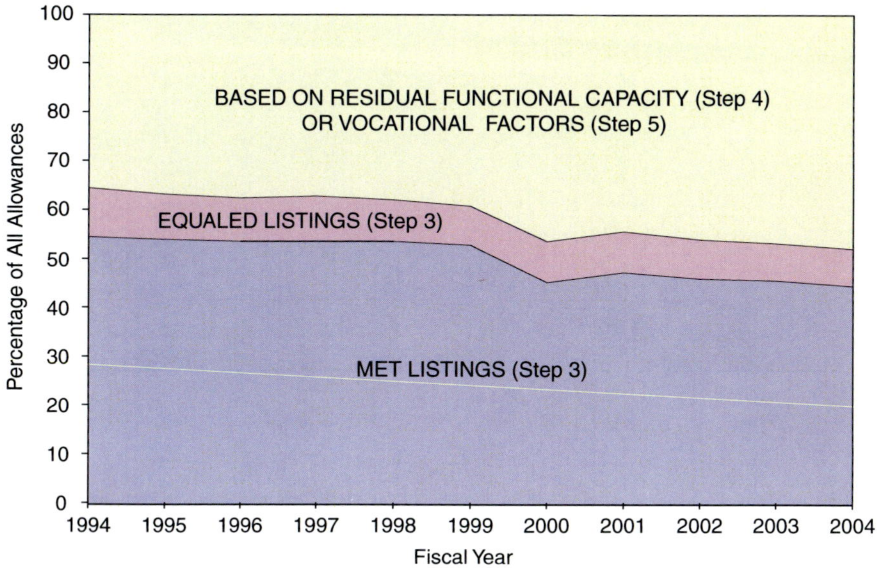

FIGURE 6-1 Basis for allowances at initial decision level, FY 1994 - FY 2004.
SOURCE: Data provided by SSA.

SSA began to investigate the validity of the Listings several years ago. In August 2001, researchers from the Disability Research Institute (DRI) at the University of Illinois at Urbana-Champaign, under contract to SSA, investigated how the Listings might be validated (DRI, 2001). In their project description, they said:

> The purpose of this project is to develop, or identify, appropriate criteria for use in validating SSA's medical listings. Any criteria that are eventually developed must withstand scrutiny by experts representing the medical, functional, vocational, research, legal, and political arenas (DRI, 2001).

As a result of their investigation, the DRI researcher concluded that because the "Listings are not a test, per se, the concepts of test validation require extension to validating a component of a larger disability determination process" (DRI, 2001:1). They suggested a four-part validation strategy relying on:

1. Assessment of face and content validity by evaluating the extent to which the Listings reflect current medical and diagnostic tests to establish actual impairments

2. Assessing predictive validity by comparing the number of people who are able to work among those who meet a listing with the number who are able to work who do not meet the listing

3. Assessment of concurrent validity by examining whether meeting a listing is a significant predictor of not engaging in substantial gainful activity (SGA)

4. Assessment of construct validity by examining the congruence of decisions made at step 3 with decisions that would be made using the medical/functional criteria at step 5

This investigation was cited approvingly on two occasions by the Government Accountability Office (GAO); first, as an example of SSA's research efforts to explore how medical advances and social changes require the disability programs to evolve (GAO, 2002:12); and again when adding SSA's disability programs to its list of high-risk government programs:

> While SSA has not fully updated its disability criteria, it has started a number of studies that recognize that medical advances and social changes require the disability program to evolve. SSA has funded a project through its Disability Research Institute (DRI) to design a study assessing the validity of its medical criteria as measures of disability . . . (GAO, 2003:9).

This effort was not continued after the initial report.

FUNCTIONING IN THE LISTINGS

The first Listings were brief and focused on clinical, diagnostic criteria. However, as the Listings have evolved, they have come to apply to a much more diverse group of applicants. They have become more elaborate and more complex, incorporating additional criteria for observations, specific signs, symptoms and laboratory findings, as well as functional outcomes. SSA has asked the committee to look into the use of functional criteria in the Listings.

SSA staff told the committee that the Listings were originally intended to be based on "medical" criteria, but they now rely more on functional criteria (Sklar, 2005a). The president of the National Council of Disability Determination Directors (representing many of the state agencies that make disability decisions on behalf of SSA) told the committee that using functional criteria in the Listings changed the Listings from "objective and simple" to "complex and subjective," causing inconsistency in decisions and increased case-processing time. He said that SSA began moving to functionally based Listings in 1985, when it published a major revision to the adult mental disorders listings. Before then, he said, the Listings only required documentation of a diagnosis, or a diagnosis plus specific clinical findings. He attributed the decline in use of the Listings to allow claims to the addition of more functional criteria that are harder to apply, observing that this creates additional work for the Disability Determination Services. He pointed to the most recent revisions to the musculoskeletal disorders listings (published on November 19, 2001, at 66 FR 58010-58046) as especially problematic (Marioni, 2005).

Although it is true that the earliest Listings (in the 1950s) were based largely on clinical and diagnostic criteria, functional criteria came into widespread usage well before 1985. The July 4, 1967, Listings (the oldest version that is readily available)[1] contained a variety of functional criteria. There were explicit measures of functional capability, such as:

- measurement of breathing capacity (respiratory impairments)
- measurement of visual acuity, visual efficiency, or visual fields (vision impairments)
- measurement of speech discrimination or hearing (hearing impairments)
- measurement of joint function (musculoskeletal impairments)

There were also more subjective functional indicators, such as:

- "History of joint pain and swelling in two or more major joints, and morning stiffness persistent on activity" (rheumatoid arthritis)
- "With well developed tremor, rigidity, and impairment of mobility" (Parkinson's disease)
- "Advanced limitation of use of hands" (scleroderma)
- ". . . nocturnal episodes which show residuals interfering with activity during the day" (epilepsy)
- ". . . marked constriction of daily activities and interests, deterioration in personal habits, and seriously impaired ability to relate to other people" (functional nonpsychotic disorders)

The mental disorders listings that were in use prior to the 1985 revision were already largely based on functional indicators of impairment severity.[2] For each of the major categories of mental disorders, the impairment listings consisted of a set of criteria that established the existence of the impairment

[1]Although this version of the Listings is long obsolete, it is preserved in SSA's operating manual at Program Operations Manual System (POMS) DI 34101.015, *Listing of Impairments as of July 4, 1967.*

[2]Available in POMS DI 34110.001, *Listing of Impairments-Part A (March 27, 1979-January 5, 1986).*

(i.e., diagnostic criteria), followed by a set of functional criteria to establish impairment severity. To meet the listing, the documented impairment had to result in persistence of "marked restriction of daily activities and constriction of interests and deterioration in personal habits and seriously impaired ability to relate to other people." (The criterion of deterioration of personal habits was not included for functional psychotic disorders.) Thus, the 1985 change was not a switch from "clinical" to "functional" criteria (or from "objective" to "subjective" standards) but, rather, a change from one set of functional criteria to another. That change was prompted by the Disability Benefits Reform Act of 1984, a law that directed SSA to revise the mental listings to more realistically evaluate the ability to engage in SGA in a competitive workplace (Collins, 1985). The functional criteria that were adopted in 1985 focused on functional outcomes that had a more direct relationship to the workplace, as illustrated in Table 6-1.

Nevertheless, it is clear that the Listings, which were originally based on little more than diagnostic criteria, now include a wide variety of both clinical and functional measures to confirm not only the existence of a particular medical condition (i.e., a diagnosis of pathology), but its degree of severity (i.e., impact of diagnosed condition on function of the claimant). SSA staff told the committee that including functional criteria in the Listings has several advantages over the use of solely clinical criteria (Eigen, 2005). They said the functional Listings criteria:

- More realistically represent the definition of disability, which is based on functional limitations.

TABLE 6-1 Comparison of Mental Impairment Severity Measures

Pre-1985 Functional Indicators	1985 Functional Indicators
Restriction of daily activities	Restriction of activities of daily living
Constriction of interests	Difficulty maintaining social functioning
Deterioration of personal habits	Deficiencies of concentration, persistence, or pace resulting in failure to complete tasks in a timely manner (in work settings or elsewhere)
Impaired ability to relate to other people	Episodes of deterioration or decompensation in work or work-like settings that cause the individual to withdraw from that situation or to experience exacerbation of signs and symptoms (which may include deterioration of adaptive behaviors)

SOURCES: POMS DI 34132.003; 50 FR 35038-35070.

- Allow SSA to devise more listings. Often there are no clinical findings that correlate with impairment severity, and the only way to devise a listing is to base it on functional indicators of severity. The only other alternative is to have no listing at all.
- Permit more allowance cases to be screened in at the Listings step.
- Permit greater parity among different listings.
- Make it possible to give meaningful consideration to an individual's symptoms and to the medical opinions of there medical treatment sources.
- Allow better evaluations of combinations of impairments.

LISTINGS REVISION PROCESS

Federal agencies, such as SSA, keep the public informed of their program rules and enable public participation in the rulemaking process under the provisions of the Administrative Procedures Act (APA). Agencies notify the public of substantive rules they propose to adopt by publishing "notices of proposed rule making" (NPRMs) in the *Federal Register* and allow members of the public an opportunity to present their views before adopting final rules. The Listings, being substantive SSA rules, are established and revised under the provisions of the APA for public notice and comment.

SSA recently began including additional steps in rulemaking for the Listings, beyond the required APA notice and comment process. The agency now publishes "advance notices of proposed rulemaking" in the *Federal Register,* seeking early input from the public on revisions to the Listings before it proposes any specific new rules. SSA is also conducting outreach meetings across the country, soliciting additional public comment and inviting input from a variety of sources, including physicians and other subject-matter experts, advocacy groups, and patients with the specific diseases or impairments under consideration. It holds these meetings before proposing any new rules (Sklar, 2005b).

SSA described these new procedures in regulations published on March 31, 2006, *Administrative Review Process for Adjudicating Initial Disability Claims* (71 FR 16425):

> As part of this effort, we have implemented a new business process to streamline the updating of our medical listings. . . .
>
> We have taken steps to increase outside participation in the development of our medical listings. As a first step, we now publish an advance NPRM to encourage members of the public to comment on the current medical criteria and to provide suggestions on how the medical criteria could be updated.
>
> In fiscal year 2005, we published advance notices involving impairments related to the respiratory and endocrine systems, growth impairments, and

> neurological impairments, as well as portions of the special senses (hearing impairments and disturbances of the labyrinthine-vestibular function). We also proposed the development of a new listing covering language and speech impairments.
>
> Following up on the advance notices, we have held numerous public outreach events. These sessions provide an opportunity for medical experts, claimants, and advocates to comment on our current policies and to advise us on the future content of the medical criteria.

SSA also told the committee that it is making regulatory updates to the Listings more frequently now. Few listings were revised between 1985 and 2005. According to GAO, SSA's listing update activities had been curtailed in the mid-1990s due to staff shortages, competing priorities, and lack of adequate research (GAO, 2002). However, as of August 2005, SSA had completed final rules updating 3 of 14 body systems, and it intends to finish a complete update of all the Listings by July 2007. SSA has also begun using an expedited internal regulatory development and clearance process, which is intended to reduce the time it takes to develop and publish a final rule by up to three and one-half months. However, the process still requires a minimum of 13 months to complete (Sklar, 2005b).

Like all other substantive agency policy, the specific criteria for all the Listings are published as regulations, using the APA regulatory process. However, SSA publishes additional guidance for its adjudicators in the form of agency rulings, called Social Security Rulings (SSRs). SSRs are agency policy interpretations, as opposed to substantive agency rules. Although they do not have the force and effect of the law or regulations, they are binding on all components of SSA (20 CFR 402.35(b)(1)). Recent examples of SSRs include:

- SSR 03-2p—Evaluating Cases Involving Reflex Sympathetic Dystrophy Syndrome/Complex Regional Pain Syndrome. This ruling provides guidance on evaluating Reflex Sympathetic Dystrophy/Complex Regional Pain Syndrome, for which there is no listing.[3]
- SSR 02-1p—Evaluation of Obesity. This ruling provides guidance on evaluation of obesity. Obesity had been deleted from the Listings on October 25, 1999.[4]
- SSR 99-2p—Evaluating Cases Involving Chronic Fatigue Syndrome. This ruling provides guidance on evaluating Chronic Fatigue Syndrome, for which there is no listing.[5]

---

[3]Available at: www.ssa.gov/OP_Home/rulings/di/01/SSR2003-02-di-01.html.
[4]Available at: www.ssa.gov/OP_Home/rulings/di/01/SSR2002-01-di-01.html.
[5]Available at: www.ssa.gov/OP_Home/rulings/di/01/SSR99-02-di-01.html.

When deciding whether to revise the Listings, SSA considers such things as specific legislation, court decisions, and congressional interest. The most important factor may be advances in medicine. It also considers its own adjudicative experiences and input from the public. To develop appropriate revisions, SSA relies on information from a variety of sources, including in-house medical experts, individual subject-matter experts from outside the agency, literature reviews, and contracted research. It receives input from agency personnel who use and apply the Listings and through the quality assurance process, and it sometimes conducts internal case reviews. SSA also receives input from the public, other government agencies, professional associations, and advocacy organizations. However, SSA does not use formal advisory committees, which are established under the Federal Advisory Committee Act (FACA), or any similar type of panel or group. In the past, SSA has assembled groups of experts to advise SSA on revisions to the Listings. However, they were not formal advisory committees as required by FACA and they are no longer used (Lively and Sklar, 2006).

REFERENCES

Barnhart, J.A. 2003. Statement of The Honorable Jo Anne B. Barnhart, commissioner, Social Security Administration. Testimony before the Subcommittee on Social Security of the House Committee on Ways and Means, September 25, 2003. Available: waysandmeans.house.gov/hearings.asp?formmode=view&id=761&keywords=Barnhart (accessed May 12, 2006).

Collins, K. 1985. Social Security Disability Benefits Reform Act of 1984: Legislative history and summary of provisions—Includes appendices. *Social Security Bulletin*. April, 1985. Available: www.findarticles. com/p/articles/mi_m6524/is_n4_48/ai_3716220/print (accessed May 17, 2006).

DRI (Disability Research Institute). 2001. *Research approaches to validation of SSA'S medical listings: Medical listings validation criteria*. Available: www.dri.uiuc.edu/research/p01-02c/default.htm and www.dri.uiuc.edu/research/p01-02c/related_project_validation_p01-02c.doc (accessed September 30, 2006).

Eigen, B. 2005. *Listings issues*. Oral presentation to the IOM Committee on Improving the Social Security Disability Decision Process. August 4, 2005. (PowerPoint presentation is in a public access file and available from the IOM on request.)

GAO (Government Accountability Office). 2002. *Social Security Administration: Fully updating disability criteria has implications for program design*. Testimony before the Subcommittee on Social Security, Committee on Ways and Means, House of Representatives. GAO-02-919T. July 11, 2002. Available: www.gao.gov/new.items/d02919t.pdf (accessed November 17, 2005).

GAO. 2003. *Major management challenges and program risks*. Social Security Administration. Available: http://www.gao.gov/pas12003/d03177.pdf.

Lively, C., and G. Sklar. 2006. *How SSA revises the Listings*. Presentation to the IOM Committee on Improving the Social Security Disability Decision Process. January 30, 2006. (PowerPoint presentation is in a public access file and available from the IOM on request.)

Marioni, A.J. 2005. Untitled oral presentation to the IOM Committee on Improving the Social Security Disability Process. January 31, 2005.

Sklar, G. 2005a. *Medical policy and medical expertise in SSA's disability programs.* Oral presentation to the IOM Committee on Improving the Social Security Disability Decision Process. January 31, 2005. (PowerPoint presentation is in a public access file and available from the IOM on request.)

Sklar, G. 2005b. *Committee tasks to improve the Listings.* Oral Presentation to the IOM Committee on Improving the Social Security Disability Decision Process. August 4, 2005. (PowerPoint presentation is in a public access file and available from the IOM on request.)

SSA. 2006. *Strategic plan FY 2006–FY 2011.* January 2006. Washington, DC. SSA Publication 04-002. Available: www.ssa.gov/strategicplan2006.pdf (accessed May 20, 2006).

SSAB (Social Security Advisory Board). 2001. *Charting the future of Social Security's disability programs: The need for fundamental change.* Washington, DC: SSAB. Available: www.ssab.gov/Publications/Disability/disabilitywhitepap.pdf (accessed November 17, 2005).

SSAB. 2003. *The Social Security definition of disability.* Washington, DC: SSAB. Available: www.ssab.gov/documents/SocialSecurityDefinitionOfDisability_002.pdf (accessed November 17, 2005).

7

Findings and Recommendations

VALUE AND UTILITY OF THE CURRENT LISTINGS

Task 1 Statement: "*. . . the committee will consider . . . [t]he value and utility of the current Listings for all users (claimants, SSA, health care professionals, state offices, and officials involved in the adjudication process).*

The Listings were originally created as a case-screening tool that would allow the Social Security Administration (SSA) to rapidly identify allowance cases without having to perform a comprehensive analysis of an individual's capacity to work. By setting the severity standard of the Listings at a higher level (inability to engage in *any* gainful activity) than its fundamental disability standard (inability to engage in *substantial* gainful activity), SSA is able to identify a significant number of allowance cases and to have some degree of confidence that these cases would be allowed if they were subject to a more comprehensive disability assessment. By relying heavily on diagnostic and clinical criteria in the Listings, SSA also ensures that disability decisions based on the Listings have a medical basis, as required by the law. By using identical and specific Listings criteria for all applicants, SSA provides equal treatment for all. So, at least on a conceptual level, using the Listings as an administrative screening tool provides significant value and utility to a variety of different constituencies:

- For SSA itself, the Listings help reduce the burden of processing millions of disability claims each year, reducing administrative costs and case-processing time.

• For individuals involved in case adjudication (SSA and Disability Determination Services [DDSs] personnel), the Listings reduce the effort and expense of processing applications by separating easy-to-approve cases from cases that require more in-depth review.
• For applicants (and their families, representatives, and health care providers), the Listings allow faster decisions in clearcut cases of inability to engage in any gainful activity and promote fairness (by providing consistent criteria and procedures).
• For the general public, the Listings promote efficiency as well as fairness in adjudication.

In addition, over several decades of use, the Listings have become an established part of the SSA disability process. They are understood and well accepted by both the legislative and judicial branches of government. Using the Listings as an administrative screening tool to identify and quickly allow obviously disabled applicants provides significant value and utility to a variety of different constituencies, including claimants, DDSs and SSA, and the general public. The committee could find no compelling reason why SSA should abandon the Listings process. However, the fact that the Listings have value and utility as a decision-making tool does not mean that they cannot and should not be improved.

Validity of the Listings as a Measure of Disability

If the purpose of the Listings is to identify quickly a subset of legitimately eligible claimants (i.e., individuals so medically impaired that they cannot be expected to achieve substantial earnings), they can be evaluated and perhaps improved as a diagnostic test whose performance is measured by its sensitivity, specificity, predictive values, and similar performance criteria (for example, examining their receiver operator characteristic curves).[1] The evaluation of the test is affected somewhat by the fact that it is the screening phase in a two-phase decision process. The goal of the overall decision process is to distinguish individuals who meet the Social Security definition of disability from those who do not, so that the people who should be awarded benefits (i.e., true positives) are allowed benefits and people who should not receive benefits (i.e., false positives) are denied. Ideally, the overall decision process has high sensitivity (i.e., ability to identify and award true positives) and high specificity (i.e., ability to identify and

[1]Receiver operator characteristic curves, developed in the 1950s as a statistical method of detecting radar and sonar signals contaminated by noise, are very useful for exploring the tradeoff between the sensitivity and specificity of diagnostic and screening tests and comparing two or more tests.

deny false positives). Because the political costs of denying benefits to applicants who meet the SSA disability standard are high, while the political and economic costs of awarding benefits to applicants who do not meet the standard are also high, SSA is willing to spend a substantial amount of time and resources to increase the sensitivity and specificity of the decision process. This, however, subjects SSA to criticism for taking too long to decide claims.

The Listings step was introduced to increase the speed of the process, even though it may reduce accuracy because it relies on less information. In theory, the accuracy problem is mitigated, because SSA uses a stricter standard (i.e., *any* gainful activity), which should increase specificity (i.e., reduce the number of false positives). Although this diminishes sensitivity, SSA can tolerate having more truly disabled claimants fail the screen, because they are not denied. Rather, they are considered in the next phase of the process (steps 4 and 5). Because these latter steps are less strict, they should be awarded benefits (this assumes that steps 4 and 5 function effectively, an issue that this committee did not address).

The use of the Listings relies on an assumption that a subgroup of individuals exists with medical impairments and associated functional limitations so severe that they are unable to work and, therefore, merely ascertaining the existence of such impairments justifies awarding them benefits. (In practice, the standard is slightly less severe and therefore more practical, because some people work despite impairments of listing-level severity—e.g., quadriplegia, total blindness; the actual standard is a medical condition so severe that the individual cannot reasonably be expected to work.) This means that the degrees of medical severity described in the Listings should be strongly correlated with not working. However, such a correlation has never been clearly established for most conditions in the Listings, and little work has been done to establish the extent to which the Listings are a valid measure of work disability.

With the exception of studies done during the development of the adult mental disorders listings implemented in 1985 (Pincus et al., 2001; reviewed in detail in Kennedy, 2002), the committee is not aware of any studies, data, or other information that establish the extent to which the Listings are a valid measure of work disability. The only validation of the decision to award benefits on the basis of a listing is the review for quality assurance of a random sample of a few percent of allowances and denials, which determines if the criteria were met, not whether they are the right criteria.

As noted above, SSA began an effort to validate the Listings in 2001. Although this initial work on validation was completed over five years ago, there does not seem to have been any follow-through. This is not to suggest that the approach proposed by the Disability Research Institute is the only possible approach or that it should be adopted. Rather, it merely illustrates that there are ways to evaluate the validity of the Listings, even in the absence of an objective "gold standard" for what constitutes disability for SSA purposes.

The lack of a gold standard—i.e., a way to identify true positives and negatives independent of SSA's process—hampers the ability of SSA to assess its decision-making process, including the effectiveness of the Listings in expediting awards at a reasonable cost. SSA should support research and perform analyses of its own program data to approximate a gold standard and better evaluate how well the Listings (and the entire decision process) work. Because there is no external objective gold standard against which the Listings can be measured, the technique of latent class analysis may be a helpful approach to refine the Listings and document their performance. Latent class analysis is a statistical technique for finding groupings of related cases (i.e., "latent classes") underlying observed categorical or nominal data (Pepe, 2003:197). One use of latent class analysis is to evaluate diagnostic tests in the absence of a gold standard, by providing estimates of sensitivity, specificity, and other properties of the tests.[2]

Inappropriate Allowances Based on the Listings

One important aspect of assessing the validity of the Listings is the extent to which they identify as disabled individuals who actually meet SSA's disability criteria (i.e., the "true positives"). An equally important issue is the extent to which they incorrectly identify as disabled those individuals who do not meet SSA's disability criteria (i.e., "false positives").

There are reasons to minimize false positives in the Listings. Most obviously, they constitute extra costs to the taxpayers in the form of benefits that should not be provided. Benefit entitlement also tends to serve as a disincentive for eventual return to work and discourages those receiving benefits from risking reentry into the labor market (primarily because of the length of time required to be out of work while qualifying for the program and the fact that applicants cannot receive vocational rehabilitation services until they are allowed cash benefits). To the extent that benefits are awarded to individuals who could otherwise work, this may remove capable workers from the labor force. It may also make it more likely that other individuals who could work will drop out of the labor force and apply for benefits, thus increasing application rates, reducing em-

[2]Examples of the use of latent class analysis in evaluating diagnostic tests in the absence of a gold standard include Albert et al., 2001; Boelaert et al., 2004; Ferraz et al., 1995; Moayyedi et al., 2004; and Young et al., 2003. Statistical methodology sources include Albert and Dodd, 2004; Hui and Zhou, 1998; Pepe, 2003; Pepe and Alonzo, 2001; Qu et al., 1996; Walter and Irwig, 1988; and Yang and Becker, 1997.

ployment, and leading to even more individuals being added to the Social Security Disability Insurance (SSDI) rolls. For society, this would mean the loss of the goods and services these workers could have produced as well as the imposition of additional taxes to pay for their benefits.

Nevertheless, given the nature of the sequential evaluation process and the Listings' "screen in" role in that process, false positives are an inevitable cost of the administrative efficiency that the Listings allow. SSA staff and executives who discussed these matters with the committee clearly recognized this fact. They also understood that false positive and false negative rates can be manipulated, to some extent, by the choice of Listings criteria. Calibrating the Listings to a fairly low degree of impairment severity will tend to increase the number of desirable true positives (i.e., screen in more applicants who deserve to receive benefits)—but at the cost of also increasing undesirable false positives. Calibrating the Listings to a higher degree of impairment severity will tend to decrease the number of undesirable false positives—but at the cost of also decreasing the desirable true positives. (SSA already does the latter to some extent by deliberately trying to set the Listings criteria to a severity level higher than the disability standard, i.e., inability to engage in any gainful activity, instead of inability to engage in any substantial gainful activity.)

If SSA makes the Listings too strict, their purpose of saving time and attendant resources is diminished. Establishing the correct balance—determining what is an acceptable rate of false positives (representing unwarranted program expenditures) as a trade-off for a desired level of true positives (representing administrative cost savings in terms of faster processing time)—is a policy issue that SSA must decide. However, to decide this SSA needs to know the false positive rate and its corresponding program costs, as well as the amount of administrative cost savings.

In discussions with the committee, SSA staff noted an isolated instance in which SSA actively investigated whether a listing was producing false positive results. In August 1999, SSA revised the Listings to remove Listing 9.09, Obesity. In explaining its removal, SSA wrote:

> . . . we reviewed a small group of cases in which individuals were found disabled based on a finding that their impairments met or equaled listing 9.09 . . . [and we found] that, in a significant number of cases, we would not have found the individuals disabled under other listings or at step 5 of the sequential evaluation process.

This was a very limited investigation into a single listing. But it is an example of the kind of investigation that could shed light onto the performance of the Listings, especially in terms of understanding the extent to which individual listings are producing inappropriate allowances.

Allowance Cases Not Identified by the Listings

The strict criteria of the Listings serve to make it highly specific, i.e., unlikely to identify and allow many false positives. Specificity is gained at some expense to sensitivity, i.e., it is likely to miss more true positives than a less strict screen. Truly disabled individuals who fail the screen and are not allowed at step 3 of the initial decision process are still considered in steps 4 and 5. If they meet the SSA definition of disability, the DDS should find they cannot do their usual work and any other work and allow them.

This is not to say that there are no undesirable consequences of an incorrect finding that an individual does not meet a listing, or that there is no reason to minimize these kinds of outcomes. Failure to identify a disabling impairment at step 3 represents a lost opportunity for adjudicative efficiency, and every such lost opportunity reduces the value and utility of the Listings. SSA should also ensure that the false negative rate at steps 4 and 5 is as low as possible, subject to the trade-off that SSA is willing to make between the sensitivity and specificity of those steps. Modifying steps 4 and 5 of the process to identify a high percentage of truly disabled (i.e., increasing sensitivity) is likely to also increase the rate of false positives (i.e., lower specificity). As with the Listings, the underlying rates of true disability and the sensitivity and specificity of the medical-vocational steps of the decision process are not known.

A decade ago, SSA asked the Institute of Medicine (IOM) to conduct an independent review of SSA's plans to redesign its disability decision process, a project that SSA had begun in 1994. After the committee deliberated and issued an interim report highly skeptical of the new plan, SSA decided to no longer pursue the new decision process; instead, it rededicated itself to improving the existing decision-making process, including "a concentrated effort to update and improve the Listings." In its 2002 final report to SSA (IOM and NRC, 2002:129-131), the committee had several observations and recommendations for SSA with respect to the Listings. Regarding SSA's plans to update the Listings, the committee observed:

> It appears likely that the agency's agenda for reform in this area will be driven as much by internal and external anecdotal concerns, including general perceptions of which Listings are the most outdated, as by any long-range strategy. Nevertheless, the committee believes that a successful process of Listings revision must be based on a systematic approach to evaluation, design, and testing. The committee has not seen any indication of a plan for determining the specificity and sensitivity parameters for any existing or proposed Listing. Developing such parameters seems critical to both the scientific and the political validation of the Listings as a decisional tool.

> Because the Listings screen is meant to be used to identify clear cases of disability, one would expect this screen to be devised such that it is highly specific (seldom identifies false positives) and relatively sensitive (identifies some substantial number of true positives). The question for SSA is how specific and how sensitive. In order to undertake meaningful research on the validity of any medical listing, SSA must be able to specify the acceptable level of specificity and sensitivity by which it can validate the screen against those criteria.
>
> SSA provided the committee with a list of ongoing projects designed to update the Medical Listings and improve their performance. The committee, however, has no information suggesting that baseline criteria were established at the outset or that any method was developed for validating the existing and proposed new Listings against those criteria. These are serious and difficult issues. As SSA moves forward to incrementally revise and reform the current decision process, it must be able to determine whether or not changes are improving the accuracy of the process. Indeed, it has to be able to make these determinations prior to the time that changes are implemented on a national basis. Whether or not specific Listings need to be improved and the direction of that improvement must await the results of the baseline evaluation and subsequent reevaluation.

The committee went on to restate and reinforce a recommendation that it had made in its interim report from years earlier:

> SSA should conduct the necessary research, prior to making changes in the Listings, to (1) determine whether or not the current Listings satisfy the agency's goals for specificity and sensitivity, (2) determine whether or not these goals are satisfied consistently across the Listings for the different body groups or conditions, and (3) evaluate the options to correct the problems detected by these evaluations, as it develops any new list of medical impairments.

That IOM committee also cited, and supported, similar recommendations that had been previously made to SSA in 1996 by the Disability Policy Panel of the National Academy of Social Insurance (NASI, 1996:22):

> Experts on SSA's medical criteria [i.e., the Listings] report that there is considerable variation among the criteria used for different body systems in terms of the severity of impairments that are presumed to constitute work disability. To date, no systematic research has been done to evaluate the consistency of the presumptions underlying the medical criteria for different body systems. Research of this kind should have a high priority.

The current committee believes that these observations and recommendations are as valid today as they were when they were first made.

Declining Use of the Listings as a Screening Tool

As noted previously, SSA is concerned that the Listings, which once formed the basis for the vast majority of the disability allowance decisions, now account for a significantly lower percentage of total allowances. While the Listings originally accounted for more than 90 percent of allowances, they are currently the basis for barely 50 percent. The agency seeks to make the Listings a more effective screening tool by increasing the rate at which allowance cases are identified by the Listings.

The extent to which the new quick disability determination (QDD) process being piloted as part of SSA's Disability Service Improvement Plan in the New England region increases the ability of the Listings to expedite cases remains to be seen. QDD should tend to increase speed by pulling allowances that can be decided quickly into a faster process of decision making, performed by more experienced adjudicators. On the other hand, the QDD process picks cases to expedite using factors in addition to medical criteria and looks for quick denials as well as quick allowances, which may slow the adjudication of cases meeting the Listings.

Ultimately, the correct rate at which allowances are made at the listings step has to be determined by carefully analyzing the actual outcomes of the disability determination process. Whether the best rate is 90 percent or 50 percent or some other figure is an empirical question. There does not appear to be any basis for assuming that the high percentage of cases identified as allowances by the Listings in the 1950s and 1960s (which unquestionably made the decision process more expeditious) were "correct" allowances, any more than it is safe to assume that it is possible to increase the rate at which allowance cases are now identified by the Listings without undesirable consequences.

In discussing these matters with the committee, SSA executives referred to a common perception that there was a change in the Listings from "medical" to "functional" standards in the mid-1980s, suggesting that this change may have significantly contributed to their declining use as a basis for allowance. These changes included a major revision to the adult mental disorders criteria that took effect in August 1985 and changes in most of the other body systems that took effect in January 1986. However, the data reviewed by the committee do not support a cause-and-effect relationship between these changes and use of the Listings. As can be seen in Figure 7-1, use of the Listings as the basis for allowance has been in decline since about 1983, when the Listings were used in 82 percent of initial allowances. Following a decline from 82 percent in 1983 to 72 percent in 1985, use of the Listings went up in 1986 and 1987, when the revised Listings were in effect, then resumed falling until the present day.

After revisions in the Listings promulgated in 1985, SSA undertook no

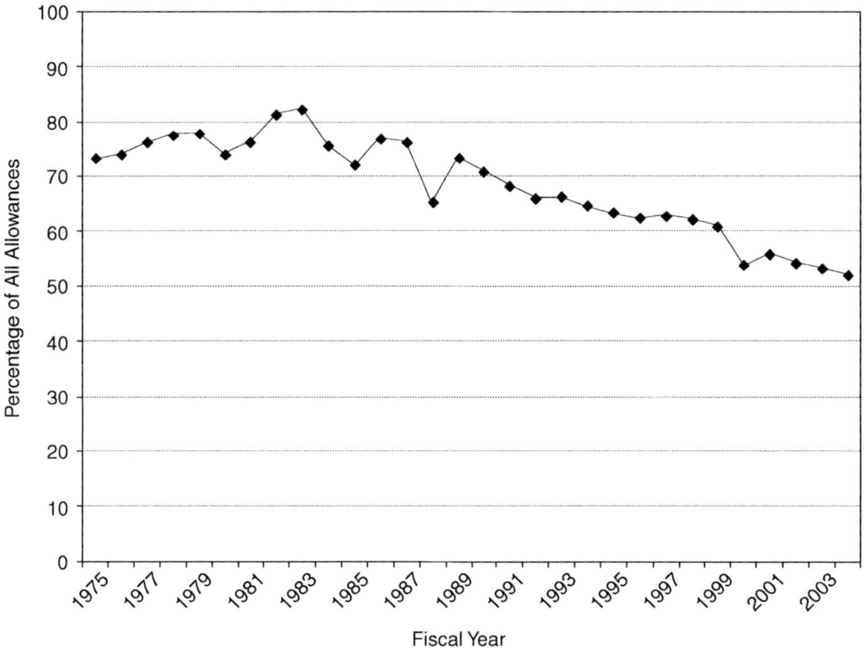

FIGURE 7-1 SSDI allowances meeting/equaling the Listings: 1975-2004 (percentages).
NOTE: Based on initial state agency determinations for SSDI-only and concurrent claims (excludes Supplemental Security Income [SSI]-only allowances and allowances made on the basis of the Listings at subsequent stages of the appeal process).
SOURCE: SSA tables.

other significant modifications until 1993 and 1994, when it revised the respiratory and cardiovascular listings, and then none again until 1999. Yet despite continuity in the Listings between 1985 and 1993, the steady decline in use of the Listings continued unchecked. The decline continued at a steady rate throughout the 1990s, with no indication that the changes in 1993 and 1994 had any effect. In addition, the sudden surge in Listings usage in 1986 is the opposite of what would be expected if the 1985 revision had been a cause of the overall decline in their usage.

Therefore, it does not seem reasonable to attribute the decline in Listings usage to any changes in the Listings themselves, either as a result of a perceived change in basic approach (functional vs. medical) or as a result of specific new Listings criteria. There are many other possible explanations for the decline. One factor might be gradual advances in medical treatment and outcomes, resulting in fewer and fewer applicants exhibiting the profound manifestations (clinical or functional) of disorders reflected in the Listings.

Another factor might be the major change in the evaluation of vocational factors SSA implemented in 1979 with the publication of the medical/vocational rules in Appendix 2 to Subpart P of 20 CFR Part 404 (the so-called "grid" rules), followed by several years in which SSA published many major policy rulings explaining the use of those new rules (especially in 1982, 1983, and 1985). Another factor could be increasing filing rates throughout the 1980s and 1990s, with a corresponding increase in the percentage of cases involving less obvious disability.

However, regardless of the reasons for the change in the rate at which the Listings are used as the basis for allowance decisions, the correct rate can only be determined through a comprehensive assessment of their performance and effectiveness.

RECOMMENDATION 1. SSA should continue to use the current Listings as a screening test in its disability decision process, but should increase their value and utility by closely examining and monitoring their performance, conducting research to evaluate and improve their effectiveness in expediting awards in obvious cases, and making timely changes in response to these evaluations.

CONCEPTUAL MODELS FOR ORGANIZING THE LISTINGS

Task 2 Statement: "*. . . the committee will consider . . . [c]onceptual models for organizing the Listings, beyond the current 'body systems' model specified in federal regulations.*"

The Listings are based on a medical model, which is not ideal, given what is known about the factors causing disability. However, a better model does not exist at this time. The bases for the listings are anatomic, diagnostic, and functional, the mix of which varies from listing to listing and body system to body system.

As medical treatments and assistive technologies advance, the anatomic and diagnostic bases for the Listings will become less and less useful as markers of disability. SSA should begin now to look for better methods of determining disability for Social Security benefits.

One alternative to a body-system-based list of diagnoses and impairments would be to develop and apply a generic functional evaluation that does not attempt to assess the severity of impairment but goes directly to the functional capacities of claimants to engage in substantial gainful activity (SGA). Of course, to meet SSA statutory requirements, such an evaluation would still have to establish a connection between the functional limitations and a "medically determinable impairment" that causes those limitations. This would be more suited to the nature of employment disability as it is understood conceptually today, i.e., not equal to a person's degree of impairment or even of functional limitation but rather the result of the interaction of a person's functional capacities with characteristics of the workplace and other external factors, such as support systems.

SSA considered developing such a screening tool in the 1990s and eventually dropped the effort (for an extensive discussion of that effort, see IOM and NRC, 2002:Chapter 6). The opinion of the committee is that a screening tool equal to the complexity of disability does not exist at this time.

A potential model for a functionally based screening tool is the current process that SSA uses to identify children applying for SSI whose impairments are "functionally equal" to the Listings. For children applying for SSI, the disability standard is stricter than the standard used for adults (under either the SSI or SSDI programs). Children must have impairments that are of listing-level severity. Because the Listings focus largely on medical criteria for many impairments, SSA developed a process by which it considers the functional consequences of a child's impairments in the context of the Listings. As with adults, SSA begins by evaluating whether the child's impairment meets any of the criteria in the Listings. If not, it next considers whether the child's impairment is equivalent to the Listings based on the medical factors, as it does for adults. However, if the impairment does not meet or medically equal the severity of the Listings, SSA then goes on to make one additional assessment for children using the Listings that it does not make for adults—functional equivalence.

With functional equivalence, SSA performs an overall functional assessment of the child using six broad domains.[3] The domains are: acquiring and using information, attending and completing tests, interacting and relating with others, moving about and manipulating objects, caring for yourself, and health and physical well-being. Each domain is scored by an SSA pediatrician on a four-point scale: no limitation, less than marked, marked, or extreme. Functional equivalence is achieved with marked limitations in two domains or an extreme limitation in one domain.

In effect, this establishes a universal "functional" listing that applies regardless of the nature of the child's impairment. A similar approach could be developed for adults, although it would most likely be a substantial undertaking for SSA to develop and validate appropriate functional criteria for adults. Established norms for the physical, mental, and social growth exist for children but not for adults.

---

[3]The childhood functional equivalence process is described in SSA's regulations at 20 CFR 416.926a.

Another alternative would be to use SSA's own program data to identify the characteristics of claims that are highly likely to be allowed and use them as a screen. Conceptually, this is the same approach as the predictive model SSA has been using to identify cases that should be reevaluated more often as part of the continuing disability review process and as the predictive model currently under development for the QDD process. It is even possible that the predictive model for QDD could be used instead of the Listings to expedite cases for claimants and reduce the cost of processing cases for SSA, if it applies to enough cases and is valid. The problem is that the predictive model is based on the assumption that SSA's current decision process is valid and reliable, which is unknown.

RECOMMENDATION 2. SSA should continue to monitor advances in assessing disability, and it should support the development of promising alternative approaches to evaluating eligibility for Social Security disability benefits. SSA also should systematically compare the new quick disability determination process with the Listings and with the final determinations of disability.

REVISING THE LISTINGS TO BE MORE CONSISTENT AND UP TO DATE

Task 3 Statement: "*. . . the committee will consider . . . [p]rocesses for determining when the Listings require revision and criteria upon which to add new listings or remove old ones.*"

Task 4 Statement: "*. . . the committee will consider . . . [f]eedback mechanisms to continuously assess and evaluate the Listings for the purpose of improving consistency in application by all adjudicators throughout the country.*"

These two tasks relate to the process that SSA uses to revise and update the Listings and the sources of information (feedback mechanisms) that are used in that process. As discussed in Chapter 6, SSA considers a number of factors in deciding whether to revise, add, or delete a listing. Unless there is some legislative or judicial action that compels a specific listing revision action, SSA considers medical advances, the experiences of its adjudicators, and input from the public (including advocacy organizations). It makes use of in-house medical experts, outside experts, and other agency personnel. These are all helpful sources of input to the listing revision process. However, SSA does not appear to make full use of its extensive program data in revising the Listings. Listings have been deleted or added based on several different scenarios, including adjudicator input about problems with specific listings, concerns from the medical or advocacy community, and political pressure. However, the committee is not aware of any listing revision that was precipitated by scientific analysis of program data or of a scientific evaluation of the effects of changes in the Listings.

SSA provided the committee with an extensive amount of highly detailed program data that could be used to assess some aspects of the performance of the current Listings, and to identify circumstances in which new listings might be appropriate. For example, these data indicated that there are impairments that are very frequently found to be disabling, but for which no listings exist. Careful analysis of these data might identify appropriate candidates for new listings. Similarly, impairments that are frequently found to be equal in severity to a listing, but seldom found to meet a listing suggest the possibility of new listings. A sudden decline in an allowance rate might signal an advance in medical treatment that has reduced the disabling effects of a listed impairment, which, in turn, might prompt revision or elimination of the listing. The same approach could be used to keep the list of presumptive disabilities up to date, as recommended in the committee's interim report (see Recommendation 3-1 in Appendix C). An analysis of these data forms claims and the claims process would provide a baseline useful in evaluating the impact of changes in the Listings and presumptive disabilities.

Feedback

One way to help improve the performance of decision making is to provide better feedback to adjudicators about the decisions they are making and about the decisions other adjudicators are making. Currently, the predominant feedback for DDSs is from the 50 percent quality review of SSDI allowances. For administrative law judges (ALJs), it is from the results of appeals of their unfavorable opinions. As noted in the interim report, these feedback arrangements provide opposing incentives to the two levels of decision making—for the DDSs to err on the side of denying claims and ALJs to err on the side of allowing claims. These incentives may not be offset by a small quality assurance sample of DDS allowances and denials (about 40,000, less than 2 percent of the total number of 2.6 million claims processed in fiscal year 2004) or an ongoing review of a sample of ALJ decisions in SSA's disability hearings quality review process (about 3,500 a year of about 500,000 hearings held). In addition, SSA does not appear to use the quality assurance process to closely examine the performance of the Listings or their application.

SSA does not systematically analyze its own programmatic data or provide feedback to adjudicators on aggregate results of their decision making. The most obvious example of this is the lack of feedback to DDS adjudicators on the results of appeals to the Office of Hearings and Appeals of their decisions. The committee suggests that SSA closely examine ways of using program information to identify listings that are not being applied consistently or to indicate possible changes in the effectiveness of listings.

RECOMMENDATION 3. SSA should develop a management information system that combines a balanced quality assurance process to promote consistency and reliability of individual allowances and denials and a program of analysis of aggregate patterns to evaluate consistency and reliability of the Listings. SSA should also develop feedback processes to inform adjudicators and program managers of decision results, including those found by subsequent adjudicators to meet or equal the Listings.

External Input Affecting the Listings

No matter how reliable and valid the Listings may be at any given moment, they are constantly affected by external developments. These include changes in disease patterns, advances in scientific knowledge and medical practice, advances in assistive technologies, and changes in the workplace affecting workers in terms of job requirements and potential sources of injury.

The most common devices that government agencies use to ensure that evidence-based regulations are kept current are:

- feedback from the regulatory process
- staff research
- external advisory committees

SSA has expanded regulatory feedback in recent years by sponsoring policy conferences and using advanced notices of proposed rulemaking (ANPRMs). At policy conferences, medical specialists present the latest research and medical practices and interact with beneficiaries, advocates, and SSA disability officials. ANPRMs solicit suggestions from all interested parties on how the Listings should be revised. The committee supports these efforts to incorporate more public and professional input into the Listings revision process.

The Office of Medical Policy, the staff component of the SSA Office of Disability Programs, is responsible for maintaining the Listings. Currently, the Office of Medical Policy has seven medical officers, who are charged with keeping abreast of the medical literature, such as the results of clinical trials, research on outcomes, and practice guidelines. Five are physicians, with expertise in psychiatry, physical medicine and rehabilitation, neurology, and pediatrics. In addition, there is a speech and language pathologist and a psychologist. This office is small and does not have experts in all the major specialties (although it can draw on the advice of specialists in the federal DDS), so its ability to supply the necessary medical expertise to the Listings revision process is limited.

RECOMMENDATION 4. SSA should ensure that its Office of Medical Policy has the expertise relevant to the full range of listed impairments and has the resources to stay knowledgeable concerning new developments in medicine and rehabilitation, for example, by conducting systematic literature reviews on a periodic basis.

Use of Medical Advisory Committees

External advisory committees are common in federal agencies. They are a way to tap expertise in the scientific and medical research community, and they also increase understanding and acceptance of government policies and programs among affected constituency groups.

Throughout its history, SSA has used a variety of different advisory committees, advisory councils, and similar groups as a source of expert advice and recommendations on difficult issues (SSA, 2001). SSA formed an external medical advisory committee in 1955 to create the original Listings. More informal medical advisory groups were used into the 1980s and were a part of the efforts to incorporate consideration of pain in the Listings, revise the cardiac listings, and revise and expand the mental listings. During that time, SSA would assemble a panel of experts from both inside the agency (including DDSs) and outside (including medical experts in the appropriate fields). The use of medical advisory groups was stopped when the Federal Advisory Committee Act (FACA) was instituted, and advocacy groups asked for representation. SSA management decided that consumer representation on medical advisory committees was not appropriate and discontinued the medical advisory committee.

Despite the strictures of FACA, other agencies with similar responsibilities to develop and apply scientifically based regulations—such as the Centers for Medicare and Medicaid Services, Food and Drug Administration, and Environmental Protection Agency—use expert advisory committees extensively to obtain advice on when and what regulatory changes are needed. They establish and operate their advisory committees under FACA. These external committees are typically balanced not just among areas of expertise but also among viewpoints, including representatives of consumers and, in some cases, affected industries as well as the relevant clinical specialties. SSA's disability programs would benefit from external advice from clinical and other experts on disability determination criteria and procedures, and the involvement of external advisory groups would also increase the understanding and acceptance of SSA disability determination requirements in the medical community.

RECOMMENDATION 5. SSA should re-establish a medical advisory committee under the Federal Advisory Committee Act to advise the commissioner on when scientifically based regulations, especially the Listings, should be revised to keep them up to date. Ad hoc advisory committees should be established under the auspices of the medical advisory committee to advise on the revision or addition of specific listings or body systems. The medical advisory committee should be multidisciplinary and include representation from all appropriate constituencies.

Responding to Advances in Medical Practice and Technology

Medicine evolves in ways that may result in the need to revise a listing, but it also makes more incremental advances that affect the way the Listings are applied. In such cases, the standard of severity in the listing does not change but the method of evaluating it may.

One way SSA has tried to make the Listings better adapt to these kinds of changes is to make the Listings themselves more generic. In the past, listings criteria have been quite specific; for example, naming particular tests, such as x-rays or diagnostic criteria, or referring to a specific edition of the *Diagnostic and Statistical Manual of Mental Disorders* (DSM). SSA has begun taking a more generic approach; for example, specifying "imaging studies" rather than x-rays or MRIs, and referring to "the latest edition" of the DSM, rather than a specific edition. This approach is helpful and should be pursued, but it is fairly limited in scope.

The greater concern is how SSA can revise the Listings fast enough to keep pace with medical advances. SSA executives expressed frustration with the formal federal rulemaking process and the length of time it takes to develop and implement new rules, and asked the committee to propose a streamlined process that would be legally acceptable.

While acknowledging that the Administrative Procedures Act (APA) places significant burdens on federal agencies to ensure that agency rules are developed in full view of the public and with full public participation, the committee fully supports the APA process. SSA has already adopted some modifications to its internal regulatory development process to expedite the development of new Listings, and the committee encourages SSA to continue those efforts, as well as its efforts to make the Listings more adaptable by providing generic rather than specific guidelines.

Another way to respond to continuing improvements in methods of treating and evaluating impairments is to use agency rulings (Social Security Rulings, or SSRs) to provide adjudicators with up-to-date methods of obtaining and evaluating evidence and up-to-date guidance in applying the Listings. The committee believes that these efforts, in conjunction with the establishment of a medical advisory committee, can help SSA keep the Listings up to date while maintaining the important protections embodied in the APA. Also, when medical advances or other changes necessitate a new SSR, the need to revise the affected listing itself should be assessed.

RECOMMENDATION 6. SSA should continue to develop procedures for expediting development of new regulations and fully involving the public and external experts in the regulatory process governed by the Administrative Procedures Act. Agency rulings, which are published in the *Federal Register* and made available on SSA's website, should continue to be used to explain and clarify the substantive rules developed in the full regulatory process.

ADAPTABILITY OF THE LISTINGS

Task 5 Statement: "*. . . the committee will consider . . . [a]daptability of the Listings, including methods to account for variable access to health care services (including diagnostics and pharmaceuticals) in determining whether an individual's condition meets or equals the Listings.*"

The criteria in some of SSA's listings are designed to apply only if an applicant is undergoing, or has undergone, specific medical treatment(s) and such medical treatment has been unsuccessful. Most listings require evidence that specific clinical or laboratory findings persist despite treatment to meet the listing. This is especially true of listings for cardiovascular impairments. For example:

> 4.10 Aneurysm of aorta or major branches, due to any cause (e.g., atherosclerosis, cystic medial necrosis, Marfan syndrome, trauma), demonstrated by appropriate medically acceptable imaging, **with dissection not controlled by prescribed treatment** (see 4.00H6). [Emphasis added]

Unfortunately, appropriate and necessary medical care and treatment for serious disorders is not readily available to everyone. For individuals who do not receive treatment, these listings may not apply. As SSA notes in the preface to the cardiovascular listings, "If you do not receive treatment, you cannot show an impairment that meets the criteria of most of these listings."[4]

---

[4]See section 4.00B.3. of Appendix 1, subpart P, 20 CFR part 404, published January 13, 2006 at 71 FR 2335.

Variable access to quality health care services throughout the country is an unfortunate fact, but it is beyond the capacity of SSA to remedy. Observation of a patient's response to medical treatment is a standard medical practice and a legitimate way for SSA to evaluate impairment severity in its rules. The fact that all applicants may not be able to document impairment severity this way does not make it any less valuable as a method to assess impairment severity in those who can, especially given that the Listings are only a screening tool to identify obvious allowances.

Ideally, individuals applying for disability benefits would be evaluated and receive the medical, vocational rehabilitation, and employment services that would enable them to resume working gainfully. Instead, in the current system, many individuals with remediable work limitations are not eligible for medical care or vocational rehabilitation until *after* they have completed the process of qualifying for cash benefits. At that point, they may become eligible for Medicaid if they are SSI recipients (unless they have already qualified under other criteria, such as those for the Children with Special Health Care Needs program). SSDI beneficiaries must wait for two years to be eligible for Medicare. Only then may these individuals be able to obtain the medical care they need.

This requirement obviously disadvantages poor people and others without adequate health care coverage, but any unfairness is the result of the social and political system that created these inequities, not SSA's Listings, which is meant to be the most efficient method available for easily identifying obvious allowance cases.

RECOMMENDATION 7. The committee recommends against attempting to consider variable access to health care at the Listings step in determining disability. It is not strictly a medical issue that can be incorporated easily in Listings criteria. Although medical evaluation is involved in gauging the severity and functional impacts of an untreated condition, the circumstances limiting access to health care and assistive technology should be considered separately.

EVALUATING MULTIPLE IMPAIRMENTS

Task 6 Statement: "*. . . the committee will consider . . . [m]ethods to assess and quantify the effects of multiple impairments that may not individually cross the eligibility threshold.*"

It is possible for claimants to have several medical conditions that together prevent them from engaging in any gainful activity, although no single impairment is of listing-level severity. SSA has a provision for considering the combined effects of multiple impairments. It is one of three circumstances in which an individual's impairment(s) may be found "medically equivalent" in severity to a listed impairment, even though no listing is met. Finding a combination of impairments equal in severity to a listed impairment would justify an allowance at step 3.

However, evaluating medical equivalence to a listing, as its name implies, is a medical judgment. It requires a medical assessment of whether the findings related to an individual's impairments are "at least of equal medical significance to those of a listed impairment."[5] As such, it does not take into account the functional consequences of the combined impairments.

In practice, determining whether multiple impairments combine to equal listing-level severity medically, i.e., considering symptoms, signs, and laboratory findings (but not age, education, and work experience) across several body systems, is very difficult and quite subjective. In some cases at least, the impairments are so different—for example, back pain, depression, and a heart condition—that combining the signs, symptoms, and laboratory tests does not provide clear guidance. Given the complexity and subjectivity of this process, and the absence of any scientific analysis of the process, it is a matter of conjecture whether adjudicators' judgments on equivalence for combinations of impairments are valid or reliable.

The committee believes that, unless SSA is able to establish scientifically the value of medical judgments on equivalence in cases involving combinations of impairments, the prudent and most practical way of deciding such cases is to assess the net functional impact that the impairments have at steps 4 and 5 of the decision process. Even where the impairments are in the same body system or otherwise related, it is difficult to determine their combined impact without reference to functional consequences.

Despite the difficulty assessing medical severity of multiple impairments, it is possible that, given a sufficiently comprehensive study of common comorbidities (which might include, for example, putting a sample of cases through medical equivalency evaluations at step 3 and residual functional capacity evaluations at steps 4 and 5 and comparing the results), some recurring patterns might occur showing frequently occurring combinations of impairments that could be described in listings that addresses those combinations. Other potential approaches to assessing combinations of impairments could include more training of adjudicators using common comorbidities as examples, mandatory review by a second medical consultant, or referral to an expert group with the appropriate specialties.

As discussed earlier, for children applying for SSI there are two different approaches to equivalence—a medical approach and a functional approach.

[5]The rules on medical equivalence are contained in SSA's program rules at 20 CFR 404.1526 and 416.926.

For functional equivalence in children, SSA assesses the net functional impact of all impairments combined. There is no similar process for adults, and developing such an approach may not be feasible.

RECOMMENDATION 8. Generally, SSA should not try to determine the medical equivalency of multiple impairments to the Listings at step 3. Such cases should be analyzed functionally. However, research may determine that some common comorbidities, each of a certain degree of severity or more, are typically allowed after going through steps 4 and 5, and these sets of conditions could be incorporated in the Listings to expedite decisions.

INTEGRATING FUNCTIONAL ASSESSMENT IN THE LISTINGS

Task 7 Statement: "*. . . the committee will consider . . . [a]dvisability of and methods for integrating functional assessment into the Listings.*"

When discussing functioning in the Listings, it is important to first define terms. The 2006 Listings use the term "function" and its different forms (e.g., functioning, functional, dysfunction, and so forth) almost 500 times. In general, the term is used in one of two distinct ways. First, there are many references to function at the body/organ level. That is, in describing how a particular organ or body part functions (e.g., "muscle function," "labyrinthine-vestibular function," "pulmonary function," "ventricular dysfunction," "cardiac dysfunction," "myocardial function," "function of the stoma," "liver dysfunction," "pancreatic dysfunction," "renal function," "hyperfunction of the adrenal cortex," "major dysfunction of a joint(s)"). References such as these to organ/body-level function are components of a clinical assessment rather than an assessment of the disabling functional consequences of the disorders.

In addition, the Listings contain references to functioning at the person level. The best example may be the musculoskeletal Listings, in which functional loss is introduced and defined in terms of the effect of the impairment on a person's normal functioning. The Listings state that ". . . functional loss for purposes of these listings [musculoskeletal] is defined as the inability to ambulate effectively on a sustained basis for any reason. . . ." Similarly, in the description of performing fine and gross movements, function is again defined at the person level, i.e., ". . . sustaining such functions as reaching, pushing, pulling, grasping, and fingering to be able to carry out activities of daily living."

It is the person-level functioning that appears to be the concern of SSA, especially to the extent that it may resemble the residual functional capacity evaluation that SSA performs at the later stages of the sequential evaluation process for individuals whose impairments are not of listing-level severity.

As discussed in Chapter 6, SSA's concerns underlying this specific task have to do with the perceived evolution of the Listings from supposedly objective, measurable clinical criteria (including organ/body-level functioning) that can be easily and quickly applied to more subjective, ill-defined functional criteria (functioning at the person level) that are difficult and time-consuming to apply. Without a doubt, the earlier listings criteria were more clinical, shorter, and easier to apply. However, the committee is not aware of any data showing that these earlier versions of the Listings were any more accurate as a screening tool than more recent versions. And, at least on an intuitive level, it would seem that Listings criteria that measure impairment severity on a functional basis would have a better chance of correlating with functional work disability than would Listings criteria that measure impairment severity on a clinical basis. As the Listings evolved from a short list of catastrophic conditions that were intended to correlate closely with inability to work, incorporating functional criteria was a natural development. As one recent historian of the Listings notes, function has been part of them for a long time, at least from the 1960s (Cowles, 2005:2). Examples of functional criteria in the 1967 Listings are cited in Chapter 6.

Recently, however, SSA has begun to incorporate function into the Listings in a more systematic way. This is clear in the 2002 musculoskeletal revision, which some see as a model for revising all the listings. The 2002 revision introduced a standardized approach to considering the functional consequences of musculoskeletal disorders, using two broad criteria, each representing the same degree of functional deficit—"inability to ambulate effectively on a sustained basis for any reason" and "inability to perform fine and gross movements effectively on a sustained basis for any reason"—as the ultimate criteria for meeting the Listings for disorders of the spine and joints, fractures of the extremities, amputation, and soft tissue injuries such as burns. As SSA noted in response to public comments expressing concern about these new functional criteria, the intent was to establish a clearer and more consistent functional standard that would "promote greater consistency in decision making."[6]

The question remains whether it is possible to identify valid functional Listings criteria that correlate highly with inability to work. Although there is no global or generic functional assessment tool that could be used for all applicants, functional assessment tools have been developed and validated

[6]See *Revised Medical Criteria for Determination of Disability, Musculoskeletal System and Related Criteria*; Final Rule. 66 FR 58023 (November 19, 2001).

for some conditions. Currently, however, functional evaluation in the Listings is not systematically based on research on such tools.

> **RECOMMENDATION 9. SSA should undertake a comprehensive assessment of the performance of both medical and functional listings, and should consider function at the Listings step when it can be shown to correlate with inability to perform substantial gainful activity (SGA). SSA should both monitor and sponsor current research regarding the extent to which medical and functional criteria are highly correlated with limitations on performance of SGA.**

RESEARCH TO SUPPORT THE LISTINGS

SSA has a disability research and demonstration program, currently consolidated in a unit of the Office of Disability and Income Support Programs (OSDIP). Moreover, SSA has authority to fund demonstrations affecting SSDI from the Social Security trust funds rather than the administrative budget, which comes from the discretionary budget.

Currently, ODISP's research is focused on return-to-work demonstrations. It would be appropriate for the program also to include research to improve the evidence base of the Listings and experiments to evaluate alternative listing criteria and procedures. This report gives examples of some experiments that could be done to improve the Listings. For example, a proposed revised listing could be tested against a sample of claims going through the regular process to compare results. This could include independent evaluations of each file, perhaps in conjunction with medical evaluations of the individuals (subject to human subjects guidelines), who would be allowed or denied under the current rules and thus not otherwise affected. SSA could also the test the effects on decision making of using functional assessment tools validated for use in particular conditions or body systems. Such testing would support the effort called for in Recommendation 9 to integrate function in the Listings to the extent functional assessments are found to be predictive of inability to engage in substantial gainful activity.

SSA is understandably concerned about the implication of a listing change and whether it will be useful for at least several years. The development of the Listings, like any regulation potentially affecting large numbers of people, is a major undertaking that takes time. There is also a benefit to having stable criteria over time, so that once a listing is revised, it is not likely to be revised again for several years. It is possible, through the use of experimentation and pilot projects, to test new regulations before they are finally adopted and applied throughout the system.

RECOMMENDATION 10. SSA, with input from the medical advisory committee, should develop a program of research to support the disability decision process, including the Listings. The research program should include experiments that test revised listings before they are adopted.

The Listing of Impairments is a screening test whose effectiveness and utility is measured by its sensitivity, specificity, predictive values, and other criteria. These in turn depend on knowledge of the validity of the test, which calls for a gold standard for comparison, and knowledge of the prevalence of listing-level disorders in the population. SSA should support research on error rates in applying the Listings, such as latent class models, which are often used when there is no gold standard measure or the results of a gold standard test are imperfect (Qu et al., 1996). SSA should also support research on the prevalence of common disorders that meet the Listings (10 impairment codes account for more than 49 percent of the applications for Social Security disability).

SSA could supplement existing surveys, such as the National Health and Nutrition Examination Survey (NHANES) or the Behavioral Risk Factor Surveillance Survey. NHANES has the advantage of using mobile examination laboratories to examine the health status of survey participants directly.

RECOMMENDATION 11. SSA, in conjunction with other agencies that assist persons with disabilities, should conduct a periodic, nationally representative sample survey of the population to determine the distribution and extent of severe impairments that might meet the Listings. This might be done by supplementing existing surveys. The results would be useful for program planning and for evaluating the effectiveness of the Listings and other aspects of the disability decision process.

REFERENCES

Albert, P.A., L.M. McShane, J.H. Shih, and the US NCI Bladder Tumor Marker Network. 2001. Latent class modeling approaches for assessing diagnostic error without a gold standard: With applications to p53 immunohistochemical assays in bladder tumors. *Biometrics*, 57:610-619.

Albert, P.S., and L.E. Dodd. 2004. A cautionary note on robustness of latent class models for estimating diagnostic error without a gold standard. *Biometrics*, 60:427-435.

Boelaert, M., S. Rijal, S. Regmi, R. Singh, B. Karki, D. Jacquet, F. Chappuis, L. Campino, P. Desjeux, D. Le Ray, S. Koirala, and P. Van der Stuyft. 2004. A comparative study of the effectiveness of diagnostic tests for visceral leishmaniasis. *American Journal of Tropical Medicine Hygiene*, 70(1):72-77.

Cowles, A. 2005. *A history of the disability listings.* March 2, 2005. Available: www.ssa.gov/history/DisabilityListings.html (accessed November 3, 2005).

Ferraz, M.B., S.D. Walter, R. Heymann, and E. Atra. 1995. Sensitivity and specificity of different diagnostic criteria for Behcet's Disease according to the latent class approach. *British Journal of Rheumatology*, 34(10):932-935.

Hui, S.L., and X.H. Zhou. 1998. Evaluation of diagnostic tests without gold standards. *Statistical Methods in Medical Research*, 7:354-370.

IOM and NRC (Institute of Medicine and National Research Council). 2002. *The dynamics of disability: Measuring and monitoring disability for Social Security programs,* edited by G.S. Wunderlich, D.P. Rice, and N.L. Amado. Washington, DC: National Academy Press.

Kennedy, C. 2002. SSA's disability determination of mental impairments: A review toward and agenda for research. In *The dynamics of disability. Measuring and monitoring disability for Social Security programs,* edited by G.S. Wunderlich et al. Washington, DC: National Academy Press. Pp. 241-280.

Moayyedi, P., J. Duffy, and B. Delaney. 2004. New approaches to enhance the accuracy of the diagnosis of reflux disease. *Gut*, 53(4):55-57.

NASI (National Academy of Social Insurance). 1996. *Balancing security and opportunity: The challenges of disability income policy.* Summary and Overview, Report of the Disability Policy Panel. Available: www.nasi.org/usr_doc/Balancing_Summary.pdf (accessed October 5, 2006).

Pepe, M.S. 2003. *The statistical evaluation of medical tests for classification and prediction.* New York: Oxford University Press.

Pepe, M.S., and T.A. Alonzo. 2001. Comparing disease screening tests when true disease status is ascertained only for screen positives. *Biostatistics*, 2:249-260.

Pincus, H.A., C. Kennedy, S.J. Simmens, H.H. Goldman, P. Sirovatka, and S. Sharfstein. 1991. Determining disability due to mental impairment: APA's evaluation of Social Security Administration guidelines. *American Journal of Psychiatry*, 148(8):1037-1043.

Qu, Y., M. Tan, and M.H. Kutner. 1996. Random effects models in latent class analysis for evaluating accuracy of diagnostic test. *Biometrics*, 52:797-810.

SSA (Social Security Administration). 2001. Research Note #13: Listing of Social Security advisory councils & commissions. Updated November 6, 2001. Available: www.ssa.gov/history/councils.html (accessed October 16, 2006).

Walter, S.D., and L.M. Irwig. 1988. Estimation of test error rates, disease prevalence, and relative risk from misclassified data: A review. *Journal of Clinical Epidemiology,* 41:923-937.

Yang, I., and M.P. Becker. 1997. Latent variable modeling of diagnostic accuracy. *Biometrics*, 53:948-958.

Young, J., H. Bucher, P. Tschudi, P. Periat, C. Hugenschmidt, and A. Welge-Lussen. 2003. The clinical diagnosis of acute bacterial rhinosinusitis in general practice and its therapeutic consequences. *Journal Clinical Epidemiology*, 56(4):377-384.

A

Biographical Sketches of Committee Members

John D. Stobo, M.D. (Chair), is president of the University of Texas Medical Branch at Galveston. Dr. Stobo graduated from medical school at the State University of New York in Buffalo in 1968. He then completed two years of training on the Osler Medical Service at the Johns Hopkins Hospital, two years as a research associate at the National Institutes of Health, and one year as chief medical resident on the Osler Medical Service at Johns Hopkins. Dr. Stobo was then an assistant professor for three years at the Department of Immunology at the Mayo Clinic. From 1976 to 1985, he served as head of the Section of Rheumatology and Clinical Immunology at the University of California, San Francisco, where he was also an investigator with the Howard Hughes Medical Institute. In 1985, he returned to Johns Hopkins as the William Osler Professor of Medicine and Physician-in-Chief of the Johns Hopkins Hospital. In 1997, Dr. Stobo assumed his present position as president of The University of Texas Medical Branch at Galveston. He is a member of the Institute of Medicine (IOM).

Frank S. Bloch, J.D., Ph.D. (Vice Chair), is professor of law, Vanderbilt University Law School. He was director of clinical education from 1979 to 2001. Before that, he taught at the University of Chicago Law School. Before he began teaching, he was a legal aid lawyer with California Rural Legal Assistance (1971-1973). Professor Bloch is an expert in social security, disability, and other benefits programs. He is also very active in the international clinical education movement. Dr. Bloch earned his B.A. from Brandeis University (1966), his J.D. from Columbia University (1969), and a Ph.D. in politics from Brandeis University (1978). Professor Bloch has served as a Fulbright Professor in India and as a research fellow at the International Social Security Association in Geneva, Switzerland. He has also served as a consultant to the Administrative Conference of the United States and the Social Security Advisory Board. He is author of *Bloch on Social Security Disability*, issued annually online since 1995, *Who Returns to Work and Why? A Six-Country Study on Work Incapacity and Reintegration* (2001), *Disability Benefit Claim Processing and Appeals in Six Industrialized Countries* (1994), and *Disability Determination: The Administrative Process and the Role of Medical Personnel* (1992). He is a former chair of the American Bar Association's Income Security Committee, Section of Administrative Law and Regulatory Practice. He is a member of the bars of California and Tennessee.

Gunnar B. J. Andersson, M.D., Ph.D., is professor and chairman, Department of Orthopedic Surgery at Rush University Medical Center. During his more than 10 years as chairman, he has also been the vice dean for surgical sciences and services, senior vice president of medical affairs and president of the medical staff, each for two-year periods. Dr. Andersson received his M.D. from the University of Goteborg, Sweden, did his residency at Sahlgren University Hospital there, and obtained a Ph.D. in Medical Science at the University of Goteborg in 1974. After a fellowship at the London Hospital, he was on the faculty at the University of Goteborg for 10 years. In 1985 he moved to the United States and Rush University Medical Center. Dr. Andersson is a member of numerous medical societies and committees, a past president of the Orthopaedic Research Society and the International Society for the Study of the Lumbar Spine, and currently chairs the Research Committee at the American Academy of Orthopaedic Surgeons. He just finished a four-year period as a member of the Council of the National Institutes of Arthritis and Musculoskeletal and Skin Diseases at the National Institutes of Health (NIH). He has been a member of the U.S. National Safety Council and on the Steering Committee of the National Research Council's Workshop on Work-Related Musculoskeletal Injuries. Dr. Andersson is a member of 15 editorial boards. He is a deputy editor for *Spine*, editor-in-chief of *Contemporary Spine Surgery*, and an associate editor of *Clinical Biomechanics*. He is the author of more than 220 original articles and 150 books and book chapters. He was the senior editor of the *Guides to the Evaluation of Permanent Impairment, 5th Edition* (2000), and co-editor of *Disability Evaluation, 2nd Edition* (2003), both published by the American Medical Association.

Richard V. Burkhauser, Ph.D., is Sarah Gibson Blanding Professor of Policy, Department of Policy Analysis and Management, Cornell University. His professional career has focused on how public policies affect the economic behavior and well-being of vulnerable populations, such as people with disabilities, older persons, and low-income households. He has published widely on these topics in journals of demography, economics, gerontology, and public policy. Dr. Burkhauser is co-principal investigator (PI) on the Department of Education-funded Rehabilitation Research and Training Center (RRTC) for Economic Research on Employment Policy for Persons with Disabilities. He is also co-PI of the RRTC on Disability Demographics and Statistics. As co-PI of these RRTCs, he has carried out an extensive program of technical assistance and presentations to government agencies, policy makers, and consumers on the employment and economic well-being of people with disabilities. Dr. Burkhauser received his B.A. from St. Vincent College (1967) and his Ph.D. in economics from the University of Chicago (1976). Before going to Cornell in 1990, he was on the faculty of Vanderbilt University and the Maxwell School at Syracuse University. His most recent work on social security policies affecting people with disabilities includes his co-authorship of *The Economics of an Aging Society* (2004) and co-editorship of *The Decline in Employment of People with Disabilities: A Policy Puzzle* (2003).

Diana D. Cardenas, M.D., is professor and chair of the Department of Rehabilitation Medicine at the University of Miami Miller School of Medicine. Her research interests include chronic pain in spinal cord injuries, prevention of urinary tract infections in people with spinal cord injuries, and bladder management. Before going to the University of Miami in 2006, Dr. Cardenas was a professor in the Department of Rehabilitation Medicine, University of Washington, and chief of service, Department of Rehabilitation Medicine, clinical director, Spinal Cord Injury Service, and director, Spinal Cord Injury Clinic, University of Washington Medical Center. She was also the project director of the Northwest Regional Spinal Cord Injury System. Dr. Cardenas earned her B.A. at the University of Texas (1969) and her M.D. at the University of Texas Southwestern Medical School (1973). She earned M.S. (1976) and M.H.A. (2001) degrees and completed her residency in PM&R (1976) at the University of Washington, Seattle. Before joining the faculty of the University of Washington in 1981, she was in the Department of Rehabilitation Medicine at Emory University. Dr. Cardenas is board certified in physical medicine and rehabilitation and in electrodiagnostic medicine. She is a fellow of the American Congress of Rehabilitation Medicine and former chair, Research Advisory and Advocacy Committee, American Academy of Physical Medicine and Rehabilitation. She is a member of the IOM.

Sheila T. Fitzgerald, Ph.D., M.S.N., is an associate professor in the Department of Environmental Health Sciences, Johns Hopkins Bloomberg School of Public Health and School of Nursing, Johns Hopkins University. Her research interests are in the occupational health of young workers, the antecedents of adult work stress, and the occupational health of women with chronic diseases. Her current research includes a longitudinal study of working adolescent and young adults and the factors, such as job stress, that contribute to the development of cardiovascular disease later in life and a study of the factors that influence return to work after diagnosis of a chronic disease. Dr. Fitzgerald received her B.S. from the University of Wisconsin (1968), M.S.N. from the University of Pennsylvania (1973), A.N.P. from the University of Maryland (1981), and Ph.D. from the Johns Hopkins School of Hygiene and Public Health (1987). She is certified as an adult nurse practitioner by the American Nursing Association. She is a member of the Johns Hopkins University Disability Advisory Committee and was a member of the Medical and Insurance Subcommittee of the President's Committee on Employment of People with Disabilities (1992-1994).

Arthur Garson, Jr., M.D., M.P.H., assumed the position of dean of the School of Medicine and vice president of the University of Virginia in June 2002. He graduated from Princeton University in 1970 and received his M.D. from Duke University in 1974, remaining there for his pediatric residency. In 1979, he completed a pediatric cardiology fellowship at Baylor College of Medicine and joined its faculty in 1985. He was named chief of pediatric cardiology in 1988. In 1992, he received a master's degree in public health, specializing in health policy and health care finance, from the University of Texas in Houston, and was recruited by Duke to be associate vice chancellor of health affairs. While there, much of his work focused on health policy. Three years later, he returned to Houston and became senior vice president and dean for academic operations at Baylor and vice president of Texas Children's Hospital. Dr. Garson has an extensive history of national and international service in the field of pediatric cardiology, specifically sudden death in children and adolescents. He was president of the American College of Cardiology from 2000 to 2001, and he continues to serve on its board of trustees and several of its committees, including government relations and quality of care. He also serves on the Agency for Healthcare Research and Quality National Advisory Council. In 2001, he was appointed to the White House Advisory Panel on Health System Improvement. Dr. Garson helps strengthen and guide medical education through his service to the Association of American Medical Colleges, the University Hospitals Consortium, and the Association of Academic Health Centers.

Kristofer J. Hagglund, Ph.D., A.B.P.P., is associate dean and professor of health psychology in the School of Health Professions at the University of

Missouri-Columbia. He was a 2000-2001 Robert Wood Johnson Health Policy Fellow in the Office of Senator Tom Harkin, where he worked on legislation addressing patients' rights, mental health parity, rural health care, community health centers, and the National Health Service Corps. Dr. Hagglund has an active research program and has published in the areas of adaptation to chronic illnesses and disabilities, health care delivery systems for people with chronic illness or disabilities, and professional issues. He is a co-principal investigator (CPI) of the Missouri Model Spinal Cord Injury System, a five-year research and demonstration project funded by the National Institute on Disability and Rehabilitation Research. He is also CPI of the Missouri Arthritis Rehabilitation Research and Training Center, where he is completing a study of health care delivery systems for people with arthritis. Dr. Hagglund also co-directs the Center for Health Policy at the University of Missouri-Columbia, which is addressing health insurance and health disparity issues in Missouri. He obtained a B.A. in psychology from Illinois State University and a Ph.D. in clinical (medical) psychology from the University of Alabama at Birmingham. He is a diplomate of the American Board of Professional Psychology and a fellow of the American Psychological Association (APA). He is immediate past president of APA'S Division of Rehabilitation Psychology.

Allen W. Heinemann, Ph.D., completed his doctoral degree in clinical psychology at the University of Kansas with a specialty focus in rehabilitation. He completed an internship at Baylor College of Medicine in Houston and was an assistant professor in the Department of Psychology at Illinois Institute of Technology. Since 1985, he has worked at the Rehabilitation Institute of Chicago (RIC), where he directs the Center for Rehabilitation Outcomes Research, a rehabilitation-focused health services research unit. He is also associate director of research at RIC and a professor in the Department of Physical Medicine and Rehabilitation at the Feinberg School of Medicine, Northwestern University. He serves on the Coordinating Committee for Northwestern University's Institute for Health Services Research and Policy Studies. His research interests focus on health services, psychosocial aspects of rehabilitation, including substance abuse, and measurement issues in rehabilitation.

Ronald Leopold, M.D., M.B.A., M.P.H., is national medical director and vice president of MetLife Disability. He is a board-certified occupational medicine physician who holds a Masters in Business Administration from The Wharton School and a Masters in Public Health from Boston University. He is an active member of the American College of Occupational and Environmental Medicine. Dr. Leopold currently serves as clinical thought leader for MetLife Disability and has recently developed the MetLife disability durations guidelines and its clinical triage claims model. His responsibilities include clinical program development, industry thought leadership, clinical data analysis, and new product development. His work also includes benefits solutions consultation with MetLife corporate customers. Dr. Leopold recently published a book, *A Year in the Life of a Million American Workers*, a visual guide to the major injuries and illnesses affecting American workers that examines industry-specific norms and suggests risk reduction programs for getting employees back to work. The book provides quantitative and qualitative information and benchmarks that employers need to identify occupational health problems in their workforce and identify intervention programs to prevent or reduce problems that result in absences. He has also worked in managed workers compensation, where he was involved in the development and management of a national provider network. In 1997, he wrote a book on the Internet for occupational health professionals.

Larry G. Massanari was acting commissioner of social security for eight months during 2001, serving until the current commissioner was appointed. Previously, he had served as the Philadelphia regional commissioner for the Social Security Administration (SSA) for 14 years, where he directed agency operations in the mid-Atlantic states. A graduate of Western Michigan University, Mr. Massanari has done graduate work at Northwestern University. He began his career at SSA in 1966 as a claims representative in a field office. He served in a variety of administrative and managerial positions in the Chicago area before moving to agency headquarters in 1979. He held several top-level positions in SSA's central office, including director of human resources and associate commissioner for policy. He was named commissioner for the Philadelphia region in 1987. Mr. Massanari was a presidential executive rank award winner in 1992, 1997, and 2002, receiving the rank of both meritorious and distinguished executive. He has been the recipient of three commissioner's citations, the highest honor conferred upon SSA employees. In 1990, he received the first Commissioner's Leadership Award. In 2003, he received the National Public Service Award from the American Society for Public Administration and the Roger W. Jones Award for Executive Leadership from American University.

Stephen G. Pauker, M.D., is vice chairman for clinical affairs and associate physician-in-chief, Department of Medicine, Tufts-New England Medical Center (NEMC), and professor of medicine and professor of psychiatry, Tufts University School of Medicine. He is an expert on clinical decision making and evidence-based medicine and founded the Division of Clinical Decision Making at Tufts-NEMC. Dr. Pauker is board certified in internal medicine and cardiovascular diseases as well as in medical hypnosis. He is a member of numerous professional societies, including the American College of Cardiology, American College of Medical Informatics, American College of Physicians, American Federation for Medical Research, American Heart Association, American Medical Association, American Society of Clinical Hypnosis, American Society of Clinical Investigation, Association of American Physicians, and Society for Medical Decision Making (which awarded him their career achievement award). Dr. Pauker is a master of the American College of Physicians. His publications and research have addressed decision making for both health policy and individual patients. He has served on a number of IOM and National Academy of Sciences committees, including the Committee to Evaluate the Artificial Heart Program of the National Heart, Lung, and Blood Institute; workshops on the National Institutes of Health Consensus Development Process and the Use of Drugs in the Elderly; Committee on Thyroid Screening Related to I-131 Exposure; Committee on Extending Medicare Coverage for Preventive and Other Services; Committee on Regulating Occupational Exposure to Tuberculosis in the Workplace; and Committee to Assess the Scientific Information for the Radiation Exposure Screening and Education Program. Dr. Pauker earned his medical degree at Harvard University in 1968 and trained in internal medicine and cardiology at Boston City and Massachusetts General Hospitals and the NEMC, all in Boston. Dr. Pauker is a member of the IOM.

Linda A. Randolph, M.D., M.P.H., currently serves as president and CEO of Developing Families Center, Inc., an innovative, comprehensive, one-stop center for childbearing and childrearing families in northeast Washington, D.C. She has spent her career working to make things happen at the community level that promote the health and well-being of mothers, children, and families, and working to make changes in public policy. She has worked in public health at the federal, state, and local government levels and in academia. She is a graduate of the Howard University College of Medicine and the University of California's School of Public Health at Berkeley. Her experience includes completing a pediatrics residency in Harlem; serving as the national director of health services for the Federal Head Start program; directing the New York State Department of Health's Office of Public Health; serving as executive director of the Carnegie Corporation of New York's "Starting Points" initiative and serving as executive director of the National Women's Resource Center for Substance Abuse and Mental Illness. Dr. Randolph served as clinical professor of community medicine, pediatrics, and psychiatry at the Mt. Sinai School of Medicine in New York and is currently adjunct research professor and senior health advisor at Georgetown University's Graduate Public Policy Institute. Dr. Randolph was the 2001 recipient of the Martha May Eliot Award of the American Public Health Association, which honors exceptional achievements in the field of maternal and child health. She was recently appointed to the board of directors of Children's Futures, a multi-million-dollar Robert Wood Johnson-funded citywide initiative in Trenton, New Jersey, that focuses on the healthy growth and development of children birth to age three. She is a member of the national advisory committee to the Community Health Scholars Program, a post-doctoral fellowship program funded by the W. K. Kellogg Foundation to meet the growing needs of schools of public health and other health professions for faculty with community competency.

Brian M. Schulman, M.D., a diplomate of the American Board of Psychiatry and Neurology in Psychiatry and a certified independent medical examiner, practices occupational and organizational psychiatry in Bethesda, Maryland. He specializes in the assessment of mental disorders and the determination of disability. Dr. Schulman has performed independent medical examinations for 25 years. He has written numerous articles and textbook chapters on assessing the medical aspects of stress, psychiatric impairment, and the determination of disability. He also co-authored a book on the self-management of chronic pain. He is on the editorial board of the *Journal of Occupational Rehabilitation* and has lectured extensively on such topics as the assessment of mental disability. He was a lieutenant commander in the Navy Medical Corps, assistant professor of psychiatry at The Georgetown University School of Medicine, and medical consultant to the Institute of Human Resources, an employee assistance program developer.

Peter W. Thomas, J.D., is a principal at the law firm of Powers Pyles Sutter & Verville, P.C. He specializes in health care, rehabilitation, and disability law and policy. He chaired the subcommittee on consumer rights, protections, and responsibilities of the President's Advisory Commission on Consumer Protection and Quality in the Health Care Industry. He has also served on advisory boards to two federal agencies, the Agency for Healthcare Research and Quality and NIH's National Center for Medical Rehabilitation Research. He currently serves on the boards of directors of the Center for International Rehabilitation and the Center on Disability and Health and co-chairs the health task force of the Consortium for Citizens with Disabilities. He previously served on the board of directors for the Commission on Accreditation for Rehabilitation Facilities from 2002 to 2004. He is a co-author of *Complying with the Americans with Disabilities Act: A Guidebook for Management and People with Disabilities* and is admitted to practice law in New York State and Washington, D.C. He attended Boston College and Georgetown University Law Center, where he was associate editor of the *Journal of Law and Technology*.

Craig A. Velozo, Ph.D., O.T.R./L, is associate professor and associate chair of the Department of Occupational Therapy, College of Public Health and Health Professions, University of Florida. His research focus is on the development of outcome measures, using Rasch measurement theory. Dr. Velozo has served as the PI on a National Institute on Disability and Rehabilitation Research field-initiated grant to develop a computerized adaptive measurement system for the activity dimension of the International Classification of Functioning Disability and Health. He also serves as research health scientist and co-director of the outcomes measurement focus of the Rehabilitation Outcomes Research Center at the North Florida/South Georgia Veterans Affairs Medical Center in Gainesville, Florida. In 2000, Dr. Velozo received the highest research recognition in the profession, selection to the American Occupational Therapy Academy of Research.

B

Committee Charge

An expert committee will provide recommendations to the Social Security Administration (SSA) on how to (1) improve the Listing of Impairments (Listings), a screening tool SSA uses as part of its process of determining eligibility for disability payments under the Social Security Disability Insurance and Supplemental Security Income programs, and (2) access and use effectively appropriate medical expertise to support the Social Security disability adjudication process at all stages, including the appeals process. Specifically, in addressing the Listings, the committee will consider:

1. The value and utility of the current Listings for all users (claimants, SSA, health care professionals, state offices, and officials involved in the adjudication process)
2. Conceptual models for organizing the Listings, beyond the current "body systems" model specified in federal regulations
3. Processes for determining when the Listings require revision and criteria upon which to add new listings or remove old ones
4. Feedback mechanisms to continuously assess and evaluate the Listings for the purpose of improving consistency in application by all adjudicators throughout the country
5. Adaptability of the Listings, including methods to account for variable access to health care services (including diagnostics and pharmaceuticals) in determining whether an individual's condition meets or equals the Listings

6. Methods to assess and quantify the effects of multiple impairments that may not individually cross the eligibility threshold (i.e., SSA's "equivalence" concept)

7. Advisability of and methods for integrating functional assessment into the Listings

In addressing the organization of medical expertise, the committee will:

8. Review SSA's list of presumptive disability conditions and suggest revisions, additions, and/or deletions. The committee will recommend essential criteria for establishing candidate conditions for presumptive disability and recommend the level of professional expertise needed to certify that a presumptive diagnosis is adequately established.

9. Advise on how best to provide medical expertise needed to support the entire disability adjudication process. This will involve describing the type of experts needed (academic specialists, practicing specialists, practicing generalists or nonphysicians), necessary credentials, and where best to locate them (from university medical centers, centers of excellence for specialized care, or community practice settings).

10. Recommend needs for standardized training and certification for consultative examiners who assess claimant's level of function based on integrated evaluation of medical impairment and functional capacity. Advise on content of a training curriculum, appropriate personnel to train, and mechanisms for the certification process.

C

Interim Report, December 2005

At the first committee meeting, held on January 30, 2005, the Social Security Administration (SSA) asked the committee to focus its attention initially on tasks 8-10 of its charge (see Appendix B) and, if possible, to issue its findings and recommendations on those tasks as soon as possible. The committee agreed that it would address these issues in an interim letter report. However, the committee also made clear that, after completing all of its deliberations, it might refine those preliminary recommendations.

The committee issued its interim report, *Improving the Social Security Disability Decision Process: Interim Report*, on these three tasks on December 21, 2005. That interim report is included in this appendix. In the interim report, the committee made 13 recommendations with respect to SSA's use of medical expertise in its disability decision-making process. Now that the committee has completed all of its deliberations, the committee adopts these recommendations as its final recommendations on these issues, subject to the following additional comments with respect to Recommendations 1-2 and 1-7 (addressing qualification requirements for physicians and psychologists who serve as medical consultants [MCs] for the state Disability Determination Services agencies and as medical experts [MEs] at administrative law judge hearings).

In recommendations 1-2 and 1-7, the committee recommended that SSA require that physicians and psychologists who serve as MCs and MEs be board certified. As the committee noted in the interim report, "board certification is rapidly becoming the standard credential for the practice of medicine or psychology." The committee realizes that, although board certification has become the norm for physicians, relatively few psychologists are board certified. The committee therefore modified its recommendation to recommend that SSA continue the current requirements for psychologists participating as MCs or MEs but establish a long-term goal requiring that psychologists be board certified.

Improving the Social Security Disability Decision Process

Interim Report

Committee on Improving the Disability Decision Process: SSA's Listing of Impairments and Agency Access to Medical Expertise
Medical Follow-Up Agency

INSTITUTE OF MEDICINE
OF THE NATIONAL ACADEMIES

THE NATIONAL ACADEMIES PRESS
Washington, D.C.
www.nap.edu

THE NATIONAL ACADEMIES PRESS 500 Fifth Street, N.W. Washington, DC 20001

NOTICE: The project that is the subject of this report was approved by the Governing Board of the National Research Council, whose members are drawn from the councils of the National Academy of Sciences, the National Academy of Engineering, and the Institute of Medicine. The members of the committee responsible for the report were chosen for their special competences and with regard for appropriate balance.

This study was supported by Contract No. SS00-04-60083 between the National Academy of Sciences and Social Security Administration. Any opinions, findings, conclusions, or recommendations expressed in this publication are those of the author(s) and do not necessarily reflect the view of the organizations or agencies that provided support for this project.

Additional copies of this report are available from the National Academies Press, 500 Fifth Street, N.W., Lockbox 285, Washington, DC 20055; (800) 624-6242 or (202) 334-3313 (in the Washington metropolitan area); Internet, http://www.nap.edu.

For more information about the Institute of Medicine, visit the IOM home page at: **www.iom.edu.**

Printed in the United States of America.

The serpent has been a symbol of long life, healing, and knowledge among almost all cultures and religions since the beginning of recorded history. The serpent adopted as a logotype by the Institute of Medicine is a relief carving from ancient Greece, now held by the Staatliche Museen in Berlin.

"Knowing is not enough; we must apply.
Willing is not enough; we must do."
—Goethe

INSTITUTE OF MEDICINE
OF THE NATIONAL ACADEMIES

Advising the Nation. Improving Health.

THE NATIONAL ACADEMIES

Advisers to the Nation on Science, Engineering, and Medicine

The **National Academy of Sciences** is a private, nonprofit, self-perpetuating society of distinguished scholars engaged in scientific and engineering research, dedicated to the furtherance of science and technology and to their use for the general welfare. Upon the authority of the charter granted to it by the Congress in 1863, the Academy has a mandate that requires it to advise the federal government on scientific and technical matters. Dr. Ralph J. Cicerone is president of the National Academy of Sciences.

The **National Academy of Engineering** was established in 1964, under the charter of the National Academy of Sciences, as a parallel organization of outstanding engineers. It is autonomous in its administration and in the selection of its members, sharing with the National Academy of Sciences the responsibility for advising the federal government. The National Academy of Engineering also sponsors engineering programs aimed at meeting national needs, encourages education and research, and recognizes the superior achievements of engineers. Dr. Wm. A. Wulf is president of the National Academy of Engineering.

The **Institute of Medicine** was established in 1970 by the National Academy of Sciences to secure the services of eminent members of appropriate professions in the examination of policy matters pertaining to the health of the public. The Institute acts under the responsibility given to the National Academy of Sciences by its congressional charter to be an adviser to the federal government and, upon its own initiative, to identify issues of medical care, research, and education. Dr. Harvey V. Fineberg is president of the Institute of Medicine.

The **National Research Council** was organized by the National Academy of Sciences in 1916 to associate the broad community of science and technology with the Academy's purposes of furthering knowledge and advising the federal government. Functioning in accordance with general policies determined by the Academy, the Council has become the principal operating agency of both the National Academy of Sciences and the National Academy of Engineering in providing services to the government, the public, and the scientific and engineering communities. The Council is administered jointly by both Academies and the Institute of Medicine. Dr. Ralph J. Cicerone and Dr. Wm. A. Wulf are chair and vice chair, respectively, of the National Research Council.

www.national-academies.org

COMMITTEE ON IMPROVING THE DISABILITY DECISION PROCESS: SSA'S LISTING OF IMPAIRMENTS AND AGENCY ACCESS TO MEDICAL EXPERTISE

JOHN D. STOBO (*Chair*), President, University of Texas Medical Branch at Galveston, University of Texas
FRANK S. BLOCH (*Vice Chair*), Professor of Law, Vanderbilt University Law School, Nashville, TN
GUNNAR B.J. ANDERSSON, Professor and Chairman, Department of Orthopedic Surgery, Rush University Medical Center, Chicago, IL
RICHARD V. BURKHAUSER, Professor and Chairman, Department of Policy Analysis and Management, Cornell University, Ithaca, NY
DIANA D. CARDENAS, Professor and Chief, Department of Rehabilitation Medicine, University of Washington Medical Center, Seattle, WA (Dr. Cardenas became a professor at the University of Florida.)
SHEILA T. FITZGERALD, Associate Professor, Division of Occupational Health, School of Hygiene and Public Health, Johns Hopkins University School of Nursing, Baltimore, MD
ARTHUR GARSON, Dean, School of Medicine, Vice President, University of Virginia, Charlottesville, VA
KRISTOFER J. HAGGLUND, Associate Dean for Health Policy and Professor of Health Psychology, School of Health Professions, University of Missouri, Columbia, MO
ALLEN W. HEINEMANN, Professor, Department of Physical Medicine and Rehabilitation, Feinberg School of Medicine, Northwestern University, Director, Center for Rehabilitation Outcomes Research, Rehabilitation Institute of Chicago
RONALD LEOPOLD, Vice President, MetLife, Alpharetta, GA
LARRY G. MASSANARI, Former Acting Commissioner, Social Security Administration, Exton, PA
STEPHEN G. PAUKER, Professor, Tufts University School of Medicine, Vice Chairman for Clinical Affairs, Department of Medicine, Associate Physician-In-Chief, Tufts-New England Medical Center, Boston, MA
LINDA A. RANDOLPH, President and CEO, Developing Families Center, Inc., Washington, DC
BRIAN M. SCHULMAN, Private Practice in Occupational Psychiatry, Bethesda, MD
PETER W. THOMAS, Principal, Powers Pyles Sutter & Verville, PC, Washington, DC

CRAIG A. VELOZO, Professor and Associate Chair, Department of Occupational Therapy, College of Public Health and Health Professions, University of Florida; Research Health Scientist, Rehabilitation Outcomes Research Center, North Florida/South Georgia Veterans Health System

Project Staff

MICHAEL McGEARY, Study Director
MORGAN A. FORD, Program Officer
SUSAN R. McCUTCHEN, Research Associate
REINE Y. HOMAWOO, Senior Program Assistant
RICK ERDTMANN, Director, Medical Follow-up Agency
PAMELA RAMEY-McCRAY, Administrative Assistant
ANDREA COHEN, Financial Associate
DAVID K. BARNES, Consultant

Reviewers

This report has been reviewed in draft form by individuals chosen for their diverse perspectives and technical expertise, in accordance with procedures approved by the National Research Council's Report Review Committee. The purpose of this independent review is to provide candid and critical comments that will assist the institution in making its published report as sound as possible and to ensure that the report meets institutional standards for objectivity, evidence, and responsiveness to the study charge. The review comments and draft manuscript remain confidential to protect the integrity of the deliberative process. We wish to thank the following individuals for their review of this report:

Veronica D. Feeg, George Mason University School of Nursing, Fairfax, VA
Claude Earl Fox, Johns Hopkins University Bloomberg School of Public Health, Baltimore, MD
Linda P. Fried, Johns Hopkins University Center on Aging and Health, Baltimore, MD
Patricia M. Owens, Consultation in Health & Disability Programs, Brooklyn, NY
James M. Perrin, Massachusetts General Hospital, Boston, MA
Harold A. Pincus, University of Pittsburgh Medical Center, Pittsburgh, PA
Glenn S. Pransky, Liberty Mutual Research Institute for Safety, Hopkinton, MA
Stephen T. Wegener, Johns Hopkins University School of Medicine, Baltimore, MD

Although the reviewers listed above have provided many constructive comments and suggestions, they were not asked to endorse the conclusions or recommendations nor did they see the final draft of the report before its release. The review of this report was overseen by **Joseph P. Newhouse,** Harvard University, and **Lee Goldman,** University of California, San Francisco. Appointed by the National Research Council and Institute of Medicine, respectively, they were responsible for making certain that an independent examination of this report was carried out in accordance with institutional procedures and that all review comments were carefully considered. Responsibility for the final content of this report rests entirely with the authoring committee and the institution.

Preface

The Institute of Medicine (IOM) Committee on Improving the Disability Decision Process has been working since it first met in January 2005 to develop recommendations to the Social Security Administration (SSA) on how to improve the medical aspects of its disability determination process. By law, Social Security can only pay benefits to those unable to engage in substantial gainful activity because of a "*medically determinable* physical or mental impairment which can be expected to result in death or which has lasted or can be expected to last for a continuous period of not less than 12 months" (emphasis added). Medical and psychological expertise is critical both in developing the criteria for measuring the severity and functional impact of an impairment or impairments on an applicant's ability to work and in applying the criteria to individual cases where the medical evidence does not clearly meet the criteria in the eyes of a nonmedical disability examiner.

The committee's final report is due in 2006, but SSA asked the committee to focus first on the expertise issues and provide early recommendations on the qualifications of the medical and psychological experts involved in the disability decision process in a short interim report. SSA is currently in the process of revamping its disability decision process and, according to a Notice of Proposed Rulemaking (NPRM) published in the *Federal Register* in July 2005, plans to establish a national network of medical and psychological experts who meet qualification standards set by the Commissioner of Social Security. The NPRM did not specify the qualification standards but noted that they would be promulgated within six months of the effective date of the final rule and that the Commissioner would consider the advice of the IOM in setting the standards.

The committee is continuing to address the remaining tasks in its charge, which focus on the medical criteria for assessing if an applicant qualifies for disability benefits. In this phase of the study, the committee is assessing the overall effectiveness of the Listing of Impairments (Listings) in the disability decision process, especially the use of the Listings as a screening tool for determining disability based on medical considerations alone. The committee's findings and recommendations concerning the screening criteria may have further implications for the expertise needed to apply the medical criteria. If so, the committee may have further recommendations about medical expertise in the final report.

In developing this interim report, the committee received input from many sources, in the form of presentations at meetings and written statements submitted for the record. Many others responded to requests for information from the committee staff. On behalf of the committee, I would like to thank those who provided information. At the first meeting on January 31-February 1, 2005, these included directors of three state Disability Determination Services (DDS) agencies—Andrew Marioni, Jr. (Delaware DDS); Tommy Warren (Alabama DDS); and Walter Roers (Minnesota DDS)—and four judges from the SSA Office of Hearings and Appeals—David B. Washington, Chief Administrative Law Judge (ALJ); Nancy Griswold, Chief ALJ, Region I, Boston; William Taylor, Executive Director, Office of Appellate Operations; and Robert Johnson, Appeals Council.

For the second meeting, in April 2005, the committee notified more than 100 organizations of the opportunity to make presentations or provide written statements at the meeting. The public forum part of the meeting was held in the Barbara Jordan Conference Center of the Kaiser Family Foundation, a very accessible facility provided for free by the Foundation. Presenters at the public forum were Eileen Sweeney, Center on Budget and Policy Priorities; Marty Ford, Disability Policy Collaboration of The Arc and United Cerebral Palsy; Ethel Zelenske, National Organization of Social Security Claimants' Representatives; Andrew Marioni, Jr., National Council of Disability Determination Directors, and Director, Delaware Disability Determination Services; David Randolph, American Academy of Disability Evaluating Physicians; and James McCarthy, National Federation of the Blind. The National Association of Disability Examiners submitted a written statement.

At the second meeting, the committee also heard from panels of experts on training and certification requirements that might improve the level of medical expertise in the disability decision process. The panelists and their organizations were Robert Robertson, Shelia Drake, Beverly Crawford and Carol Dawn Petersen, Government Accountability Office; John

Pro, American Board of Independent Medical Examiners; Douglas Martin, American Academy of Disability Evaluation Physicians; Steve Geiringer, Wayne State University and American Academy of Physical Medicine and Rehabilitation; Elizabeth Genovese, American College of Occupational and Environmental Medicine; Sandra Hall, American Association of Occupational Health Nurses; Joanne Ebert, Association of Rehabilitation Nurses; Michael Borek, Medical Director, Delaware DDS; Joseph Aaron, Chief Medical Officer, New Jersey DDS; William Humphreys, former medical consultant, Virginia DDS; Barry Eigen, Office of Disability and Income Security Programs; Monte Hetland, Pediatric Medical Officer, Office of Medical Policy, SSA; George Jesien and Rhoda Schulzinger, Association of University Centers on Disabilities; Howard Goldman, University of Maryland School of Medicine; and Thomas Yates, Health and Disability Advocates, Chicago.

At its fourth and fifth meetings in August and October 2005, the committee heard from Christine Hartel, National Research Council (NRC); Susan Van Hemel, NRC; Kristin Johnson, Charles Sweet, and Katherine Edwards, Disability Evaluation Services, University of Massachusetts Medical School; Jo Anne Barnhart, Commissioner of Social Security; Patricia Owens, Consultation in Health and Disability Programs, Brooklyn, New York; and Ethan Balk, AHRQ Evidence-based Practice Center, Tufts-New England Medical Center.

I would like to thank the SSA officials who not only requested the study, made presentations and answered questions at committee meetings, and met with committee staff, but also contributed information, documents, and statistics and made available the directors and medical directors of state DDS agencies and administrative law judges in the Office of Hearings and Appeals who met with the committee (listed above). These officials are Jo Anne B. Barnhart, Commissioner of Social Security, who met with the committee on October 6, 2005, to describe her plans for improving the disability decision process and answer questions from committee members; Martin H. Gerry, Deputy Commissioner for Disability and Income Security Programs; Glenn Sklar, Associate Commissioner for Disability Programs; Pamela Mazerski, Associate Commissioner for Program Development and Research; and Nancy Schoenberg, Office of Disability Programs, the project officer for this study who greatly facilitated responses to the committee's requests for information.

The staff would like to thank the following for providing information or other assistance: Bob L. Appleton, Office of Disability Programs, SSA; Barbara Barzansky, American Medical Association; Kathleen M. Bernett, American Board of Independent Medical Examiners; Howard Bradley, Office of Research, Evaluation and Statistics, SSA; Shari Bratt, National Association of Disability Examiners (NADE); Dean M. Burgess, American Association of Occupational Health Nurses; Shanklin Cannon, Northwestern Mutual; Lenore Carlson, Office of Disability Determinations, SSA; Winthrop S. Cashdollar, America's Health Insurance Plans; Joanne Castello, Office of Disability Programs, SSA; Thomas Charest, Jefferson Pilot Financial; Mary Chatel, Office of the Commissioner, SSA; Carol G. Cook, U.S. Office of Personnel Management; Deborah A. Cotter, American Psychological Association; Ann R. Cox, American Association of Occupational Health Nurses; Beverly Crawford, Government Accountability Office (GAO); Susan David, Office of Disability Programs, SSA; Laurence Desi, Office of Medical Policy, SSA; Anne Deutsch, Northwestern University; Terry Dodson, Office of Disability Programs, SSA; Shelia Drake, GAO; Dan Dougherty, Prudential Disability Management Services; Barry Eigen, Office of Disability Programs, SSA; Barry Eisenberg, Academy of Occupational and Environmental Medicine; Judith Feder, Georgetown University; Angela Foehl, American Psychiatric Association; Claire Green, Office of Hearings and Appeals (OHA), SSA; David Hatfield, OHA, SSA; Michael Heitz, OHA, SSA; Monte Hetland, Office of Medical Policy, SSA; Jay Himmelstein, University of Massachusetts Medical School; Deena Howell, Florida Retirement System; Sunmee Jo, OHA, SSA; Carol Jones, Office of Disability Programs, SSA; Patricia Jonas, Assistant Deputy Commissioner for Disability and Income Security Programs, SSA; Jim Julian, Office of Medical Policy, SSA; Karen Kadell, Minnesota State Retirement System; Cille Kennedy, Department of Health and Human Services; Theresa Klubertanz, NADE; Joseph LaDou, University of California Medical School-San Francisco; Susanne Lapierre, Liberty Mutual; Joni Lavery, National Academy of Social Insurance (NASI); Barry S. Levy, Tufts University; Cathy Lively, Office of Medical Policy, SSA; Jeffrey S. Lubbers, Washington College of Law, American University; Margaret Malone, Office of the Commissioner, SSA; Martha Marshall, NADE; Kathleen H. McGinley, National Association of Protection and Advocacy Systems; Paul Martin, Aetna Insurance Company; Jill F. Mocarski, Northwestern Mutual; Mark Nadel, Georgetown University; William E. Narrow, American Psychiatric Institute for Research and Education; Dorothy Nettles, Office of Disability Determinations; Paul Newacheck, University of California-San Francisco; Barbara Otto, Health & Disability Advocates, Chicago; Georgann Ozanich, Minnesota State Retirement System; Diane M. Pedulla, American Psychological Association; Carol Dawn Petersen, GAO; Clark Pickett, Office of Research, Evaluation and Statistics, SSA; Marquita Rand, Office of Medical Policy, SSA; Virginia Reno, NASI; Robert Rich, University of Illinois at Urbana-Champaign; Robert E. Robertson, GAO; John M. Rogers, The Hartford Life Insurance Companies; Gloria Barone Rosanio, CIGNA Disability Management Solutions; Jane Ross, NRC; Vince Sabatino, Office of Program Development and Research, SSA; Sandra Z. Salan, Office of Medical Policy, SSA; Stephen

Schmidt, Office of Workers' Compensation Programs, U.S. Department of Labor; Frank Schuster, Office of Medical Policy, SSA; Art Spencer, Office of Disability Programs, SSA; Steven Sperka, Northwestern Mutual Life; Kaye Sullivan-McDevitt, UnumProvident Portland Disability Benefits Center; Lauren Swanson, CIGNA Disability Management Solutions; Patricia Thomas, MetLife Disability; Tiana Tozer, The Standard; Michael Weinrich, National Center for Medical Rehabilitation Research, National Institutes of Health; Mimi Wirtanen, NADE; Gooloo Wunderlich, NRC; Sandra Yost, American Academy of Disability Evaluating Physicians; and Barry Zevin, Tom Waddell Health Center, San Francisco Department of Public Health.

Finally, I would like to thank the staff members who have worked hard to help the committee organize its meetings and produce this interim report on a compressed time schedule. They are Michael McGeary, Study Director; Rick Erdtmann, Director, Medical Follow-up Agency; Morgan Ford, Program Officer (since October 2005); Susan McCutchen, Research Associate; Reine Homawoo, Senior Program Assistant; and David K. Barnes, Consultant.

John D. Stobo, M.D.
Chair

Contents

Figures and Tables

FIGURES

TABLES

ANNEX TABLES

Abbreviations and Acronyms

AAMRO	American Association of Medical Review Officers
ABMS	American Board of Medical Specialties
ABPP	American Board of Professional Psychologists
ACUS	Administrative Conference of the United States
AHC	academic health center
ALJ	administrative law judge
ALS	amyotrophic lateral sclerosis
AMA	American Medical Association
AME	aviation medical examiners
AUCD	Association of University Centers on Disabilities
CE	consultative examination
CFR	Code of Federal Regulations
CME	continuing medical education
COPD	chronic obstructive pulmonary disease
CPP/OAS	Canada Pension Plan/Old Age Security
CPT	Current Procedural Terminology, AMA
CY	calendar year
DDS	Disability Determination Services
DE	disability examiner
DHHS	U.S. Department of Health and Human Services
DOL	U.S. Department of Labor
DOT	U.S. Department of Transportation

Ed.	Edition
eDib	electronic disability process
ESRD	end stage renal disease
FAA	Federal Aviation Administration
FEU	Federal Expert Unit
FY	fiscal year
GAO	Government Accountability Office
HIV	human immunodeficiency virus
IME	independent medical examination
IOM	Institute of Medicine
MC	medical consultant
M.D.	doctor of medicine
ME	medical expert
MRO	medical review officers
NIH	National Institutes of Health
NIOSH	National Institute for Occupational Safety and Health
NPRM	Notice of Proposed Rulemaking
OHA	Office of Hearings and Appeals, SSA
OWCP	Office of Workers' Compensation Programs, DOL
PD	presumptive disability
PER	pre-effectuation review
Ph.D.	doctor of philosophy
POMS DI	Program Operations Manual System—Disability Insurance, SSA
Psy.D.	doctor of psychology
QA	quality assurance
QME	Qualified Medical Examiner
RVU	relative value unit
SDM	single decision maker
SSA	Social Security Administration
SSAB	Social Security Advisory Board

SSDI	Social Security Disability Insurance
SSI	Supplemental Security Income
TERI	terminal illness
U.S.	United States
VA	Department of Veterans Affairs

Improving the Social Security Disability Decision Process
Interim Report

EXECUTIVE SUMMARY

Overview of Social Security Disability Programs

The Social Security Administration (SSA) provides Social Security Disability Insurance (SSDI) benefits to disabled persons of less than full retirement age and to their dependents. SSA also provides Supplemental Security Income (SSI) payments to disabled persons who are under age 65. For both programs, disability is defined as a "medically determinable physical or mental impairment" that prevents an individual from engaging in any substantial gainful activity and is expected to last at least 12 months or result in death.

As of December 2004, SSA was making disability payments to 10.8 million adults and children based on their own disability and 1.5 million dependents of disabled adults. In fiscal year (FY) 2005, SSA estimated it would process approximately 2.5 million initial claims for disability benefits, 25 percent more than in FY 2000.

Assuming that an applicant meets the nonmedical requirements for eligibility (e.g., quarters of covered employment for SSDI; income and asset limits for SSI), the file is sent to the Disability Determination Services (DDS) agency operated by the state in which he or she lives for a determination of medical eligibility. SSA reimburses the states for the full costs of the DDSs.

The DDSs apply a sequential decision process specified by SSA to make an initial decision whether a claim should be allowed or denied. If the claim is denied, the decision can be appealed through several levels of administrative and judicial review. On average, the DDSs allow 37 percent of the claims they adjudicate through the five-step process. A third of those denied decide to appeal, and three-quarters of the appeals result in allowances. Nearly 30 percent of the allowances made each year are made during the appeals process after an initial denial.

In 2003, the Commissioner of Social Security announced her intent to develop a "new approach" to disability determination. The goals of the new approach are to (1) make the correct decision as early in the claims process as possible and (2) foster return to work at all stages of the process.

IOM Study Charge

In late 2004, SSA asked the Institute of Medicine (IOM) to help in two areas related to its initiatives to improve the disability decision process.

1. Improvements in the criteria for determining the severity of impairments. Currently, SSA uses a Listing of Impairments (the Listings) to identify impairments and associated medical findings that are so severe that SSA can consider individuals with one of these impairments, or their equivalent in severity, to be disabled without additional evidence of their inability to work.
2. Improvements in the use of medical expertise in the disability decision process. Currently, each DDS has medical consultants on staff and a roster of outside medical sources it uses to conduct independent medical examinations, called consultative examinations, and each regional office of the Office of Hearings and Appeals has a roster of medical experts who have agreed to provide their opinions in cases being heard by administrative law judges. Other than state licensure, SSA does not have national qualification standards or training and certification requirements for any of these medical sources.

SSA's request to IOM was broken down into 10 specific tasks. The first seven tasks pertain to the Listings, and the final three—tasks 8, 9, and 10—pertain to presumptive disability categories, organization of medical expertise, and training and certification of consultative examiners, respectively (see Annex). The last three tasks are addressed in this interim report.

In July 2005, SSA published a notice of proposed rulemaking (NPRM) that included establishment of a Federal Expert Unit that would set up and administer a national network of medical, psychological, and vocational experts to support the disability decision process at the initial decision point and subsequent levels of appeal. In the NPRM, SSA announced that it is looking to the IOM committee's interim report for advice on the qualifications of the medical and psychological experts to be recruited for the national network.

The final report will address the remaining tasks, which pertain to the criteria and procedures of the disability decision process. It is possible that after further information gathering and analyses of the effectiveness of the disability decision process in identifying those who qualify for benefits and excluding those who do not, the committee may refine its recommendations concerning medical and psychological expertise in the final report.

It should be noted that, in this interim report, tasks 9 and 10 are presented before task 8. This is because, due to the NPRM, the recommendations on the qualification standards and training requirements for medical experts are of immediate importance while presumptive disability is not the subject of rulemaking at this time.

Constraints on the Disability Decision Process

The committee supports the primary goals of SSA's new disability decision process—to make the right decision as early in the claim process as possible, and to improve the accuracy, consistency, and timeliness of disability decisions at all levels of the disability process. Because the agency has not adopted the final version of its new plan, it is too early to reach any conclusions about the new process itself. Nevertheless, the committee believes that several factors significantly limit SSA's ability to make the correct decision early in the process and these factors contribute to error, inconsistency, and delay in decision making.

One factor is the lack of emphasis on developing a complete record at the beginning of the disability decision process, although fuller case development has been recommended in a number of reports. More complete case development at the front end of the process may not be essential for an accurate initial disability decision in every case, but overall it should reduce the impetus for appeals, reduce the number of reversals on appeal, and shorten the average length of time before reaching final adjudication. This is difficult to accomplish, however, because disability decision makers in the DDSs are subject to strong pressures from SSA to decide cases quickly and to reduce administrative costs (including medical costs) per case.

A second factor is a contrasting set of incentives for DDSs and administrative law judges, which has the effect of pushing decision outcomes in different directions at different levels of adjudication. By law, DDSs are subject to a "pre-effectuation" review by SSA regional offices of 50 percent of all decisions to allow claims in SSDI cases. Denials are not reviewed for correctness. SSA's quality assurance system, which does look at denials as well as allowances after the fact, reviews only one percent of the cases. Although a third of the denials are appealed for review by an administrative law judge, and the majority of those appeals result in allowances, the costs of decisions reversed by the administrative law judges are not internal to the DDS. In addition, there is no information feedback loop from the appeals process on the results of hearings, especially on the characteristics of cases allowed on appeal that were denied initially. In contrast, administrative law judges have incentives to allow claims. The chances of having an allowance decision subsequently reviewed are very small, while more than half of all denial decisions are appealed to the Appeals Council, the next level of review.

The new disability plan recently set forth by the Commissioner describes SSA's intent to "create and operate a comprehensive and multidimensional approach to quality assurance" in order to improve quality and accountability throughout the disability process. The committee agrees that fundamental change is needed in the SSA quality review process to place equal emphasis on allowances and denials. The committee plans to address the role of balanced incentive systems in its final report.

Organization of Medical Expertise

> **Task 9:** "*Advise on how best to provide medical expertise needed to support the entire disability adjudication process. This will involve describing the type of experts needed (academic specialists; practicing specialists; practicing generalists or non-physicians); necessary credentials and where best to locate them (from university medical centers, centers of excellence for specialized care, or community practice settings).*"

Claimants must have a medical basis for impairments disabling them from work to qualify for benefits. Accordingly, SSA relies on medical experts to provide medical evidence (including treating physicians and independent medical examiners), analyze the evidence, and determine if it justifies an allowance (the last two activities are performed by medical and psychological consultants in the DDSs).

DDSs collectively have more than 2,100 *medical and psychological consultants* (hereafter, MCs), most of them part-time contractors. In most DDSs, the MC works with a lay disability examiner to make the disability decision jointly.

The applicant's own medical providers, called *treating sources* by SSA, are the primary source of medical evidence throughout the entire disability decision-making process. By regulation, DDSs must seek medical evidence and opinions from treating sources and, unless there are inconsistencies or ambiguities, give their evidence controlling weight.

Medical expertise is also provided by medical personnel who perform consultative examinations (CEs)—i.e., examinations and tests—on claimants at SSA's request, when needed information is not available from existing medical records. Although the claimant's own treating source is the preferred *CE provider*, SSA usually uses providers that it recruits specifically to perform these examinations and tests.

For cases appealed for a hearing, administrative law judges may request the presence of a *medical expert* (ME) to serve as an expert witness at a hearing. MEs are private practitioners who agree to serve for a fee and are recruited by the regional offices of the Office of Hearings and Appeals (OHA).

SSA also has MCs in a federal DDS and in the regional offices, where they are involved in quality review and case consultation.

Specialization of Medical Consultants

At committee meetings, SSA staff raised concerns that not all DDSs have a full range of medical specialists among their MCs. The committee also heard from organizations representing the state DDS directors and the disability examiners and MCs that not all DDSs always have all the specialties desired. The committee also heard from administrative law judges that they are not always able to find certain specialists to serve as medical experts at hearings. According to DDSs and administrative law judges, the main reasons for lack of access to all specialties are inadequate compensation to attract higher-paid specialties and scarcity of specialists in rural areas and less populous regions of the country.

> **Recommendation 1-1. SSA should make arrangements to ensure that the state Disability Determination Services (DDS) agencies and the Office of Hearings and Appeals (OHA) have ready access to the full range of physician specialties and other health professionals needed to evaluate cases. These experts should be available to consult with adjudicators in the DDSs and OHA on the development and evaluation of medical and functional information needed to reach a decision.**

There are several possible arrangements for ensuring DDSs access to specialists, including the establishment of a national network of experts coordinated by a Federal Expert Unit (FEU), as proposed by the July 2005 NPRM. An FEU organized as a decentralized network of medical, psychological and vocational experts could play several roles. First, network experts could serve as consultants to adjudicators at the DDSs and OHA, similar to what MEs do for OHA currently, which would provide adjudicators with access to expertise that is not otherwise available. Second, network experts could serve as MCs in the adjudication process and make the disability determination in conjunction with the disability examiner. Third, network experts could perform CEs (this is not proposed in the NPRM).

However, establishing a national network of experts who would play different roles at different points in the process (e.g., acting as agency adjudicators in initial decisions and providing expert opinions to administrative law judges in de novo proceedings) will require arrangements that ensure that the same medical expert does not serve as adjudicator and expert witness in the same case. Likewise, if members of the network perform CEs, they should be instructed to be impartial and not be permitted to serve in other roles in the same case.

Qualifications of Medical Consultants

Currently, DDSs rely on state licensure or, in the case of psychologists and speech-language pathologists, certain alternative qualification requirements, to ensure a minimum level of medical expertise and competence among MCs. MCs are not required to be board certified, possess any additional credentials, or have an active practice in patient care.

Board certification is rapidly becoming the standard credential for the practice of medicine and psychology. Certification also has the benefit of requiring periodic recertification to demonstrate continued competence.

Recommendation 1-2. SSA should make board certification of physicians and psychologists* mandatory. This will necessitate an increase in compensation in order to recruit and retain qualified physicians and psychologists as MCs and MEs or as members of the national network of experts, if it is established. SSA also should allow current MCs with qualified program experience who are not board certified to continue for a time period of five years.

The committee recognizes that requiring a higher level of qualification (i.e., board certification) may affect SSA's ability to attract and retain experts. Historically, SSA has had difficulty recruiting qualified experts given the nature of the work and comparatively low reimbursement rates. Therefore, if SSA is to attract enough candidates, a requirement for higher qualifications must be accompanied by increased compensation.

Training of Medical Consultants

Board certification represents mastery of a specific body of knowledge and continuing education, but the certification process alone does not en-

---

*In its final report, the committee affirmed its recommendations in the Interim Report except for two. It dropped those parts of Recommendations 1-2 and 1-7 that recommended board certification of psychologists, because at this time there are too few board-cetified psychologists to meet the demand that would be created. The committee still recommends board certification of physicians.

sure that an individual is qualified to provide expertise in SSA's disability programs. Currently, SSA has no standardized national training program for MCs, to ensure a reliable level of knowledge and promote consistency in decision making, although it has been working on an MC training program for several years.

> **Recommendation 1-3. SSA should continue to develop and implement a mandatory national training program for all MCs, including those in the national network of experts outside the DDSs. The training program should focus on how to evaluate disability and on Social Security disability policies and procedures, be competency-based, and be coupled with ongoing assessment of MC competency as part of the quality assurance process.**

The training program should concentrate on the aspects of the MC role that are not usually learned in medical school or residency programs, namely, evaluation of work disability and Social Security disability program policies and procedures. The training should be ongoing, it should be competency based, and SSA should perform an ongoing assessment of MC competency as a component of its revised quality assurance program.

Better Use of Medical Expertise

Many of the Listings have a substantial functional component and at least half the adult claims are decided on the basis of the interaction of medical and vocational factors, not on severity of impairment alone. Under current procedures, MCs must be physicians, psychologists, or other "acceptable medical sources" (i.e., podiatrists, optometrists, speech-language therapists). This policy has the effect of excluding from DDSs many medical personnel who could contribute to the disability decision-making process, including personnel trained to evaluate functional limitations and their impact on ability to work (e.g., nurse practitioners, occupational therapists, physical therapists, registered nurses, psychiatric social workers).

> **Recommendation 1-4. SSA should expand the range of expertise available in DDSs and implement alternative methods of developing and adjudicating cases within DDSs that would make more efficient and effective use of existing sources of expertise, and SSA should require these additional types of experts to undergo the same training as MCs.**

For example, DDSs could use registered nurses who are certified as nurse practitioners or case managers to help triage cases, advise disability examiners on what is needed to complete development of the medical record, and help decide when a case should be referred to a MC for review or to a specialist.

Other Sources of Medical Expertise

Using technology (e.g., electronic case files and video hearings) to make medical experts more widely available, establishing rigorous, standardized qualification requirements for all experts, and compensating experts at a level commensurate with their expertise will help to ensure that disability adjudicators have sufficient expertise to help them address complex medical issues in most cases. However, there will still be circumstances in which SSA needs more specialized expertise than the network of experts may have. Examples include more complex or rare cases, newly developing conditions (e.g., emerging infectious diseases), or conditions for which research is rapidly changing the state of the art in clinical practice.

Recommendation 1-5. SSA should consider developing formal working relationships with specialized clinical research centers to review and evaluate the medical record in difficult cases, provide feedback on how well SSA is evaluating certain disabling conditions, and identify improvements that should be made in evaluation criteria (including the Listings) and procedures.

SSA should consider developing demonstration projects with academic clinical research centers that focus on conditions that are difficult to evaluate, similar to the demonstration project that SSA currently has with the Association of University Centers on Disabilities, even though few medical experts in academic research centers will be familiar with the SSA disability program or with evaluating the work capacities and limitations of patients. The centers would nevertheless be an excellent source of medical expertise in reviewing complex cases, a means of learning how to improve adjudicative evaluation and decision making and improving the training of disability examiners, MCs, and administrative law judges, and an input to the revision and updating of the Listings.

Involvement of Treating Physicians and Other Treating Sources

Greater participation by treating sources is an excellent means of obtaining all the relevant medical and functional information early in the disability decision process, which speeds the process, leads to more informed decisions, and saves the costs of going back to the treating physician for additional information or of having to order a CE.

Recommendation 1-6. SSA should take steps to improve the flow of medical information from treating sources, especially by asking for the specific information wanted, making it easier to furnish the information, and reimbursing for the full cost of collecting the information and for producing and transmitting the report.

Efforts should focus on making treating sources more knowledgeable about SSA rules and procedures and what is expected of them, providing protocols and forms that elicit and organize relevant information, making it easier technologically for treating sources to provide the information, and compensating them adequately for the extra practice expenses involved in providing records and a useful report.

Current rates of compensation for providing records and preparing reports significantly affect both treating source participation and report quality. Rates are generally low relative to fees paid by other disability benefit agencies, which discourages the participation of treating sources.

Qualifications of OHA Medical Experts

MEs function as independent expert witnesses in a quasi-judicial process. They have no direct adjudicative function, and they do not examine the claimant. They use their medical expertise at hearings to help the administrative law judges and other participants understand complex medical issues of the case in layman's terms. SSA has not required specific qualification standards for MEs.

Recommendation 1-7. Medical experts (MEs) used by administrative law judges should be board certified if they are physicians or psychologists.* SSA should encourage the use of licensed medical personnel other than physicians or psychologists as MEs in appropriate cases. All MEs should be adequately compensated for the time and effort required to serve in this capacity.

Regardless of whether MEs are drawn from existing rosters, or some newly established network as is proposed in the July 2005 NPRM, SSA should establish consistent national qualification standards for MEs to ensure a level of uniformity across the country. As discussed earlier, board

*In its final report, the committee affirmed its recommendations in the Interim Report except for two. It dropped those parts of Recommendations 1-2 and 1-7 that recommended board certification of psychologists, because at this time there are too few board-cetified psychologists to meet the demand that would be created. The committee still recommends board certification of physicians.

certification is fast becoming the standard credential for the practice of medicine and psychology.

The fee schedule for ME services is low compared with fees paid for expert witnesses by other programs and has not been increased for some time. More adequate compensation will help increase the participation of MEs from higher-paid specialties and specialties with relatively few members.

Training and Certification of Consultative Examiners

Task 10: *"Recommend needs for standardized training and certification for consultative examiners who assess claimant's level of function based on integrated evaluation of medical impairment and functional capacity. Advise on content of a training curriculum, appropriate personnel to train, and mechanisms for the certification process."*

DDSs purchase CEs to obtain or clarify information that is missing, conflicting, or ambiguous in a claimant's medical records. CE providers are asked to report examination and test results, a diagnosis and prognosis, and an opinion on what the claimant can do despite his or her impairment or impairments.

Each DDS is charged with recruiting and orienting medical personnel who agree to be available to perform CEs in return for a fee set by each state. CE providers are not required to be what SSA defines to be an "acceptable medical source," if a medically determinable impairment is established and the issue at hand is the severity of the impairment and how it affects an individual's functioning. CE providers may be what SSA calls "other sources," who may be other medical practitioners such as nurse-practitioners, physical therapists, occupational therapists, chiropractors, and audiologists, or nonmedical sources such as teachers, day care providers, social workers, and employers.

Training and Certification Requirements for Consultative Examiners

SSA requirements for CE providers are minimal. They must be currently licensed to practice medicine in the state and have the training and experience to perform the type of examination or test being requested. They are not required to have training or certification specifically in the evaluation of disability.

Currently, each state makes its own arrangements for orienting and training CE providers. SSA furnishes CE providers with a guide, known as the Green Book, which provides general information about the Social Security disability programs and how claims are adjudicated, including the role of CEs, how CE providers are selected, and what the DDSs look for in a report of a CE.

Recommendation 2-1. SSA should establish reasonable requirements for training and certification of consultative examination providers. The training and certification should focus on two competencies: evaluation of limitations on ability to work resulting from impairments, and evidentiary and other requirements of SSA's disability decision-making process.

The ability to diagnose and treat diseases and injuries is fulfilled by the current requirement that CE providers be licensed or certified in their area of expertise. However, licensure and board certification do not necessarily ensure that CE providers are expert in evaluating how a person's impairment limits his or her functioning in employment settings or that providers know how to provide medical evidence in a form useful for evaluating whether someone meets Social Security's definition of disability. Accordingly, CE providers should be required to demonstrate competence in these subject areas, namely, functional assessment of disability and SSA disability program policies and procedures.

Adequate Reimbursement for CE Providers

A comprehensive disability examination entails much more than a standard medical examination. The clinician must assess the nature and severity of the impairment or impairments by reviewing medical records, taking a history, performing an examination, and if needed, administering a diagnostic test or tests, and then he or she must evaluate the functional consequences of the impairment or combination of impairments, determine what the claimant's capabilities are to work (in adults) or engage in age-appropriate activities (in children), and prepare a report that helps the DDS determine the nature, severity, and duration of the impairment and the claimant's residual functional capacity (or, in SSI children, functional limitations).

The median fee that DDSs pay for an examination and report is approximately $130. Few pay more than $165. These fees are quite low compared with the fees that other disability benefit programs pay for disability evaluations and reports, including the federal and state workers' compensation programs and private disability insurers.

Recommendation 2-2. Reimbursement should be adequate to cover the full costs of a consultative examination, which involves more than a standard examination, whether it is focused or comprehensive in scope. This will require a substantial increase in fees over the amounts cur-

rently paid in most states. There also should be adequate compensation for time spent in orientation and training activities.

SSA should conduct market studies and studies of fees that other public programs pay for similar services to determine a national fee schedule for CEs, adjusted for geographic differences in practice costs, with several fee levels depending on how focused or comprehensive the examination is. The fee schedule should be updated annually.

Higher fees should increase the pool of medical sources willing to perform CEs, especially in harder-to-recruit specialties such as orthopedics. It should also provide the incentive for more treating physicians to be willing to perform CEs.

Requests for CEs Focused on What Is Needed in Each Case

Improving the quality of CEs depends not only on the skill and knowledge of the CE providers but also on whether they have been asked for the right information.

Recommendation 2-3. SSA should ensure that requests for consultative examinations indicate clearly what is needed in each case rather than making general requests for records and opinions.

SSA could develop templates for CE request letters for common types of cases that can be easily individualized. In addition to a checklist of standard items to consider, each request letter should contain a *narrative* paragraph to provide further guidance to the CE provider that describes what the disability examiner is concerned about and thinks is needed to evaluate the claim in question.

Presumptive Disability Categories

Task 8: *"Review SSA's list of presumptive disability conditions and suggest revisions, additions, and/or deletions. The committee will recommend essential criteria for establishing candidate conditions for presumptive disability and recommend the level of professional expertise needed to certify that a presumptive diagnosis is adequately established."*

An applicant for SSI based on disability or blindness may receive up to six months of payments prior to the final determination of disability or blindness if he or she is determined to be "presumptively disabled" or "presumptively blind" (hereafter presumptive disability) and meets all other (i.e., financial) eligibility requirements. SSA field offices can make presumptive disability determinations in cases involving certain impairments specified by SSA. DDSs can make presumptive disability findings in any case in which the available evidence indicates a "strong likelihood" that the claim will be allowed after going through the regular formal determination process.

Revising the Presumptive Disability Categories with Explicit Criteria

Presumptive disability is primarily a social policy which recognizes that applicants for SSI have little or no income or assets and probably need immediate assistance with the costs of living. Therefore, the committee is unable to recommend specific categories to include or delete because the selection criteria are not solely medical.

The nonmedical criterion in selecting presumptive disability categories is the degree of risk, i.e., the reversal rate because of false positives for which SSA is willing to pay in order to reach all true positives. Early in the SSI program, SSA determined that a reversal rate of more than 10 percent over several months made a category a candidate for deletion. Only 9 of the 15 current categories meet this criterion, however. A reversal rate of 20 percent or less would bring the total to 13. At the same time, the presumptive disability categories do not include conditions that consistently have high allowance rates, which therefore on equity grounds could be considered as candidates for inclusion as presumptive disability categories. In 2004, for example, cases with 1 of 12 primary impairment codes had a 90 percent chance of approval, and only 4 of those codes corresponded closely to existing presumptive disability categories.

Recommendation 3-1. SSA should consider dropping some current presumptive disability categories, and perhaps adding some, after deciding on explicit criteria for including categories.

Calculations based on SSA allowance rates by impairment category indicate that there are a number of conditions in which the probability is high that a claimant who alleges he or she has one of the conditions will end up being allowed, which makes them good candidates to be presumptive disability categories. The question the committee cannot answer is whether that probability should be 90, 85, 80 percent, or some other number. The answer depends on the trade-off society wishes to make between helping groups of low-income persons with a given probability of being determined disabled by SSA and the cost of paying for cases that end up being disallowed.

Increasing Consistency in Presumptive Disability Decision Making

The percentage of SSI claims that are granted presumptive disability status varies widely across SSA field offices and DDSs, a situation that SSA could improve. The percentage of field office presumptive disability cases ranges from 0.1 percent to 3.5 percent of SSI claims. The range for DDSs is from 0.6 percent to 34.6 percent. The majority of field offices do not use all 15 presumptive disability categories.

Recommendation 3-2. SSA should mandate the use of the presumptive disability procedure by, and take other administrative steps to achieve more consistency among, the SSA field offices and DDSs in the implementation of the presumptive disability policy.

Currently, the use of the presumptive disability procedure is voluntary, which leads to large differences in practice from office to office that are not just the result of inherent difficulties in assessing cases. If SSA has a presumptive disability process, and it is part of national social policy, it should be applied uniformly from place to place. This is primarily a matter for administrative policy to achieve.

Learning from Terminal Illness (TERI) Procedures

Presumptive disability is a policy to expedite *payments*. TERI (**TER**minal **I**llness) cases involve expedited *decisions*. According to the SSA program operations manual, "Cases where there is an indication of a terminal illness (TERI) are to be handled in an expeditious manner because of the sensitivity involved."

Recommendation 3-3. SSA should look at TERI procedures for lessons in making expedited decisions on cases that must meet specific medical criteria. These include uniform special procedures throughout the decision process that promote consistency as well as speed.

TERI cases are subject to special procedures through which the case is expedited through every step of the disability determination process, including the appeals process and the payment process. The issue is whether field office interviewers are able to identify TERI cases with some accuracy. This would involve determining the percentage of cases flagged as TERI cases that turn out to meet the criteria and also the percentage of cases that were not flagged that should have been. Differences between types of cases and offices could be analyzed for better understanding of TERI decision making and ways to improve it.

INTRODUCTION

Overview of Social Security Disability Programs

The Social Security Administration (SSA) provides Social Security Disability Insurance (SSDI) benefits to disabled persons of less than full retirement age and to their dependents. SSA also provides Supplemental Security Income (SSI) payments to disabled persons who are under age 65. For both programs, adult disability is defined as a "medically determinable physical or mental impairment" that prevents an individual from engaging in any substantial gainful activity and is expected to last at least 12 months or result in death. Childhood disability under SSI is defined as a physical or mental condition or combination of conditions that causes "marked and severe functional limitations" and is expected to last at least 12 months or result in death. As of December 2004, SSA was making disability payments under the SSDI and SSI programs to 9.8 million people aged 18-64 and 1.0 million children based on their own disability, as well as payments to an additional 1.5 million dependents of disabled individuals in the SSDI program (SSA, 2005c:31-33).

SSDI and SSI disability account for 22 percent of SSA's benefits payments each year (SSA, 2005a:147). Yet, they account for 57 percent of SSA's administrative costs, because determining disability status is much more complicated than verifying a worker's work records to compute Social Security retirement benefits (SSA, 2005a:161).

In fiscal year (FY) 2005 SSA expected to process approximately 2.5 million initial claims for disability benefits, 1.6 million continuing disability reviews, and 600,000 appeals hearings (SSA, 2004a:4-5). The annual number of claims, which was 2.1 million in FY 2000, is expected to continue to increase as baby boomers age into their 50s and early 60s and become more prone to disabling impairments.

Claimants file applications through one of 1,300 SSA field offices, over the telephone, by mail, or on the Internet. Interviewers in the field offices apply the nonmedical eligibility criteria to determine insured status and ask claimants to provide supporting medical documentation. The case files are then sent to a state Disability Determination Services (DDS) agency, which makes the initial decision as to whether the individual is disabled based on medical and, if needed, vocational criteria provided by SSA.

The DDSs use a five-step decision process, called the sequential evaluation process by SSA, for each claim for disability benefits, whether under SSDI or SSI.[1] The first decision is whether the applicant is currently engaged in substantial gainful employment, which is defined as earning more than

[1]For overviews written for physicians, see Nibali (2003) and Robinson and Wolfe (2000).

a certain amount per month ($830 a month in 2005 except for statutorily blind beneficiaries).[2] If yes, the application is denied. Step two is to determine whether the applicant has a medically determinable impairment that is severe, i.e., significantly limits the applicant's physical or mental ability to engage in basic work activities, and that will last 12 months or longer. If no, the claim is denied. If yes, step 3 is a determination of whether the applicant's impairment meets or equals one of the more than 100 conditions listed in a Listing of Impairments (Listings), which are assumed to be so severe that SSA accepts that the applicant cannot work. If yes, the claim is allowed. If not, step 4 involves an assessment of the applicant's residual functional capacity to do past work. If yes, the claim is denied. If no, step 5 looks to see if the applicant can engage in any employment in the U.S. economy. If yes, the claim is denied. If no, it is allowed. On average, the DDSs allow approximately 37 percent of the claims they adjudicate through the five-step process.

The share of claims that are allowed at step 3 by meeting or equaling the Listings has declined over the years, to about half currently. This means that a growing percentage of cases must undergo intensive medical-vocational evaluation during steps 4 and 5, which require more time and DDS staff resources to perform.

Currently, approximately 70 percent of the allowances that are eventually made are made at the initial level, a process that takes about 97 days (SSA, 2004a:Appendix A). About a third (36 percent) of the applicants whose claims are initially denied decide to file an appeal. Of those, approximately 67 percent result in allowances at some point in the multistep appeals process, which averages more than a year to complete. Ultimately, slightly more than half of the claims (52.3 percent) are approved.[3]

On September 25, 2003, the Commissioner of Social Security told the Subcommittee on Social Security of the House Committee on Ways and Means of her intent to develop a "new approach" to disability determination (Barnhart, 2003). The goals of the new approach are to (1) make the correct decision as early in the claims process as possible and (2) foster return to work at all stages of the process. On July 27, 2005, after consulting with a variety of groups, SSA published a notice of proposed rulemaking (NPRM) describing specific regulatory changes it plans to make to implement the Commissioner's new approach to the disability decision-making process (SSA, 2005e). Among the initiatives proposed in the NPRM was the establishment of a Federal Expert Unit that would set up and administer a national network of medical, psychological, and vocational experts to support the disability decision process at the initial decision point and

[2]The statutorily blind are subject to different earnings rules.

[3]These calculations are based on FY 2003 data.

subsequent levels of appeal. The NPRM also proposes establishment of a Quick Disability Determination Process that would use a predictive statistical model to identify cases likely to be allowed and send them to a special unit to be adjudicated within 20 days. The NPRM includes other changes that are not addressed in this report.

IOM Study Charge

SSA asked the Institute of Medicine (IOM) to help in two areas related to its initiatives to make the disability determination process more efficient and accurate. First, SSA asked IOM to recommend improvements to the Listing of Impairments, which contains impairments and associated medical findings that SSA considers so severe that individuals with them (or with conditions equal to them in severity) are considered disabled without additional evidence of their inability to work. Among other things, the IOM will look at alternative conceptual models for organizing the Listings (currently based on 14 body systems), processes for determining when the Listings require revision, and the advisability of integrating functional assessment into the Listings.

Second, SSA asked IOM to recommend ways to improve the use of medical expertise in the disability determination process, including the appeals process. Subsequently, in the July 2005 NPRM, SSA announced it is looking to the IOM for advice on the qualifications of the medical and psychological experts to be recruited for the national network.

SSA's requests to IOM are broken down into 10 specific tasks. The first seven pertain to the Listings, and the final three—tasks 8, 9, and 10—pertain to presumptive disability categories, organization of medical expertise, and training and certification of consultative examiners, respectively (see Annex). The last three tasks are addressed in this interim report.

It should be noted that tasks 9 and 10 are presented before task 8 because, due to the NPRM, the recommendations on the qualification standards for medical experts are higher priority than those on presumptive disability, which is not the subject of rulemaking at this time.

IOM Committee

The IOM formed a committee to conduct the study. The 16 committee members are experts in clinical decision making, physical medicine and rehabilitation, orthopedic surgery, occupational medicine and nursing, psychiatry and psychology, pediatrics, public health, functional assessment, occupational rehabilitation, legal and economic aspects of disability, social security disability administration, claimant advocacy, and private disability insurance. The committee expects to issue its final report in 2006.

The committee was asked by SSA to operate under certain assumptions:

1. The existence of a national electronic disability records system that allows claims folder documents to be transmitted electronically and viewed by all employees and medical personnel, regardless of their location;
2. The existence of a national video hearing capability;
3. An unchanged statutory definition of disability; and
4. That beneficiary return-to-work, vocational rehabilitation, and work incentives for applicants are outside of the scope of the committee's deliberations.

Interim Committee Report

SSA asked the committee to prepare preliminary recommendations, prior to the final report, addressing the three tasks that relate to medical expertise issues, with a special focus on the appropriate qualifications of medical and psychological experts involved in disability decision making. Therefore, the committee agreed to issue this interim report, which provides the committee's initial impressions on those tasks. This report, based on preliminary information gathering and analyses, and deliberations at the committee meetings, is in some respects an interim report. After further information gathering and analyses of the effectiveness of the disability decision process in identifying those who qualify for benefits and those who do not, the committee may refine its recommendations concerning medical and psychological expertise in the final report.

The final report will address a number of issues with potential implications for the qualifications of the medical experts involved in the disability decision process. These include the extent of knowledge about differences in decision outcomes depending on the qualifications of decision makers; research on inter-rater reliability of decision criteria; comparisons of evaluations of samples of cases by different groups of SSA adjudicators or by adjudicators compared with outside medical experts; results of long-term follow-ups of applicants who were allowed and denied; evaluations of alternative decision making models, such as the single decision maker model; studies of sources of variation in allowance rates among DDSs and Office of Hearings and Appeals (OHA) hearing offices; and in-depth analyses of program statistics about the outcomes of applications for benefits at different levels of decision making. The final report will summarize what is known about how well the disability determination process serves as a screening tool to avoid false positives and false negatives and the factors that affect its sensitivity and specificity, in epidemiologic terms.[4] In the absence of such

[4]Sensitivity is the measure of a screen's ability to detect true positives, i.e., those the test is seeking to screen in, and specificity is the measure of its ability to detect true negatives, i.e. those the test is seeking to exclude.

information and analysis, this report is based mostly on the judgment of the committee of the qualifications, training, and certification that should be expected of medical participants in the disability decision process.

SSA's Proposed Disability Decision Process Changes

SSA's requests to IOM are closely related to the agency's plans to institute a new approach to improve the SSDI and SSI disability process. For purposes of the medical expertise issues addressed in this interim report, the relevant aspect of the plan is the intent to establish a national network of medical and psychological consultants who would be used by all adjudicators, including disability examiners in the DDSs and administrative law judges (ALJs) in the OHA. In the July 2005 NPRM, SSA proposed establishing "a Federal Expert Unit to augment and strengthen medical and vocational expertise for disability adjudicators at all levels of the disability determination process," and creating "a national network of medical, psychological, and vocational experts who will be available to assist adjudicators throughout the country" (SSA, 2005e:43593). SSA explained that:

. . . [U]nder our current disability adjudication process, medical, psychological, and vocational experts are not consistently available to all adjudicators at every level or in all parts of the country.

> We are therefore proposing to establish and operate a Federal Expert Unit, which we believe will help to ensure the full development of the record, enable adjudicators to make accurate determinations or decisions as early in the process as possible, and facilitate subsequent review should a case be appealed to a higher level. We propose to create a national network of medical, psychological, and vocational experts who will be available to assist adjudicators throughout the country. This national network may include experts employed by or under contract with the State agencies; however, all experts affiliated with the national network must meet qualifications prescribed by the Commissioner.
>
> The Federal Expert Unit will organize and maintain this network comprised of medical, psychological, and vocational experts who will provide medical, psychological, and vocational expertise to State agencies, reviewing officials, administrative law judges, and the Decision Review Board. We want to ensure that the right set of medical eyes reviews medical records and answers questions about the wide variety of impairments seen in disability claims. We believe that the expert network affiliated with the Federal Expert Unit will help ensure that a medical, psychological, and vocational expert who has the qualifications required by the Commissioner

> assists in adjudicating disability claims. With the assistance of the Institute of Medicine, we plan to develop standards that define the medical and psychological expertise necessary for experts to qualify for participation in the national network (SSA, 2005e:43594).

In discussions with SSA staff, the committee was asked to assume that, under the new plan, there would be a national pool of medical experts and that there would be flexibility in payment rates for expert medical advice. The committee was not to assume that the experts would necessarily be centrally located.

The plan for achieving process improvements is also predicated on successful implementation of SSA's electronic disability system (eDib), which is currently being rolled out nationwide. SSA expects all DDSs and OHA hearing offices to be processing their workloads with electronic disability folders on a regular basis by the end of 2006 (Barnhart, 2005). Although SSA refers to eDib as an electronic disability system, it is not a true electronic medical record, in which all information would be stored as structured data. In such a system, the data could be manipulated for purposes such as policy analysis or management information. SSA's eDib system includes a mixture of structured data and images, with the medical evidence portion of the file consisting of images of paper medical records. This will make it possible for medical experts in remote locations to review medical records, assuming that arrangements to keep claimant files secure are made.

TRENDS IN THE DISABILITY DECISION PROCESS

The Social Security disability programs have grown rapidly in recent years, and several problems have come with this growth—problems that promise to become worse as the baby boomer generation reaches the age when disability becomes more likely (the oldest baby boomers will turn 60 in 2006). These problems, which have been documented in a number of reports,[5] include:

- significant growth in applications;
- variability in decision making at each stage in the adjudication process;
- high rate of appeals and of reversals of initial decisions to deny benefits; and
- long length of time to reach a final decision.

---

[5]See reports of the Social Security Advisory Board (SSAB) and the Government Accountability Office (GAO), for example, GAO (2003, 2004) and SSAB (1998, 2001a).

Program Growth

Historically, both the SSDI and SSI disability programs have experienced steady, although not consistent, program growth. The causes for this growth and fluctuation are complex and not fully understood, and may include the broader socioeconomic and demographic environment as well as programmatic actions and court decisions (IOM, 2002:42). Even in the context of historical program growth, recent increases in application rates have had significant workload implications for SSA. According to SSA statistics, 1,041,362 workers applied for SSDI in 1998. The number of applications grew steadily to 1,485,482 in 2004, an increase of 42.6 percent in six years (Zayatz, 2005:Table 2). Applications have also increased in the SSI program. Applications by adults for SSI disability payments increased from 1,108,957 in 1998 to 1,438,992 in 2004 (29.8 percent increase), and applications for SSI childhood disability payments went from 335,732 in 1998 to 402,218 in 2004 (20.1 percent increase) (SSA, 2005b:Appendix C).[6]

Variability in Disability Decisions

As noted above, the initial disability allowance rate is approximately 37 percent. However, this rate varies significantly from DDS to DDS, and from region to region. In calendar year (CY) 2004, the initial allowance rate for individual states ranged from 25.3 percent to 61.1 percent. An SSA study of initial allowance rates in the late 1990s analyzed a similar spread of about 30 percentage points across DDSs. It found that statistically controlling for economic conditions, demographic factors, prevalence of SSDI and SSI beneficiaries, health status, and other external factors explained only half of the variance across the states (Strand, 2002). This finding suggests that up to half of the variance in allowance rates among the states may be due to differences in state administrative practices (e.g., use of consultative examinations, involvement of doctors in making disability decisions, payment amounts for medical evidence of record and consultative examinations, salaries and qualifications of disability decision makers, and training practices), quality assurance practices of state agencies and SSA regional offices, and/or state program policies (e.g., requiring individuals to file for SSA disability as a condition of eligibility for state benefits).[7]

Allowance rates at the ALJ hearing level also vary widely from state to state. In FY 2002, the overall hearing allowance rate was about 66 percent but, at the state level, the rate varied from 35 to 86 percent (SSAB, 2001b:70).

---

[6]The three categories of applications total more than 2.5 million—the number of applicants—because some adults apply for SSDI and SSI benefits concurrently.

[7]These factors are listed in SSAB (2001b:5).

Appeals and Allowances on Appeal

About a third of the claims denied initially by the DDSs are appealed to the ALJ hearing level, after being denied at reconsideration level. By way of comparison, 8 percent of the claims for disability compensation from the Department of Veterans Affairs (VA) are appealed to the hearing level, even though VA, like SSA, allows less than half the claims initially.[8] At UnumProvident, a provider of private long-term disability insurance, 10 to 15 percent of cases initially denied are appealed (Lewin, 2001:42). In Canada, approximately 20 percent of the disability applicants denied by the Canada Pension Plan appealed for a hearing in FY 2003.[9]

The appeal rate of one-third contributes to the lengthy average time it takes to make a final decision. Many applicants must wait an average of more than one year from the time they are denied by a DDS until an ALJ decides their case (see next section, below, on timeliness). There also are financial implications of the high rate of appeals. According to GAO, the average cost of processing an appeal hearing ($2,157 in 2001) is much greater than the average cost of processing an initial claim ($583 in 2001) (GAO, 2004:11).

The 1,200 ALJs who hold hearings on disability cases are employees of SSA, and although they operate separately from the DDS adjudicators, they are supposed to apply the same rules and regulations. Nevertheless, ALJs allow 61 percent of the claims that are appealed to them and deny or dismiss the rest. At the VA, 22 to 26 percent of the appeals are successful, 29 to 36 percent are remanded back for reconsideration, and 40 to 42 percent of the initial decisions are upheld (Lewin, 2001:42). At UnumProvident, 7 to 12 percent are reversed (Lewin, 2001:42). About half of the denials for disability benefits from the Canada Pension Plan are reversed (CPP/OAS, 2004:Figure 8). Possible reasons for the high allowance rates by ALJs in appeals cases include (SSAB, 2001b:5-6):

- The fact that most claimants are never seen in person by an adjudicator until they have an ALJ hearing;
- Rules that allow claimants to introduce new evidence and allegations at each stage of the appeals process;
- The time lag between the initial denial and the hearing, during which a claimant's condition may worsen;

[8]VA pays for partial permanent disability, and the 8 percent includes those appealing for a higher disability rating as well as those denied any benefits.

[9]In 2002-2003, 31,200 applicants (51.4 percent of all applicants) were denied at the initial or reconsideration levels. During the same period, there were 6,300 (20.2 percent of the denials) appeals for a hearing before a hearing tribunal (Canadian Parliament, 2003:Chapter 4).

• Administrative differences between the DDSs and hearing office, including their access to and use of medical and vocational expertise;

• Greater involvement of attorneys and other claimant representatives at the ALJ hearing, who help claimants assemble a more complete case record;

• Differences in the quality assurance procedures applied to initial decisions and hearings-level decisions, which may bias DDS examiners to deny claims and ALJs to allow claims; and

• Differences in the training given to ALJs and state DDS examiners.

Decision Timeliness

In FY 2004, average processing times for disability claims at each level of the decision process were (Figure 1):

- 95 days for initial disability claims;
- 97 days for reconsiderations;
- 394 days for hearings; and
- 251 days for decisions on appeals of hearings at the Appeals Council.

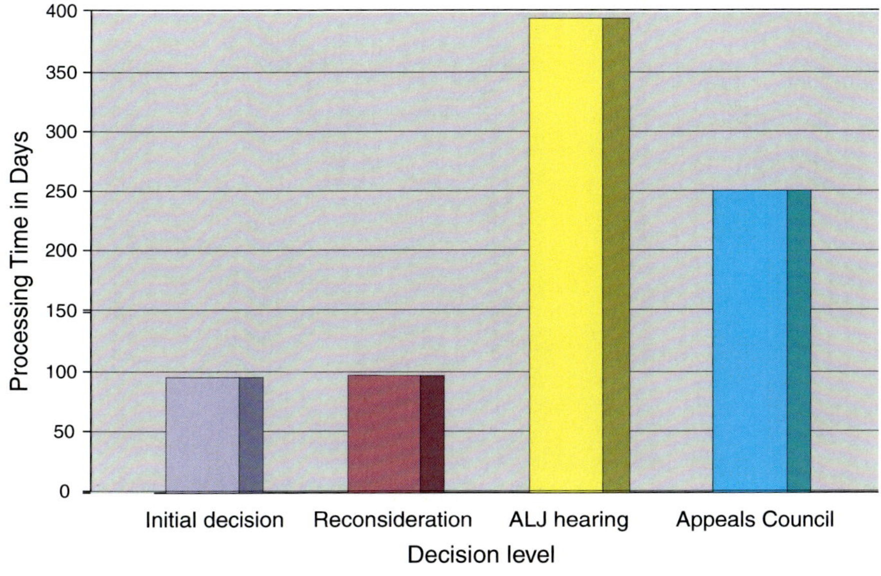

FIGURE 1 Processing time for disability claims in days, CY 2004.
SOURCE: SSA, 2005a:17.

Although the DDSs processed 2.6 million initial disability cases in FY 2004, the backlog was 625,000. ALJs issued 497,000 hearing decisions, but the number of pending hearing requests was 636,000 (SSA, 2005a:45-50).

Nevertheless, most of the disability allowance decisions in FY 2004 were made at the initial level of the decision process (Figure 2):

- 71.0 percent of the claims eventually allowed were allowed at the initial level;
- 6.2 percent of the claims eventually allowed were allowed at reconsideration;
- 22.6 percent of the claims eventually allowed were allowed at an ALJ hearing; and
- 0.2 percent of the claims eventually allowed were allowed at the Appeals Council.

Given that nearly a quarter of the claims were allowed after a hearing or an appeal of a hearing, the overall weighted average time until an allowance was made was 204 days. As noted above, appeals add substantially to the administrative costs of the program. Making the correct decision initially will require more resources at the front end of the disability

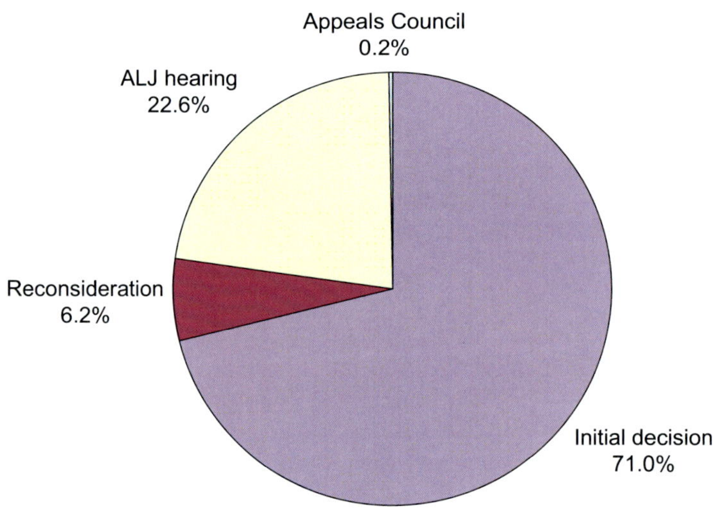

FIGURE 2 Percentage of allowed claims by decision level, CY 2004.
SOURCE: SSA, 2005d.

decision-making process, but these costs could be offset by savings from lower appeals rates.

Implications of Trends for the Interim Report

The increasing caseload makes it desirable to make the disability decision process as efficient as possible. One way to increase efficiency would be to find ways to make the Listings a more effective screening tool at step 3 of the sequential decision process, which will be addressed in the second phase of the study and the final report. A more effective screening tool could reduce the number of false negatives, i.e., cases that, although they meet the definition of social security disability, fail the screen and therefore have to undergo a more intensive and time-consuming medical-vocational analysis at steps 4 and 5 before they are allowed. The variability in allowance rates from DDS to DDS and between DDSs and OHA might be reduced if all had access to the same or equivalent expertise. If cases could be better evaluated and the medical record more fully developed at the beginning of the process, there might be fewer appeals and fewer allowances on appeal.

Equalizing access to medical expertise across decision-making units could help ameliorate the trends in case loads, processing time, appeal and reversal rates, and variability in decision making, but it is also justified on the grounds that every applicant for disability benefits should have the benefit of the expertise needed to evaluate their case regardless of where they live. Although it cannot be proven with available information, the committee finds it logical to expect that this will result in improved evaluations of complex cases, leading to more accurate decisions, which in turn will have beneficial effects by reducing the need for lengthy appeals and improving the case record for appeals that are filed. In the final report, the committee will analyze existing data and past research and identify research and experiments that SSA could sponsor to see what difference that different types and amounts of medical expertise make in decision outcomes.

The committee also notes in this interim report that several other factors are important in improving decision making. These include fuller development of cases before the initial decision and a quality assurance system with incentives that balance the need for making the right decision with the need for making decisions as quickly as possible.

CONSTRAINTS ON THE DISABILITY DECISION PROCESS

The committee supports the primary goals of SSA's new disability plan—to make the right decision as early in the claim process as possible, and to improve the accuracy, consistency, and timeliness of disability decisions at all levels of the disability process. Because the agency has not adopted the final version of its new plan, it is too early to reach any conclusions about the plan itself. Nevertheless, the committee believes that several factors significantly limit SSA's ability to make the correct decision early in the process, and these factors contribute to error, inconsistency, and delay in decision making.

The development of a full record at the beginning of the disability decision process and evaluation of the record by appropriate experts, including medical experts, may not be essential for an accurate initial disability decision in every case. However, fuller case development at the front end of the process should reduce the impetus for appeals, reduce the number of allowances on appeal, and shorten the average length of time before reaching final adjudication. Full case development at the front end of the process has been recommended in a number of reports.[10] This is difficult to accomplish, however, because disability claim-processing personnel, especially in DDSs, are subject to strong pressures to make decisions quickly and to reduce administrative costs (including medical costs) per case.

These time and cost pressures are reflected in SSA's Performance and Accountability Report for FY 2004, wherein SSA identifies four strategic goals. The first goal is "To deliver high-quality, citizen-centered service." Within each strategic goal, the report identifies specific strategic objectives. The first strategic objective under this first strategic goal is "To make the right decision in the disability process as early as possible." To measure achievement in reaching this goal and this objective, SSA identifies six key performance indicators. Yet, despite the emphasis on high-quality service and making the right decision early in the process, none of these key performance indicators measures either the accuracy of the decisions or whether the decision was made as early in the process as possible. All six performance indicators focus on making decisions quickly and reducing the caseload (SSA, 2005a:45-51):

1. Number of initial claims processed by DDSs;
2. Number of SSA hearings processed;
3. Average processing time for initial disability claims;
4. Average processing time for hearings;
5. Number of initial claims pending; and
6. Number of hearings pending.

Within the context of these pressures to move cases quickly, DDSs and ALJs are also subject to a contrasting set of incentives that have the effect of pushing decision outcomes in different directions at different levels of adjudication.

---

[10]See, for example, ACUS (1989) and Bloch et al. (2003).

In addition to tight time and resource constraints, DDSs are subject by law to a 50 percent "pre-effectuation" review by SSA regional offices of all decisions to allow claims in SSDI cases before payment is made. These factors create a disincentive to performing complete claim development because the chances of having a denial decision subsequently reviewed are slight. SSA's quality assurance (QA) system reviews both SSDI and SSI cases, including allowances and denials, but the sample size is approximately 1 percent of the cases.[11] About a third of the denials are appealed for review by an ALJ, but the costs of decisions reversed by the ALJ are not internal to the DDS. In addition, there is no information feedback loop from the appeals process on the results of hearings, especially on the characteristics of cases allowed on appeal that were denied initially.

In contrast, ALJs have incentives to allow claims. First, they are permitted to make use of several processing expedients that apply only to allowance cases (e.g., short-form decisions, "bench" decisions, on-the-record decisions). These make allowances easier and faster to process than denials, which require full development and a comprehensive written decision. Second, the chances of having an allowance decision subsequently reviewed are very small. On the other hand, more than half of all denial decisions are reviewed by the Appeals Council at the claimants' requests.

The new disability plan recently set forth by the Commissioner describes SSA's intent to "create and operate a comprehensive and multidimensional approach to quality assurance" in order to improve quality and accountability throughout the disability process. The committee agrees that fundamental change is needed in the SSA quality review process. An essential component of that change must be to promote not only quality and accountability, but consistency throughout the disability claims process. Another essential feature would be to place equal emphasis on allowances and denials. The committee will address the role of balanced incentive systems in improving the disability decision process in its final report.

ORGANIZATION OF MEDICAL EXPERTISE

Task 9: *"Advise on how best to provide medical expertise needed to support the entire disability adjudication process. This will in-*

---

[11]In FY 2004, just over 40,000 cases (both allowances and denials) were reviewed for QA, of which 1,500 (3.6 percent) were returned to correct errors or for better documentation; 335,000 cases of allowances were subjected to pre-effectuation review (PER), of which 13,000 (3.8 percent) were returned due to error or inadequate documentation. QA reviews cover initial claims, reconsiderations, and determinations of continuing eligibility; PER covers favorable initial and reconsideration decisions in title II and concurrent claims (SSA, 2005a:215-216).

volve describing the type of experts needed (academic specialists; practicing specialists; practicing generalists or non-physicians); necessary credentials and where best to locate them (from university medical centers, centers of excellence for specialized care, or community practice settings)."

Medical Expertise and the Disability Adjudication Process

Under the law, impairments cannot qualify a claimant for disability benefits unless they have a medical basis. SSA's disability decision-making process relies on several types of medical expertise to provide medical evidence (including treating physicians and independent medical examiners), analyze the evidence, and determine if it justifies an allowance. Medical experts help to establish the medical basis of claimants' impairments, evaluate whether they meet or equal the listings, and if not, evaluate the impact of the impairment or impairments on their functional capacity. For claim adjudication, there are four principal types of medical expertise, some internal and some external to SSA and the DDSs:

1. Medical Consultants (MCs).

Initial disability decisions are made by personnel in state DDSs (as well as one federal DDS, operated by SSA). Every DDS has a complement of medical and psychological consultants (hereafter, MCs) who help determine whether claims meet SSA criteria. Currently, the DDSs collectively have more than 2,100 MCs, most of them part-time contractors. In most DDSs, the MC works with a trained layperson, called a disability examiner (DE), on a two-person team to make the disability decision jointly (unless there are nonmedical grounds for denial, such as a failure to undergo a consultative examination, which the DE can make alone). MCs also play an important role in assembling and interpreting the medical record that is the basis for a disability determination decision. By law, the MC must be a pediatrician (or other specialist appropriate to the child's impairment) in child disability cases and a psychiatrist or psychologist in denials of mental disability cases. (In 10 states where SSA has been testing an alternative disability adjudication process, DEs can make the disability decision alone, unless it is a child or denial of a mental disability case.) In addition to reviewing cases, MCs may also perform other functions at a DDS, including training of DEs and other staff and developing and maintaining relationships with the medical community.

2. Treating Medical Sources.

An applicant's own medical providers, called treating sources by SSA, are the primary source of medical evidence throughout the entire disability decision-making process. By regulation, DDSs must seek medical evidence and opinions from treating sources and, unless there are inconsistencies or ambiguities, give their evidence controlling weight. DDSs also must ask treating sources first to conduct a consultative examination, if one is needed, and if the treating sources meet SSA's criteria for doing the examination.

3. Consultative Examination (CE) Providers.

Medical expertise is also provided by medical personnel who perform examinations and tests on claimants at SSA's request when needed information is not available from existing medical records. Although the claimant's own treating source is the preferred source for a CE, SSA usually uses providers that it recruits specifically to perform these examinations and tests.

4. Medical Experts (MEs).

For cases appealed to a hearing, medical expertise can come from MEs, who generally appear and testify as expert witnesses at hearings. They respond to questions from ALJs, who conduct the hearings and make the decisions, and from claimants (or their representatives). MEs are private practitioners who agree to serve for a fee. They are recruited by expert witness coordinators in the regional offices of the OHA. Currently, the regional offices have nearly 1,600 MEs on their rosters.

There are several additional sources of medical expertise for SSA, although they are not directly involved in claim adjudication:

- Physicians and psychologists who assist in quality assurance review of claim adjudications. For cases reviewed in SSA central office, the physicians and psychologists are MCs in the federal DDS. In the regional offices, SSA relies on part-time MCs, who do not work in DDSs; and
- Physicians, psychologists, and other medical personnel who are involved in policy development in SSA's Office of Disability Programs.

Specialization of Medical Consultants

In meetings with the committee, SSA staff raised concerns that not all DDSs have a full range of medical specialists among their in-house MCs. They also referred to a major imbalance between alleged impairments and the areas of expertise of DDS MCs, citing, for example, a high percentage of claims involving musculoskeletal disorders, but relatively few DDS MCs who are orthopedic specialists. Most MCs are in generalist specialties such as internal medicine, pediatrics, and family medicine (35 percent) or in mental health specialties (47 percent). SSA staff also expressed concern about state-to-state variation in the mix of different areas of medical expertise.

The committee also heard from organizations representing the state DDS directors and the DEs and MCs that not all DDSs had all the specialties desired.[12] The main obstacles they reported were inadequate compensation to attract higher-paid specialties and lack of supply in certain regions of the country. Although the organizations testified that most cases can be adjudicated by generalists, they expressed support for arrangements enabling them to access hard-to-recruit specialists. The committee also heard from ALJs that they were not able to find certain specialists to serve as medical experts at hearings. The ALJs cited similar obstacles as DDS officials did: the low fees they can pay and the lack of certain specialists in rural areas.

Medical Consultants

In June 2004, the most prevalent specialties among medical consultants were (in descending order) psychology, internal medicine, psychiatry, pediatrics, and family practice. These five specialties account for three-quarters of the 2,136 MCs in the DDSs nationwide (Figure 3). Of these, the only specialty represented among MCs in all 52 DDSs was psychology.[13]

Other than 59 speech-language pathologists, no other specialty numbered more than 38 nationally. As a result, 29 DDSs had no MCs specializing in cardiology, 28 had no neurologists, and 25 had no orthopedic surgeons or orthopedic specialists. Ten DDSs had just one or two specialists other than the most prevalent five listed above. Another six only had three other kinds of specialists.

Each of the 10 regions had at least one cardiologist, neurologist, and orthopedist among its DDSs, however, and nine had at least one of the 25 ophthalmologist MCs in the country. Other scarcer specialties (and the number of regions with one or two DDSs that had them) were: endocrinology (4), gastroenterology (4), hematology (4), infectious disease (3), oncology (5), otolaryngology (2), pulmonology (6), and rheumatology (6) (Annex Table 2).

If each case had to be evaluated by a specialist in the alleged impairment, there would be a large mismatch between the mix of impairments among cases and the distribution of MCs among specialties. A recent analysis by SSA found, for example, that nearly 20 percent of decisions

[12]The National Council of Disability Determination Directors and the National Association of Disability Examiners, respectively.

[13]There are DDSs for each of the 50 states, the District of Columbia, and Puerto Rico, which are grouped under 10 regions headquartered in Boston, New York City, Philadelphia, Atlanta, Chicago, Dallas, Kansas City, Denver, San Francisco, and Seattle.

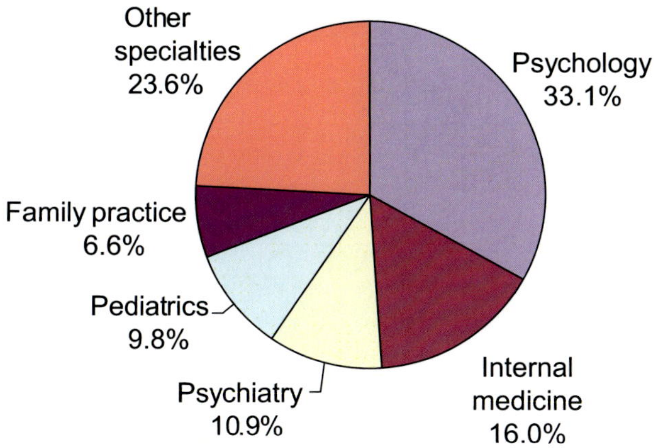

FIGURE 3 Medical consultants by specialty, June 2004.
NOTE: Each MC is classified by one primary specialty.
SOURCE: Annex Table 1.

involve musculoskeletal impairments while 2.5 percent of MCs are orthopedists (Figure 4). Nearly 4 percent of decisions are on cases involving the endocrine system, primarily diabetes mellitus, and 0.2 percent of MCs are endocrinologists. It is not known, however, how many of the decisions in these cases could have been handled by a more general specialist, such as an internist or family medicine physician, versus how many could have

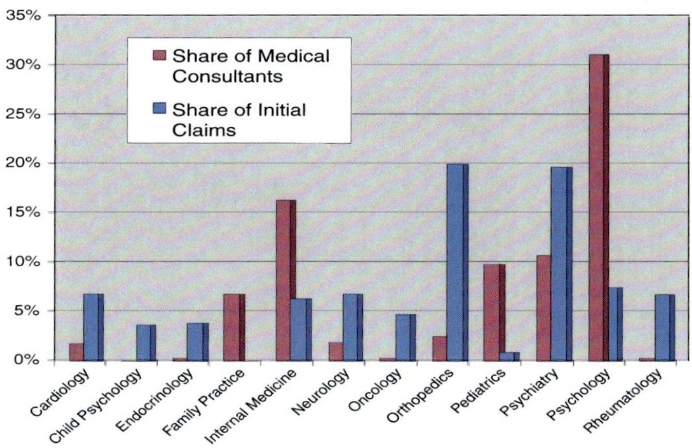

FIGURE 4 Comparison of MC specialty mix with initial case mix.
NOTE: Each MC is classified by one primary specialty.
SOURCE: Annex Table 3.

benefited from more specialized evaluation. These would be "close call" cases in which the claimant is on the boundary of "able to work" and "not able to work" or the medical evidence is complex and could be interpreted either way.

Medical Experts

In June 2005, the OHA regional offices had blanket purchase agreements with 1,575 MEs representing 1,861 specialties (some MEs were specialists in more than one field of medicine). Most of the physicians were board certified, although it is not a requirement. The most common specialties (in descending order) were clinical psychology, internal medicine, psychiatry, orthopedic surgery, and pediatrics, which accounted for two-thirds of the total (Figure 5). Physicians in these specialties were on the rosters of at least 9 of the 10 regions, along with neurology, cardiovascular diseases, ophthalmology, family practice, and rheumatology.

The number of different ME specialties varies by region (Figure 6). Some ALJs have access to a large number of specialties, for example, in the Atlanta region (41 specialties), Philadelphia region (36 specialties), and Chicago region (34 specialties). Others have access to few, such as the Denver region (12 specialties) and the Seattle region (17 specialties). Three regions lack access to MEs specializing in endocrinology (Dallas, Denver, Seattle), hematology (Atlanta, Dallas, Denver), gastroenterology (Dallas,

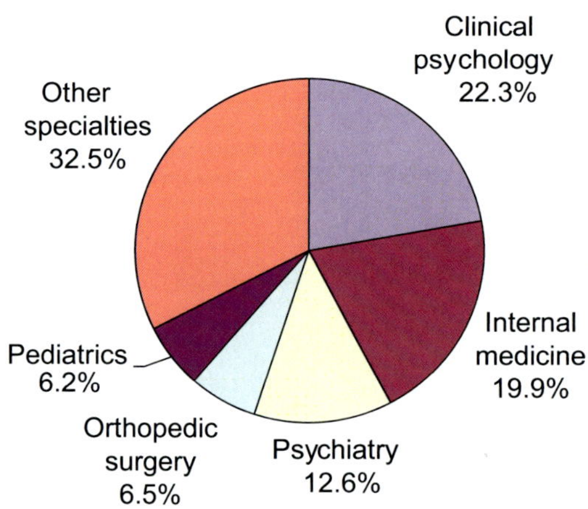

FIGURE 5 Medical experts by specialty, June 2005.
NOTE: This is the distribution of the 1,861 specialties; some MEs practice in more than one specialty and are counted more than once.
SOURCE: Annex Table 4.

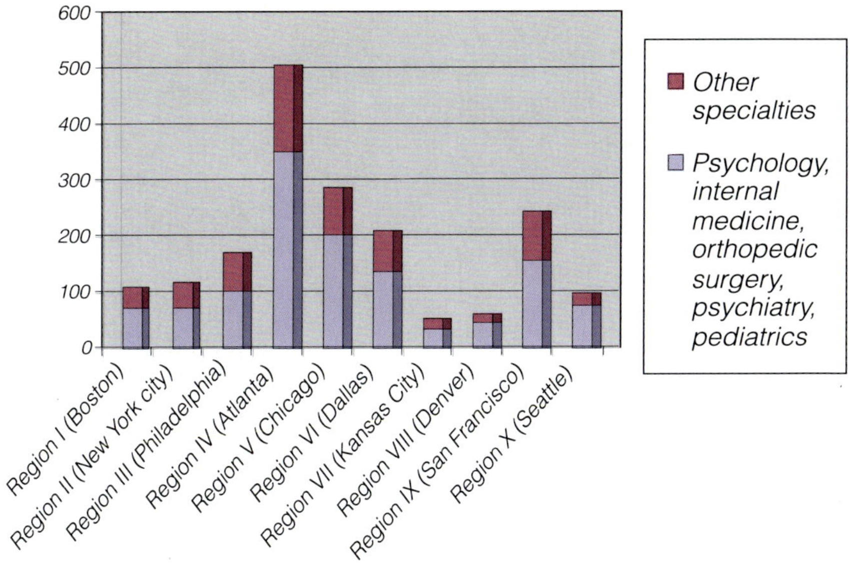

FIGURE 6 Number of different medical expert specialties, by region, June 2005. NOTE: This is the distribution of specialist categories, not the number of MEs in each specialty.

Kansas City, and Denver), and physical medicine and rehabilitation (Boston, Denver, Seattle). For a number of specialties, there were only one or two MEs in each of a few regions. These included infectious diseases, immunology, podiatry, gynecology, speech-language therapists, and a number of pediatric subspecialties (e.g., pediatric neurology, endocrinology, allergy, and pulmonology).

DDSs need to have access to a full range of medical expertise, although the committee did not find a need for a close match between the distribution of impairments among applicants and the mix of specialties among MCs. Most people go to an internist, gynecologist, or pediatrician for medical care and are referred to more specialized experts when needed. Similarly, most private insurers take a stepped approach to medical expertise, in which only those cases needing more specialized knowledge and judgment are referred on by the claims examiners or case managers.[14] Initial evaluations are often performed by a nurse, nurse practitioner, or in-house generalist physician, with relatively few cases needing to go to a specialist or subspecialist. The use of generalists to handle most situations and call on

[14]See, for example, Anfield (2002), for a description of UnumProvident's use of "the appropriate level of medical expertise" for each case.

specialists when needed allows for the most efficient use of costly specialist resources. It also helps ensure that the evaluation addresses the whole person, rather than focusing narrowly on one disorder. Such a model should also be effective for disability determinations in SSA, and it is quite similar to the way DDSs currently operate in relying on generalist specialists to evaluate the less complicated cases.

If the case record is fully developed, a trained DE should be able to make the disability determination in many cases without MC involvement, as currently occurs in SSA's prototype process being tested in 10 states. In the prototype process, many decisions are made by DEs alone, i.e., as single decision makers (SDMs). The committee understands that SSA has evaluated the quality of SDM decisions as compared to team decisions, but the results of this evaluation were not available to the committee. Several sources told the committee that the results of the analysis showed that SDM decision quality was comparable to DE-MC team decision quality. In more complex cases, the DE could consult with a generalist MC, usually in a situation where face-to-face discussion is possible. However, only the most complex cases need to be evaluated by a specialist physician or multiple specialists. This is where the current DDS process can break down, because many DDSs have few, if any, MCs in certain specialty areas.

For cases requiring physician input, most MCs can be primary care physicians, such as internists, family practitioners, pediatricians, psychiatrists, and psychologists. These kinds of experts, who constitute three-quarters of the MCs at DDSs currently, are best equipped to handle the broad range of cases presented, including those with multiple impairments or co-morbid disorders. Additional specialist MCs, such as cardiologists, oncologists, endocrinologists, ophthalmologists, and rheumatologists, who would be appropriate for more complex cases, could be accessed through the national network if the DDS does not have an MC with the needed specialty.

Nevertheless, it is vital that all SSA adjudicators have a full range of medical expertise available. Currently, DDSs must rely on cumbersome and time-consuming ad hoc arrangements to have a case file reviewed by an MC in another state DDS, the federal DDS, the SSA regional or central office, or elsewhere, if the originating DDS does not have an MC with the appropriate expertise.

Recommendation 1-1. SSA should make arrangements to ensure that the state Disability Determination Services (DDS) agencies and the Office of Hearings and Appeals (OHA) have ready access to the full range of physician specialties and other health professionals needed to evaluate cases. These experts should be available to consult with adjudicators in the DDSs and OHA on the development and evaluation of medical and functional information needed to reach a decision.

Better availability of specialty expertise could be accomplished in several ways, which are not mutually exclusive, including:

- formalizing and expanding the currently ad hoc cooperative arrangements among the DDSs to share experts;
- having SSA hire or contract for the services of MCs in specialties that individual states find hard to recruit (or that are needed in low volume by any single state) and assign them to work in a few DDSs around the country but to serve all the DDSs in their region; and/or
- having SSA establish federal regional units or national networks of medical experts in all specialties to whom complex cases could be referred for review and consultation and, perhaps, adjudication. SSA has already proposed this sort of arrangement in the Commissioner's new disability plan (SSA, 2005e:43594-43595).

The Commissioner's plan, as outlined in the NPRM published in the July 27, 2005 *Federal Register*, would establish a Federal Expert Unit (FEU). The FEU would create and maintain a national network of medical, psychological, and vocational experts[15] who would be available to adjudicators through the entire disability decision process, including DEs in DDSs and the administrative judges in OHA.[16] These experts would be recruited and paid by SSA at rates to be established by the Commissioner.[17]

The Commissioner evidently intends to recruit members of the national network of experts from practitioners in private practice, who would agree to review medical evidence in case files and either consult to MCs in the DDS and ALJs in OHA or participate as an MC in the disability determination decision, depending on the case. Assuming they are reimbursed at market rates, medical experts from specialties that DDSs and OHA have found hard to recruit would be more likely to participate and provide expertise that is not available currently. Medical and other experts could potentially be recruited from the academic health centers (AHCs). Many health profes-

---

[15]The question of vocational expertise was outside the scope of this study and is not addressed in this report.

[16]This includes ALJs and administrative appeals judges. The latter are part of the Appeals Council, the next level of appeal above ALJs.

[17]The plan also proposes to abolish the reconsideration step and establish a new federal position, a reviewing official, between the DDS and the ALJ hearing. The reviewing official would review the file if requested by a claimant denied at the initial level and either allow or deny the claim. If a denial, the claimant could appeal for an ALJ hearing. The plan would also replace the Appeals Council with a Decision Review Board consisting of ALJs and administrative appeals judges who would review cases in which quality control staff disagreed with the decision of the ALJ. If theses proposals are adopted in the final rules, the medical experts in the national network would provide expert advice to reviewing officials and the Decision Review Board.

sionals employed by AHCs are highly trained, salaried, and might have an interest in evaluating complex cases and earning additional income.

The July 2005 NPRM is not entirely clear on the role of the experts in the FEU network, in particular, whether they are consultants to adjudicators, including MCs in the DDSs, or are themselves MCs who participate in the adjudication decision, or both, depending on what is needed in each case. The NPRM says the experts "will be available to assist adjudicators throughout the country," "provide medical, psychological, and vocational expertise to state agencies, reviewing officials, administrative law judges, and the Decision Review Board," and "ensure that the right set of medical eyes reviews medical records and answers questions about the wide variety of impairments seen in disability claims." In summary, the experts would be available to assist adjudicators by providing the medical, psychological, and vocational expertise they may need to help decide a case. This implies that the experts will act in a consulting role, advising adjudicators on what the evidence means in terms of severity and impact on function, especially in complex cases or rare conditions.

The consulting role appears to be similar to the role that MCs play in the prototype decision process being tested in 10 states, in which DEs may act as single decision makers or, if they deem it necessary to evaluate the medical evidence properly, involve an MC in the decision process. But the NPRM proposes to abolish the prototype process demonstrations. This would appear to restore the DE-MC team in the adjudication of every case nationally. If the national experts are meant to serve as consultants to adjudicators, they would be available to consult with these adjudication teams when the DDS does not have the appropriate specialist or specialists to evaluate a claim, similar to when a treating physician refers a case to a specialist for review and advice.[18]

At times, however, the NPRM indicates that the national experts would act as the MC in the initial decision cases whose files they are reviewing. For example, it says that the DDSs should continue to employ MCs but they would be required to meet the same qualification standards as the experts in the federal network "in order to participate in the disability adjudication process."[19] This implies that if the DDS MCs do not meet the qualifications to be part of the national network, they will not be able to act as MCs and presumably the adjudication role would be filled by non-DDS members of

[18]The nomenclature can be confusing. DDS MCs are adjudicators, not consultants, except in the 10 prototype states. The medical experts at ALJ hearings, however, are consultants, not adjudicators.

[19]In testimony to Congress on September 27, 2005, the Commissioner put it this way: "The NPRM provides that state agencies may continue to use state medical and psychological consultants in the disability determination process, as long as they meet SSA's qualification standards" (Barnhart, 2005).

the national network. The new regulatory language proposed in the NPRM says that if a DDS refers a claim to the FEU, a medical or psychological expert affiliated with the national network will evaluate the evidence to determine the medical severity of the impairment or impairments (proposed sec. 405.14). An advantage of having members of the national network act as MCs is that SSA could pay a rate high enough to attract experts in specialties that are typically paid more than internists, family doctors, and pediatricians and who DDSs find it difficult to recruit.

Members of the national network would clearly serve as consultants when acting as expert witnesses at ALJ hearings or reviewing medical records in cases before the Appeals Council (or before reviewing officials and the Decision Review Board, if they are implemented as proposed in the NPRM). In these situations, they would be providing opinion evidence requested by the adjudicator, as the MEs currently signed up the OHA regional offices do. There will be two advantages to using the national networks members as experts. First, the use of the same experts by the DDSs and OHA should increase consistency in decision making. Second, the hearing offices will have access to a greater range of specialties, especially if SSA pays the national network experts more than OHA does now. ALJs could also have medical records reviewed by anyone in the country rather than be restricted to the specialties that happen to be in the local area.

The NPRM does not address CEs, but the medical and psychological experts in the national network are obvious candidates to be CE providers, assuming that arrangements are made to ensure they act as independent evaluators when acting in the CE provider role. This topic is addressed more fully below in the discussion of Task 10.

In conclusion, an FEU organized as a decentralized network of medical, psychological and vocational experts could play several roles. First, network experts could serve as consultants to adjudicators at the DDSs and OHA, similar to what MEs do for OHA currently. In this role, they would review medical records and provide expert opinions about how to develop a case (what tests or examinations to look for or have done), interpret medical evidence (whether the diagnosis, findings, and symptoms are consistent with the severity of impairment), and provide opinions on functional limitations. This would provide adjudicators with access to expertise that is not otherwise available but that is needed to evaluate complex cases or rare diseases. A common pool of consultants with uniform training also should promote greater consistency in decision making. Network consultants could also improve the evaluation of functional capacity if membership were expanded to include additional health professionals (see "Better Use of Medical Expertise," below).

Second, network experts could serve as MCs in the adjudication process and make the disability determination in conjunction with the DE. This would be especially helpful in complex, difficult-to-evaluate cases requiring subspecialty expertise. There are some practical problems to overcome, however, when the DE and MC are in different locations. Communication will be an issue, as will be the resolution of conflicting opinions. Also, if the MC is highly specialized, multiple impairments or co-morbidities will require evaluation by additional experts and pose a problem of integrating the results into an overall assessment.

Third, network experts could perform CEs (this is not proposed in the NPRM).

Establishing a national network of experts who would play different roles at different points in the process (e.g., acting as agency adjudicators in initial decisions and providing expert opinions to ALJs in de novo proceedings) will require arrangements that ensure that the same medical expert does not serve as adjudicator and expert witness in the same case. Likewise, if members of the network perform CEs, they should be instructed to be impartial and not be permitted to serve in other roles in the same case.

Qualifications of Medical Consultants

Current qualification standards for MCs in SSA's regulations require that MCs must be a:[20]

- Licensed physician (medical or osteopathic doctor);
- Licensed or certified psychologist who also meets other specific qualification standards;
- Licensed optometrist;
- Licensed podiatrist; or
- Qualified speech-language pathologist.

MCs who are not physicians are limited to evaluating the specific impairments for which they are trained. Only physician MCs perform the full range of duties of an MC. Although referred to as MCs in this interim report, psychological consultants may only participate in cases involving the evaluation of mental impairments. Similarly, optometrists may only establish visual acuity and visual fields, podiatrists may only establish impairments of the foot and ankle, and speech-language pathologists may only establish speech and language impairments.

Currently, MCs are not required to be board certified, possess any additional credentials, or have an active practice in patient care.

Fully performing the MC role requires mastery of three domains of knowledge. First, MCs must be expert in their medical field (e.g., medicine,

[20] 20 CFR 404.1616 and 416.1016.

psychology, speech-language pathology). Second, they need to understand how to evaluate disability. This is a skill not usually learned as part of standard medical education and training curriculum, which focuses on diagnosis and treatment.[21] Disability evaluation, i.e., understanding how the functional limitations imposed by impairment affect ability to work, is a subject usually learned by taking additional courses or through on-the-job experience, preferably both. Third, MCs must be knowledgeable about Social Security policies and procedures for determining eligibility for disability benefits. (See "Training of Medical Consultants," below, for additional discussion on this topic.)

Currently, DDSs rely on state licensure or, in the case of psychologists and speech-language pathologists, certain alternative qualification requirements, to ensure a minimum level of medical expertise and competence. DDSs also try to assign complex cases to MCs with more specialized expertise, although this is not required. It is also not always possible, because some specialties are not widely available. In June 2004, for example, there were 38 neurologists, 36 cardiologists, 25 ophthalmologists, and 18 orthopedic surgeons serving as MCs in DDSs nationally. Five states had none of these specialties represented among their MCs, and 25 states had between one and five.

Each DDS has a training program for its MCs to educate them on disability evaluation and Social Security program definitions and requirements. This typically includes working at first on easier cases with a more experienced MC and gradually taking on harder cases as experience is gained.

The committee finds the current qualification standards to be adequate for purposes of ensuring a minimum level of competence and qualification for speech-language pathologists, optometrists, and podiatrists. However, for physicians and psychologists, board certification is rapidly becoming the standard credential for the practice of medicine or psychology. Virtually everyone entering medical practice today is board certified. Currently, board certification is a common prerequisite for hospital privileges and other professional activities, such as participation in a provider network.

A number of studies have found a relationship between board certification of physicians and better outcomes, although other studies have not or had mixed results (Brennan et al., 2004). There is evidence that quality of physician performance (as measured by currency of knowledge, standards of practice, and patient outcomes) tends to decline with experience (as

[21]For example, according to the 2004-2005 survey of U.S. medical schools by the Liaison Committee on Medical Education, 66 (52.4 percent) of the 126 schools reported that occupational medicine was a required part of the curriculum. 64 of the 66 reported the number of curricular hours, which ranged from 0.5 to 47.0. The median number of hours was 3.0 (Barzansky, 2005).

measured by the number of years in practice or age).[22] Certification boards have addressed the possibility of decline by requiring periodic recertification and are moving to a more continuous process of assessing competence (Steinbrook, 2005).

Recommendation 1-2. SSA should make board certification of physicians and psychologists* mandatory. This will necessitate an increase in compensation in order to recruit and retain qualified physicians and psychologists as MCs and MEs or as members of the national network of experts, if it is established. SSA also should allow current MCs with qualified program experience who are not board certified to continue for a time period of five years.

The basic training for a physician specialist includes four years of premedical education in a college or university, four years of medical school, and after receiving the M.D. degree, three to five years of residency (i.e., specialty training under supervision). After residency training, physicians are considered to be specialists and are board eligible. Approximately 30 percent elect to pursue additional training to become subspecialists. Training in a subspecialty can take another one to three years to complete. Certification boards generally require that a person seeking certification have an unrestricted state license to practice medicine to qualify to take the certification examination. Finally, a candidate for certification must pass a written and, in some cases, an oral examination. Most subspecialties require additional board exams qualifying the physician to be a board certified subspecialist. Subsequently, most boards require periodic recertification every six to 10 years, which involves continuing education, review of credentials, and further examination.

The basic training for a psychologist specialist includes a bachelor's degree, four or more years of psychology graduate school and one year of clinical internship. After receiving the Ph.D. or Psy.D. degree, one to two additional postdoctoral fellowship years are required to be eligible for spe-

---

[22] A review of 62 empirical studies relating currency of medical knowledge/health care quality to years in practice/physician age found that 32 studies reported decreasing performance with increasing years in practice for all outcomes assessed; 13 reported the same for some outcomes but not others; and 2 found increased performance with experience that peaked and then declined. Of the 15 remaining studies, 2 found increasing performance with increasing years in practice for some or all outcomes assessed, and 13 found no association (Choudhry, et al., 2005).

*In its final report, the committee affirmed its recommendations in the Interim Report except for two. It dropped those parts of Recommendations 1-2 and 1-7 that recommended board certification of psychologists, because at this time there are too few board-cetified psychologists to meet the demand that would be created. The committee still recommends board certification of physicians.

cialty certification. Additional years of clinical practice are often required to be eligible for board certification by the American Board of Professional Psychology. Board certification also requires psychologists to have an unrestricted state license to practice psychology and they must pass a written and an oral examination (ABPP, 2005).

The member boards of the American Board of Medical Specialties (ABMS) have issued more than 800,000 certificates in 36 specialties and 88 subspecialties. Approximately 30 percent were issued in the past 10 years (ABMS, 2005:Table 2). ABMS and the American Medical Association estimate that 89.2 percent of physicians with current licenses were board certified in 1999, up from 76.1 percent in 1989.[23] The number certified in a subspecialty (e.g., cardiology, infectious diseases, rheumatology, child and adolescent psychiatry, pain medicine) is still small, however.

The committee recognizes that establishing a higher level of qualification (i.e., board certification) may affect SSA's ability to attract and retain experts. SSA has historically had difficulty recruiting qualified experts given the nature of the work and comparatively low reimbursement rates. Establishing a firm requirement for higher qualifications must be accompanied by increased compensation rates if SSA is to attract enough candidates. A requirement for board certification that is not accompanied by compensation at the full market rate could have the paradoxical effect of decreasing the overall quality of the expert pool. On the one hand, it would exclude uncertified experts who are highly capable. On the other hand, it might attract only those who may be board certified but whose capabilities do not command market-rate fees.

The fact that compensation rates for current DDS MCs are set by the states may complicate the implementation of a uniform national payment system. However, given that the July 2005 NPRM indicates that SSA plans to pay DDS MCs in the national network the same as non-DDS MCs, the committee assumes that SSA has the ability to overcome this complication.

Of course, board certification only addresses physician/psychologist competence in a field of medicine (diagnosis, treatment practices, disease course). It does not ensure that they are skilled in evaluating disability or knowledgeable of Social Security disability program requirements, which is the basis for Recommendation 1-3, below. Experienced current MCs have these qualifications. Therefore, depending on the eventual structure of the medical expertise pool that is the subject of SSA's current proposed rulemaking, SSA should establish a phase-in period or grandfathering provision for some individuals who are currently providing program medical expertise. For example, SSA could require all members of a newly organized

[23]www.abms.org/Downloads/Statistics/Table9_Chart1.pdf.

FEU to be board certified as of a certain date (e.g., implementation of the FEU), while still allowing current program physicians/psychologists who become members of an affiliated national network a period of five years to acquire the necessary qualifications. The committee recognizes that implementing a board certification requirement will pose practical problems but believes that it should be the standard for medical experts in SSA's disability decision process.

In discussions with the committee, SSA staff also raised the issue of whether there should be a requirement that program physicians, psychologists, and others be currently (or recently) engaged in direct patient care. Although recognizing the advantages of current involvement in active patient care, the committee believes that such a requirement would exclude otherwise highly qualified and needed experts who do not (or no longer) engage in direct patient care for a variety of reasons, such as high malpractice insurance and other practice costs, engagement in research, and administrative duties.

Training of Medical Consultants

Board certification and recertification represent mastery of a specific body of knowledge and continuing education, but the certification process alone does not ensure that an individual is qualified to provide expertise in SSA's disability programs. As noted above, disability evaluation expertise and program knowledge are also essential, and ongoing training is necessary to ensure competence.

Currently, SSA has no standardized national training program for MCs, which would ensure a reliable level of knowledge and promote consistency in decision making. Such a training course exists for DEs. It was developed in conjunction with the DDSs, and the DDSs are required to use it.

Many DDSs have their own programs for training MCs. A comprehensive, standardized MC training program should be based on the best of the current DDS training programs and developed with input from the DDSs. It should not only address SSA program rules, but also include a comprehensive component on disability assessment. The same program should be required for MCs in the Federal DDS and for those who review cases for PERs and QA in the regional offices.

Recommendation 1-3. SSA should continue to develop and implement a mandatory national training program for all MCs, including those in the national network of experts outside the DDSs. The training program should focus on how to evaluate disability and on Social Security disability policies and procedures, be competency-based, and

be coupled with ongoing assessment of MC competency as part of the quality assurance process.

SSA has been developing a standard training curriculum for MCs for the past several years. The curriculum was developed by a committee with representatives of the DDSs and SSA national and regional offices and is currently under review. The training program should be completed and implemented as soon as possible. It should concentrate on the aspects of the MC role that are not usually learned in medical school or residency programs, namely, evaluation of work disability and Social Security disability program policies and procedures. There also should be an ongoing training component. The training should be competency based, and SSA should perform an ongoing assessment of MC competency as a component of its revised quality assurance program.

Better Use of Medical Expertise

Under current procedures for the development and evaluation of disability claims MCs must be physicians, psychologists, or other "acceptable medical sources" (i.e., podiatrists, optometrists, speech-language therapists). This policy has the effect of excluding from DDSs many medical personnel who could support the disability decision-making process, for example, personnel trained to evaluate functional limitations and their impact on ability to work (e.g., nurse practitioners, occupational therapists, physical therapists, registered nurses, psychiatric social workers).[24] Many of the Listings have a substantial functional component (e.g., mental and childhood Listings) and at least half the adult claims are decided on medical-vocational factors (i.e., an evaluation of the interaction between functional limitations and ability to work at steps 4 and 5 of the sequential evaluation process). Medical expertise in evaluating functioning is, therefore, vital to accurate claim adjudication. Currently, few if any DDSs make use of the wide range of medical expertise available beyond the currently acceptable medical sources that could both expedite case processing and improve the quality of the initial decisions.

Recommendation 1-4. SSA should expand the range of expertise available in DDSs and implement alternative methods of developing and adjudicating cases within DDSs that would make more efficient and effective use of existing sources of expertise, and SSA should require these additional types of experts to undergo the same training as MCs.

---

[24]Talmadge (2003) discusses the contributions of physical therapists, occupational therapists, occupational nurses, and other disciplines make to the disability evaluation process.

Expanding the range of expertise available in case adjudication would help DDSs implement the proposed "quick disability determination process" and make it more effective. The DDSs could triage cases more extensively, identifying not only the easy cases that can be expedited by the quick decision process, but also the hard cases that need more focused attention. In addition, it would allow DDSs to use interdisciplinary teams in appropriate cases.

For example, DDSs could use registered nurses certified as nurse practitioners or case managers to help triage cases, advise DEs on what is needed to complete development of the medical record, and help decide when a case should be referred to an MC for review and advice and/or referral to a specialist. SSA might also consider encouraging DDSs to employ nurses as DEs, as has been done in the New York DDS. If a quick decision process is developed, nurses could have the expertise, with physician backup, to identify suitable cases. This option is constrained, however, by a shortage of registered nurses in most states that is projected through at least 2020 (DHHS, 2002:Table 6).

A disability case evaluation process that makes use of a variety of expertise could look something like this:

- Cases are initially handled by a triage unit staffed by trained personnel (similar to current DEs) who sort cases according to complexity and identify the specific expertise needed.
- Cases are referred to one of several units, such as for:
  - Apparent simple allowances (e.g., presumptive disability, quick decision cases),
  - Uncomplicated cases that may be decided by a nonphysician professional (e.g., experienced DE, registered nurse),
  - Cases with complex medical issues requiring physician MC review,
  - Cases with complex functional issues requiring evaluation by a professional skilled in functional evaluation, or
  - Cases requiring an interdisciplinary team evaluation.
- All these units have the ability to consult with experts in other units on an as-needed basis, or to transfer cases to another unit, as appropriate.
- Expertise that is not available in the DDS (e.g., medical specialists and subspecialists) is made available via referral to:
  - Another DDS,
  - An MC in the national network, if it is established, or FEU, or
  - A specialized clinical center in a medical center (see Recommendation 1-5, below).

Other Sources of Medical Expertise

Using technology (such as electronic case files and video hearings) to make agency experts more widely available, establishing rigorous, standardized qualification requirements for all experts, and compensating experts at a level commensurate with their expertise will help to ensure that disability adjudicators have sufficient expertise to help them address complex medical issues in most cases. However, there will still be circumstances in which SSA needs more than a network of individual experts. Examples include more complex or rare cases or newly developing conditions (e.g., emerging infectious diseases). SSA would also benefit from having external resources that can help with program evaluation and provide analyses useful for policy development.

There are many specialized clinical research centers that focus on specific diseases and their functional consequences. The National Institute of Disability and Rehabilitation Research funds a number of specialized centers, including model programs in spinal cord injury, brain injury, and work rehabilitation, and research and training centers in a variety of disability areas. The National Institutes of Health (NIH) funds dozens of clinical research center programs, each with multiple centers (IOM, 2004). NIH-funded centers include Autoimmunity Centers of Excellence, Asthma and Allergic Diseases Centers, Comprehensive Sickle Cell Centers, Multidisciplinary Clinical Research Centers for Arthritis and Musculoskeletal and Skin Diseases, Alzheimer's Disease Centers, Vision Research Centers, Diabetes Research and Training Centers, Autism Research Centers of Excellence, Parkinson's Disease Research Centers of Excellence, Digestive Diseases Research Centers, a Rare Disease Clinical Research Network, and Specialized Centers of Research on various types of cancer and chronic heart and lung diseases, to name some. These centers are in academic medical centers across the country.

Recommendation 1-5. SSA should consider developing formal working relationships with specialized clinical research centers to review and evaluate the medical record in difficult cases, provide feedback on how well SSA is evaluating certain disabling conditions, and identify improvements that should be made in evaluation criteria (including the Listings) and procedures.

SSA should consider developing demonstration projects with academic clinical research centers that focus on conditions that are difficult to evaluate. Academic research centers focus on improving diagnosis and treatment and few medical experts in them will be familiar with the SSA disability program or with evaluating the work capacities and limitations of patients. The centers would nevertheless be an excellent source of medical expertise in reviewing complex cases, a means of learning how to improve adjudicative evaluation and decision making and improving the training of DEs, MCs, and ALJs, and an input to the revision and updating of the Listings (policies and procedures for evaluating and updating the Listings will be addressed fully in the final report of this committee).

For example, SSA currently has a demonstration project with the Association of University Centers on Disabilities (AUCD) in which sets of SSI childhood cases with certain conditions (e.g., school-age children with mental retardation; children with low birth weight; adolescents with cognitive, psychiatric, or emotional impairments) are referred to AUCD centers for evaluation after they have been evaluated and a preliminary denial determination made by the DDS. This process has helped to improve the evaluation of children with mental conditions and problems with language development, and it has improved the process of gathering evidence of adaptive functioning. This project has made suggestions for improving the procedures and criteria for evaluating childhood disability, developed training for DEs, drafted national age-specific function forms, and produced an electronic database of appropriate assessment instruments for assessing children (e.g., instruments for measuring cognitive ability, adaptive behavior, speech and language skills, etc.). This arrangement is a model for similar arrangements in other areas of impairment. However, one significant limitation of the AUCD project was that it focused only on denial decisions. Any similar future projects need to look at examples of both allowances and denials.

Similar arrangements could be made with other research centers that focus on vocational rehabilitation or functional aspects of disability. This would be especially appropriate if SSA increases its efforts to return claimants to work by assessing their functional capacity earlier in the process.

Involvement of Treating Physicians and Other Treating Sources

Treating sources are an important component of SSA's disability decision process. Under its rules, SSA develops evidence from a claimant's own medical sources before evaluating evidence obtained on a consultative basis. It must give some deference to a treating source's opinion and even "controlling weight" in cases where a treating source's opinion is well supported by medically acceptable clinical and laboratory diagnostic techniques and is not inconsistent with the other substantial evidence in the case record. This deference to the treating source acknowledges that he or she has a longitudinal picture of the claimant from an on-going treatment relationship, which is desirable in documenting the severity and functional consequences of impairment or impairments.

In addition, it is SSA policy that, when a CE is required (e.g., because the evidence is incomplete or inconsistent), the treating source is the preferred source for the CE.

Despite the clear preference for treating source evidence in SSA's rules, the committee heard testimony that treating physicians and psychologists and other medical sources who provide treatment to applicants are not used as sources of medical information as often or as well as they could be and that many treating sources who do respond to requests for medical evidence only provide copies of records, not their judgment of the patient's functional capacities. The committee also learned that treating sources seldom perform consultative examinations, although SSA does not track this statistic. Greater participation by treating sources is an excellent means of obtaining all the relevant medical and functional information early in the disability decision process, which speeds the process, leads to more informed decisions, and saves the costs of going back to the treating physician for additional information or of having to order a CE.

Recommendation 1-6. SSA should take steps to improve the flow of medical information from treating sources, especially by asking for the specific information wanted, making it easier to furnish the information, and reimbursing for the full cost of collecting the information and for producing and transmitting the report.

Obtaining fuller and better medical evidence and opinions from treating providers, and obtaining it as early in the process as possible, would lead to more accurate and better substantiated decisions, making it possible for those who qualify for benefits to do so sooner. It would also reduce the need for costly, time-consuming, and sometimes poor quality consultative examinations.

Nevertheless, reliance on treating sources has limitations. Treating sources may unduly promote the interests of their patients, and SSA disability decision makers must take this into account in evaluating their opinions. This is why a treating source's opinion must be well supported by the evidence. Some treating sources will be reluctant to provide more than the records, even if assured they are not making a decision affecting the well-being of a patient. They may fear that assessing the impairment or disability status of a patient seeking benefits may interfere with the clinician-patient relationship, especially if the patient is denied.[25]

---

[25]The ethical and practical concerns of treating physicians asked to evaluate their patients seeking disability benefits are discussed in Mischoulon (2002), Pransky et al. (2002), Leo and Del Regno (2001), Himmelstein et al. (2000), and Zinn and Furutani (1996).

Performing a proper disability evaluation or providing a complete report with a well-substantiated medical source opinion requires a great deal of time, often poorly remunerated. Evaluating patients with impairments for disability program eligibility takes more time, and therefore more practice expense, than most other types of patients (Lewin, 2005). Disability management and return-to-work issues are often present, and patients with severe impairments are often more psychologically stressed than other patients because of employment and financial concerns. In addition, clinical staff must spend additional time analyzing the medical history and records and completing a report.

Finally, treating sources may not have adequate training or experience in evaluating disability or understanding of SSA criteria and procedures to provide relevant information or opinions that squarely address DDS needs for decision making.

Ways to improve the amount and quality of input from treating sources can be identified through analysis of best practices in DDSs, which can be implemented more consistently throughout the country. Efforts should focus on making treating sources more knowledgeable about SSA rules and procedures and what is expected of them, providing protocols and forms that elicit and organize relevant information, making it easier technologically for treating sources to provide the information, and compensating them adequately for the extra practice expenses involved in providing records and a useful report. Obtaining sufficient information from treating sources at the initial level is the best way to improve the accuracy and timeliness of the decisions and to make the right decision as early in the process as possible. Examples of actions needed to be taken to improve the process include:

- Providing higher compensation for the costs of providing records and preparing a proper report;
- Providing materials—written, audio, and audiovisual—developed to communicate what is expected from treating sources with regard to patients who apply for social security disability benefits, similar to *Understanding SSI Disability for Children*, a booklet and video developed with the American Academy of Pediatrics as an educational tool for pediatricians who have patients with disabilities.[26]

[26]The booklet and video were designed to be used for continuing education. Pediatricians who use them are eligible for up to two hours of American Medical Association Physician's Recognition Award category 1 credit (www.pedialink.org/cme/_coursefinder/CMEdetail.cfm?aid=14720&area=liveCME).

• Making sure that the letters asking for medical evidence explain clearly what is needed and are specific enough that the treating physician responds with useful information;

• Providing standard protocols or guidelines online for evaluating the most common conditions similar to the protocols developed by the SSA-AUCD Children's SSI Project for assessing cognitive impairments, low birth weight, speech/language deficits, and other conditions in different age groups;

• Developing standardized forms for reports that are formatted to elicit relevant information, like the Psychiatric Review Technique form (SSA-2506-BK), which was designed with the assistance of the American Psychiatric Association and other professional groups to improve the quality of evaluations of mental impairments (Pincus et al., 1991);

• Emphasizing the need to obtain physicians' statements about the functional aspects of the disability, in addition to the clinical information;

• Providing standardized forms to gather information on functional limitations. Some hearing offices currently use this kind of form;

• Making available free dictation services (as some DDSs already do) and web-based "smart" forms as well as traditional paper forms to fill out;

• Providing flexibility for reporting physicians. For example, some physicians might prefer providing a narrative report while others may prefer checklists; and

• Encouraging claimant participation in obtaining treating source cooperation.

Current reimbursement rates significantly affect both treating source participation and report quality. Reimbursement rates are generally low relative to market rates. For example, reimbursement for providing medical records is about $20. As will be discussed in the section on consultative examinations, below, reimbursement for performing a disability examination is also low, especially compared with comparable examinations performed for workers' compensation and for private disability insurance carriers.[27]

Qualifications of OHA Medical Experts

At the hearing level of the disability claim process, ALJs are solely responsible for making the disability decision, including all medical, functional, and vocational aspects. MEs are not directly involved in the decision

[27]Each state sets its own rates for CEs. According to fee schedules from 48 DDSs supplied by SSA, the median fee for an internal medicine examination and report was $126 in 2004 (five states paid less than $100; four states paid more than $165). The median rate was $129 for a cardiology—and $132 for an orthopedic—examination and report.

making. However, they are called on to testify at hearings as expert witnesses or, occasionally, to respond to written interrogatories from ALJs.

MEs provide assessments of the medical evidence in response to specific questions from the ALJ. In FY 2001-2002, ALJs used MEs in 11 percent of cases, down from 14 percent of cases in FY 1999-2000. Judges conducting peer reviews of a sample of cases found that allowance decisions made in hearings with ME testimony were slightly better supported than those made in hearings without ME testimony (SSA, 2003:41-42).

To some extent, MEs serve a role similar to that of MCs at the initial decision step. However, there are significant differences. In most states, MCs function as decision makers (albeit on a team) and they are, for all practical purposes, employees of the DDS (even though technically most are contractors). MEs function as independent expert witnesses in a quasi-judicial process. They have no direct adjudicative function, and they do not examine the claimant. They provide needed medical expertise to the proceedings to help the parties to the hearing understand complex medical issues in the case in layman's terms. They may also be asked to provide an expert opinion on other issues, such as whether the claimant's impairments meet or equal the severity of the Listings; the claimant's ability to perform work-related activities; or expected impairment duration.

At the present time, SSA has not defined specific qualification standards for MEs, as it has for MCs. In addition, MEs receive no formal training from SSA, although they may receive basic program information. This is intended to ensure their independence and impartiality as expert witnesses.

Recommendation 1-7. Medical experts (MEs) used by ALJs should be board certified if they are physicians or psychologists. SSA should encourage the use of licensed medical personnel other than physicians or psychologists* as MEs in appropriate cases. All MEs should be adequately compensated for the time and effort required to serve in this capacity.

Regardless of whether MEs are drawn from existing rosters, or some newly established network as is proposed in the July 2005 NPRM, SSA should establish consistent, national qualification standards for MEs to ensure a level of uniformity across the country. As discussed earlier, board

---

*In its final report, the committee affirmed its recommendations in the Interim Report except for two. It dropped those parts of Recommendations 1-2 and 1-7 that recommended board certification of psychologists, because at this time there are too few board-cetified psychologists to meet the demand that would be created. The committee still recommends board certification of physicians.

certification is fast becoming the standard credential for the practice of medicine and psychology. Therefore, physicians and psychologists who serve as MEs should be required to be board certified. Having a high level of qualification for MEs who testify at hearings is essential to the integrity of the hearing process. In addition, given the nature of the hearing process, the committee does not believe it would be appropriate to grandfather in existing MEs who are not board certified.

Despite the absence of formal qualification standards for MEs, there appears to have been a de facto requirement that MEs be either physicians or psychologists. According to data provided by SSA, the current roster of MEs includes only a handful of "acceptable medical sources" who are not physicians or psychologists (i.e., podiatrists, optometrists, or speech and language pathologists) or other qualified health professionals. As discussed previously, there are other health professionals (e.g., occupational therapists, physical therapists, registered nurses, psychiatric social workers) who could support the disability decision-making process by providing expert assessment of impairment severity and functional limitations, including functional components of Listings. These experts would be a valuable source of information at the ALJ hearing level, as well as at the DDS level.

Although the committee has recommended additional training for DDS MCs in disability evaluation and program requirements, it does not see a similar need for MEs, given that they are not directly involved in adjudication. If the national network proposed in the NPRM is established and network experts become the pool for MEs, then MEs will receive MC training, as called for in Recommendation 1-3.

As is the case with DDS MCs, SSA has difficulty recruiting well-qualified ME candidates in certain specialties, in large part because the compensation is too low. MEs are usually paid $160 a case, $80 for reviewing the file and $80 for attending a hearing.

According to a recent survey of OHA regional offices, every region had shortages of MEs in at least some specialties (SSA, 2004b). The regional offices consistently reported that the main reason for lack of access to medical expertise was the low fees they could offer, although some said MEs were also quitting because of the recent requirements of Central Contract Registration and fingerprinting. The result is that hearings cannot be scheduled, or cases wait until enough accumulate that need the same type of specialist to make it worthwhile for the ME to appear, or MEs in other than the needed field of expertise are used. A substantial fee increase to market rates, similar to the one recommended for CEs in Recommendation 2-2, below, in conjunction with higher qualification standards, would attract more and better candidates.

TRAINING AND CERTIFICATION OF CONSULTATIVE EXAMINERS

> **Task 10:** "*Recommend needs for standardized training and certification for consultative examiners who assess claimant's level of function based on integrated evaluation of medical impairment and functional capacity. Advise on content of a training curriculum, appropriate personnel to train, and mechanisms for the certification process.*"

Each DDS purchases CEs to obtain or clarify information that is missing, conflicting, or ambiguous in claimant's medical records. They also purchase CEs when claimants do not have a regular source of treatment and thus have fragmented records that are difficult to locate. CE providers are asked to report examination and test results, a diagnosis and prognosis, and an opinion on what the claimant can do despite his or her impairment.

Each DDS is charged with recruiting and orienting medical personnel who agree to be available to perform CEs in return for a fee set by each state. If the claimant's treating source is qualified, equipped, and willing to perform the examination or test and generally furnishes complete and timely reports, the treating source is the preferred source for the CE, because "The individual's treating source is often in the best position to provide detailed longitudinal information about the individual."[28] If the treating source prefers not to do the CE, there are conflicts and inconsistencies in the file that cannot be resolved by going back to the treating source, or the DDS knows from prior experience that the treating source has consistently failed to provide complete or timely reports, the DDS can obtain the CE from a nontreating source. Currently, SSA keeps track of the number and costs of CEs purchased by each DDS but does not know the percentage of cases in which a CE or CEs is ordered or the percentage that is performed by the treating source.

CE providers are not required to be what SSA defines to be an acceptable medical source,[29] if a medically determinable impairment has been established and the issue at hand is the severity of the impairment and how it affects an individual's functioning. CE providers may be what SSA calls "other sources," who may be medical practitioners such as nurse-practitioners, physical therapists, occupational therapists, chiropractors, and audiologists, or nonmedical sources such as teachers, day care providers, social workers, and employers. The committee was told that few CEs

---

[28]POMS DI 22510.010.

[29]Currently, acceptable medical sources are limited to licensed physicians, licensed or certified psychologists, licensed optometrists, licensed podiatrists, and licensed or certified speech-language pathologists.

are purchased from sources who are not acceptable medical sources, which SSA refers to as "other sources," although these other sources are often in a better position to provide evidence about how well their patients function than are treating physicians who may see the patients infrequently (Talmadge, 2003). Other sources will become more important if SSA changes the emphasis from proving inability to work to encouraging return to work, which will require determination of what an applicant can do, not of what they cannot do.

Training and Certification Requirements for Consultative Examiners

Current SSA requirements for CE providers are minimal. They must be currently licensed to practice medicine in the state and have the training and experience to perform the type of examination or test being requested. They are also supposed to have the facilities and equipment needed to perform the examinations or tests being requested and have a good understanding of SSA's disability programs and their evidentiary requirements.[30] CE providers are not required to have training or certification specifically in the evaluation of disability.

The DDS adjudicator is supposed to select a specialist to perform the CE when the nature or complexity of a particular impairment or impairments warrants it, although there are no guidelines for which specialist to choose. According to SSA's program operations manual, a CE provider usually does not have to be a specialist in the medical field relevant to the individual's impairment or impairments. For example, an internist could be asked to perform an examination involving impairments of the musculoskeletal, cardiovascular, neurological, and other body systems.[31]

The DDSs are required to have an ongoing program to recruit CE providers; a process for orientation, training, and review of new CE providers on the content of CE reports; and an oversight program for CE providers, with special emphasis on "key" providers (those who bill at least $100,000 for CEs annually, or have a practice directed primarily towards independent medical examinations rather than the treatment of patients, or are one of the top five CE examination providers in the state by dollar volume). These requirements were contained in the Social Security Disability Benefits Reform Act of 1984, in response to complaints about the quality of CEs, especially those performed by so-called bulk providers (Bloch, 1992:98-108). (The preference for CEs by treating sources was also mandated by this law.)

---

[30]20 CFR 404.1519g(b) and 416.919g(b).

[31]POMS DI 22510.010.

Currently, each state makes its own arrangements for orienting and training CE providers. SSA requires DDSs to submit documentation that they have conducted annual oversight visits to key providers, but data on the findings are not systematically gathered and analyzed.

SSA furnishes CE providers with a guide, known as the Green Book, which was developed to give basic information about the CE process to physicians and other health professionals (SSA, 1999). The guide, which is available online as well as on paper, provides general information about the Social Security disability programs and how claims are adjudicated, including the role of CEs, how CE providers are selected, and what the DDSs look for in a report of a CE.

Although SSA does not currently have specific training and certification requirements for CE providers, there are training and certification requirements in other federal and nonfederal medical evaluation programs. For example,

Federal Aviation Administration (FAA)

The FAA requires pilots to be medically certified to fly. This is done by Aviation Medical Examiners (AMEs). To become an AME, the FAA requires physicians to complete Medical Certification Standards and Procedures Training and a basic AME seminar and to attend a three-day AME Seminar or equivalent training at three-year intervals thereafter.

U.S. Department of Transportation (DOT)

DOT has a drug testing program for individuals in safety-sensitive positions in the transportation industry. This function is performed by Medical Review Officers (MROs). Beginning in 2001, DOT has required training and certification of MROs and 12 hours of continuing medical education (CME) related to MRO practice every three years. Rather than provide the training and certification itself, DOT recognizes training and CME courses given by the American College of Occupational and Environmental Medicine, American Society of Addiction Medicine, and American Association of Medical Review Officers (AAMRO) and the written certification examination given by AAMRO.

U.S. Department of Labor (DOL)

DOL provides benefits to workers who have contracted pneumoconiosis from coal dust or asbestosis. The pneumoconiosis must be confirmed by a radiograph. The radiograph is read first at a facility approved by the National Institute for Occupational Safety and Health (NIOSH) and confirmed by a physician "B Reader" engaged by NIOSH. NIOSH requires B Readers to be certified and recertified every four years. The certification examinations are held at NIOSH's Appalachian Laboratory for Occupational Safety and Health in Morgantown, West Virginia. NIOSH suggests that applicants use NIOSH's home self-study syllabus or attend the American College of Radiology Symposium on Radiology of the Pneumoconioses held every two years.

State Workers' Compensation Programs

California requires those who evaluate injured workers in disputed state workers' compensation cases to be certified as Qualified Medical Evaluators (QMEs). To be certified means passing a test for knowledge and skills in clinical assessment/evaluation; medical treatment; disability issues/vocational rehabilitation/maximum medical improvement; causation; apportionment; basic workers' compensation laws and regulations; and report writing. The QME test was developed and is administered by CPS Human Resource Services. Eligibility to be a QME also requires completion of a 12-hour course in disability evaluation report writing approved by the state.

Several other states, for example, Texas, also require state-approved training courses and written certification examinations of physicians who evaluate impairment in workers' compensation cases. The courses are given by the American Academy of Disability Evaluating Physicians and the written examination by the American Association of Expert Medical Evaluators.[32]

If not board certified, QMEs have to have completed an accredited residency program. Both California and Texas require approved continuing education courses and periodic recertification.

Recommendation 2-1. SSA should establish reasonable requirements for training and certification of consultative examination providers. The training and certification should focus on two competencies: evaluation of limitations on ability to work resulting from impairments, and evidentiary and other requirements of SSA's disability decision-making process.

The ability to diagnose and treat diseases and injuries is fulfilled by the current requirement that they be licensed or certified in their area of medical expertise. Physicians, for example, should be licensed and, if specialists, board certified. Licensure and board certification do not necessarily ensure,

[32] www.tdi.state.tx.us/wc/dwc/divisions/irtraining.html.

however, that CE providers are expert in evaluating how a person's impairments limits their functioning in employment settings or that they know how to provide medical evidence in a form pertinent to evaluating whether someone meets Social Security's definition of disability. Physicians, with the exception of those trained in occupational medicine, usually do not learn how to evaluate work disability during medical school or residency or for board certification (Scheer, 2000:121) and are often not confident about their ability to determine who is disabled (Zinn and Furutani, 1996). Accordingly, CE providers should be required to demonstrate competence in these subject areas, namely, functional assessment of disability and SSA disability program policies and procedures.

The committee realizes that such requirements increase the costs of serving as a CE provider and, all other things being equal, would reduce the availability of medical sources to perform CEs. Other programs, however, such as the California and Texas workers' compensation programs, require training and certification of medical evaluators and have no problem recruiting. The higher compensation for CEs recommended below, if brought in line with the fees in workers' compensation and other disability benefit programs, should offset the cost to potential CE providers of reasonable training and certification requirements.

SSA should:

- Develop a training curriculum on disability evaluation and SSA disability policies, rules, criteria, and procedures for CE providers, including both acceptable medical sources and other providers who evaluate function, such as nurses, occupational and physical therapists, and psychiatric social workers. This curriculum should be consistent with but less in depth than the one for MCs called for in Recommendation 1-3, above.
- Provide the training curricula as online modules with pre- and post-test questions.
- Require CE providers to complete the appropriate training module and pass the post-test with a certain minimum score.
- Develop continuing education modules and require CE providers to take them and pass a post-test every two years.

The training and certification requirement should be phased in over several years after the curriculum has been well tested and adequately piloted in a few locations. This must be done in conjunction with the implementation of a fee schedule commensurate with the work involved in performing CEs, to prevent CE providers from dropping out of the program in great numbers.

An additional option would be to use members of the national network of medical and psychological experts to supplement the pool of CEs, assuming that there are enough experts to accommodate this as well as advise DDS and OHA decision makers. The advantage of using national network experts is that they will have mastered the curriculum for MCs, which will focus on disability evaluation and on SSA program rules and practices (see Recommendation 1-3, above). There is a potential down side. SSA should be mindful that national network experts paid to serve as CE providers by SSA may not be seen as impartial as CE providers who are otherwise independent of the agency. Policies should be instituted, therefore, so that an expert who reviews the medical record in a case cannot also perform a CE in the case or serve as an expert witness if the case goes to an ALJ hearing. The national network experts should receive training that clarifies the different roles they would have as consultants to MCs, as MCs themselves, as CE providers, and as expert witnesses (MEs) at ALJ hearings. In the last case, for example, experts are involved in a de novo proceeding in which previous medical opinions are not taken for granted.

SSA should exempt treating physicians who perform CEs of their patients from these training requirements. Few if any will have more than a few patients a year needing a CE, which would not justify the time it would take to become certified. However, the longitudinal knowledge they have of a patient's functional impairments would help offset their lack of training in disability evaluation and SSA program rules. SSA should provide guidelines to treating physicians who perform CEs and notify them that SSA will reimburse them for time spent in orientation and training activities, as called for in Recommendation 2-2, below.

Adequate Reimbursement of CE Providers

In a standard medical examination, the clinician diagnoses the problem and develops a treatment plan. In a comprehensive disability examination, the clinician not only diagnoses and assesses the nature and severity of the impairment or impairments by reviewing the medical records in the claimant's file, taking a history, performing an examination, and if needed, administering a diagnostic test or study, he or she also:

- Evaluates the functional consequences of the impairment or combination of impairments.
- Determines what the claimant's capabilities are to perform work-related activities (in adults) or to engage in age-appropriate activities, such as school, physical activities, and social activities (in children).
- Prepares a report complete enough to help the DDS determine the nature, severity, and duration of the impairment and the claimant's residual functional capacity and that includes the objective medical facts as well as observations and opinions.

An adequate CE examination should include the following:[33]

- Review of the claimant's medical records;
- Taking of a medical history;
- Examination of the patient, including the administration of any needed tests;
- Interpretation of test results;
- Preparation of a report detailing findings from the history, examination, and tests;
- Diagnosis and prognosis; and
- Medical source statement.

A medical source statement is the CE provider's opinion of the claimant's ability to do work-related activities, such as sitting, standing, walking, lifting, carrying, handling objects, hearing, speaking, and traveling. In cases of mental impairment or impairments, the CE provider is expected to give an opinion on the claimant's ability to understand, carry out and remember instructions, and respond appropriately to supervision, coworkers, and work pressures in a work setting. In childhood cases, the CE provider gives an opinion on how appropriately, effectively, and independently the child can perform activities compared to the performance of other children the same age who do not have impairments.

Recommendation 2-2. Reimbursement should be adequate to cover the full costs of a consultative examination, which involves more than a standard examination, whether it is focused or comprehensive in scope. This will require a substantial increase in fees over the amounts currently paid in most states. There also should be adequate compensation for time spent in orientation and training activities.

SSA should consider adopting a standard fee schedule for DDSs to use in purchasing CEs, adjusted for geographic differences in practice costs, with several fee levels depending on how focused or comprehensive the examination is. The maximum fees should be substantially higher than Medicare's fees for regular office visits, because of the increased time it takes to perform a disability evaluation.[34] This could be done in several ways. First, SSA could mandate the use of Current Procedural Terminology

[33]See, for example, Demeter (2003), Demeter and Washington (2003), and Geiringer (2000), on the elements of a disability evaluation and report.

[34]A recent study found that the relative value units (RVUs) for the work involved in the medical evaluation of workers' compensation claimants in California were 24 to 25 percent greater than the RVUs for regular office visits of moderate or high severity used by the Centers for Medicare and Medicaid Services for its Medicare Physician Fee Schedule (Lewin, 2005).

(CPT) codes in the Medicare fee schedule that are more appropriate for a disability evaluation and that have higher relative value units (RVUs) than regular office visits. Codes 99244 and 99245, for example, are for "consultations," which are defined as "a type of service provided by a physician whose opinion or advice regarding evaluation and/or management of a specific problem is requested by another physician or other appropriate source" (AMA, 2004). Code 99244, with an RVU of 4.56, is for patients who present with problems of moderate to high severity requiring approximately 45 minutes of face-to-face time with the physician, and 99245, with an RVU of 5.90, is for patients who present with problems of moderate to high severity requiring approximately 60 minutes of face-to-face time with the physician.[35] Medicare currently pays up to $173 and $224, respectively, for these services, compared with $137 and $174 for the parallel office visit codes (99204 and 99205).

Second, SSA could use a higher conversion factor than Medicare uses to multiply the RVUs for each code. Medicare's current conversion factor is $37.89. The Federal Employee's Compensation Act program, for example, uses a conversion factor of $50.58. This translates into maximum fees of $231 and $298, respectively, for the consultation codes mentioned above (99244 and 99245). The Texas workers' compensation program pays 125 percent of the Medicare rate.

Alternatively, SSA could use CPT codes 99455 and 99456, which are for "work-related or medical disability evaluation services." Medicare does not use these services and therefore has not assigned a relative value to them, but the federal Office of Workers' Compensation Programs (OWCP) has assigned them RVUs of 6.96 and 9.16, respectively.[36] This would mean fees up to $264 and $347, respectively, using the Medicare conversion factor, and up to $352 and $463 using the OWCP conversion factor.[37] These fees are paid to treating physicians for an examination at the time of maximum medical improvement to assess permanent disability. OWCP pays more for second opinions from independent medical examiners (IMEs). It has competitive contracts with IME companies in each region of the coun-

[35]According to the AMA, "moderate severity" means a moderate risk of morbidity or mortality without treatment; an uncertain prognosis, or an increased probability of prolonged functional impairment. "High severity" means a high to extreme risk of morbidity without treatment; a moderate to high risk of mortality without treatment; or a high probability of severe, prolonged functional impairment.

[36]A number of state workers' compensation programs use these codes to pay for disability evaluations, for example, Texas, Maryland, Louisiana, North Carolina, and Michigan.

[37]It should be noted that all these fees are adjusted by a geographic practice cost index by both Medicare and OWCP so, for example, OWCP's geographically adjusted fee for CPT code 99456 would be $445 in Boise, Idaho, and $505 in Boston, Massachusetts.

try and currently pays between $600 and $685 per examination and report, depending on the region (Schmidt, 2005).

In California's workers' compensation program, in the event of a dispute, a QME is called on to evaluate the worker. QMEs have passed a state-administered competency based examination, take state-approved continuing education courses, and are paid through a special fee schedule.[38] The fee for a basic comprehensive medical-legal evaluation, which includes record review, examination, report, and overhead expenses) is $500; the fee for a complex evaluation is $750. The Texas workers' compensation program pays $350 for an examination and report at the time of maximum medical improvement (the fee is more if an impairment rating is performed).[39]

SSA should conduct market studies and studies of fees that other programs pay for similar services to determine the new national fee schedule for CEs. The fees should probably vary by specialty and geographic location. They should be updated annually.

Higher fees should increase the pool of medical sources willing to perform CEs, especially in harder-to-recruit specialties such as orthopedics. This will help ensure that the appropriate specialist or specialists can be assigned in each case. It should also provide the incentive for more treating physicians to be willing to perform CEs. Higher fees should also increase the quality of CEs, although that is based on the judgment of the committee, not hard evidence.

Focused Requests for CEs Based on What Is Needed in Each Case

Improving the quality of CEs depends not only on the skill and knowledge of the CE providers but also on whether they have been asked for the right information. DEs, in consultation with MCs, if needed, are supposed to develop a complete medical history for at least the preceding 12 months; evaluate the medical evidence to identify missing, inconsistent, or ambiguous information; and, if the treating physician does not supply the missing information or clarify inconsistencies and ambiguities, purchase a CE to obtain the information. Once a CE is indicated, the goal is to obtain needed information quickly and avoid having to ask the CE provider for additional information or order another CE.

Recommendation 2-3. SSA should ensure that requests for consultative examinations indicate clearly what is needed in each case rather than making general requests for records and opinions.

[38]www.dir.ca.gov/IMC/physicians.html.

[39]www.tdi.state.tx.us/wc/dwc/divisions/irtraining.html.

SSA could develop templates for CE request letters for common types of cases that can be easily individualized. Templates for commonly encountered disabling conditions (e.g., lower back pain, asthma, osteoarthritis, chronic pulmonary insufficiency/chronic obstructive pulmonary disease, low birth weight, loss of hearing, developmental disabilities) would contain a comprehensive list of examinations, tests, diagnostic procedures, and other questions concerning the condition in question. These would serve as a checklist to remind DEs what is typically needed in each type of case and help them identify which questions and requests need to be made in each specific case, depending on what is already in the record. The unneeded items could be deleted and the now individualized letter could be printed. However, the DE should include a *narrative* paragraph in the request letter describing what the DE is concerned about and thinks is needed, to provide further guidance to the CE provider.

The cooperative effort with AUCD to develop an electronic database of all appropriate assessment instruments for assessing development and functioning in children should help DEs and MCs determine what test or tests are needed in childhood cases. Similar databases could be developed of appropriate tests for other common medical conditions that are the subjects of disability claims.

Many DDSs have developed standard request letters and forms. SSA should establish a process to identify best practices currently in use among the DDSs for facilitating useful CE examinations and reports. Experienced DEs and MCs should be involved, along with outside medical experts knowledgeable about current clinical practice and research.

PRESUMPTIVE DISABILITY CATEGORIES

Task 8: "*Review SSA's list of presumptive disability conditions and suggest revisions, additions, and/or deletions. The committee will recommend essential criteria for establishing candidate conditions for presumptive disability and recommend the level of professional expertise needed to certify that a presumptive diagnosis is adequately established.*"

An adult or child applying for SSI based on disability or blindness may receive up to 6 months of payments prior to the final determination of disability or blindness if he or she is determined to be "presumptively disabled" or "presumptively blind" (hereafter, presumptive disability) and meets all other (i.e., financial) eligibility requirements.

SSA field offices are authorized only to make presumptive disability determinations for certain specified impairments. DDSs can make presumptive disability findings in any case in which the available evidence indicates a "strong likelihood" that the claim will be allowed after going through the regular formal determination process.

Initially, the list of presumptive disability categories, because it was meant for use by field office personnel with no medical training, was confined to conditions that were either (1) easily verifiable by direct observation during the claims interview (e.g., amputation) or (2) easily confirmed by a telephone call to an appropriate authority, such as the treating physician or school official (e.g., total deafness). Over time, as presumptive disability categories were added to the original three, the evidence requirements became more complex. In some categories, a document is now needed. For example, in low-birth-weight cases, a birth certificate or hospital admission summary is required. In end stage renal disease (ESRD) cases, Medicare form CMS-2728 is needed. For allegations of HIV infection, SSA developed a special check-block form for the treating source or CE provider to complete. Field office interviewers use the completed form to confirm the diagnosis and see if the checked items indicate that disease manifestations are of listing-level severity.

The impairment categories for which field offices may make presumptive disability decisions currently are:

1. Amputation of a leg at the hip.
2. Allegation of total deafness.
3. Allegation of total blindness.
4. Allegation of bed confinement or immobility without a wheelchair, walker, or crutches, allegedly due to a long-standing condition, excluding a recent accident and recent surgery.
5. Allegation of stroke (cerebral vascular accident) more than three months in the past and continued marked difficulty in walking or using a hand or arm.
6. Allegation of cerebral palsy, muscular dystrophy or muscular atrophy and marked difficulty in walking (e.g., use of braces), speaking or coordination of the hands or arms.
7. Allegation of Down syndrome.
8. Allegation of severe mental deficiency made by another individual filing on behalf of a claimant who is at least seven years of age.
9. Birth weight below 1200 grams (2 pounds, 10 ounces) for a child claimant who is less than one year old, according to the birth certificate or other evidence, such as the hospital admission summary.
10. Human immunodeficiency virus (HIV) infection confirmed by a medical source.
11. Available evidence such as the hospital admission summary which shows a gestational age at birth and a certain corresponding birth weight

for a child claimant who is less than one year old (e.g., 35 weeks and 1700 grams of less).

12. Confirmation from physician or hospice official that an individual is receiving hospice services for a terminal illness.

13. Allegation of spinal cord injury producing the inability to ambulate without the use of a walker or bilateral hand-held assistive devices for more than two weeks which is confirmed by an appropriate medical professional.

14. ESRD with ongoing dialysis where file contains an ESRD Medical Evidence Report-Medicare Entitlement and/or Patient Registration.

15. Allegation of amyotrophic lateral sclerosis (ALS, Lou Gehrig's disease).

According to SSA statistics, field offices and DDSs granted presumptive disability status in 135,603 cases in CY 2004, constituting approximately 7.7 percent of the 1.76 million SSI claims made that year. Field offices accounted for 17,191 (13 percent) of the 135,603 presumptive disability decisions made in CY 2004 (the rest were made by DDSs). The field office presumptive disability cases constituted 1.0 percent of the applications for SSI benefits in 2004. The rate of presumptive disability varied from field office to field office, from 0.1 to 3.5 percent (a difference of 35 times).

Looking at field offices as a group, half of all presumptive disability decisions were in the two low-birth-weight categories (categories 9 and 11 in Table 1, column 2). Three other categories accounted for another 25 percent: category 6 (allegation of cerebral palsy, muscular dystrophy, or muscle atrophy), category 7 (allegation of Down syndrome), and category 19 (HIV infection).

Ultimately, 10.3 percent of the field office presumptive disability cases were not allowed at the initial decision level after going through the regular disability determination process (Table 1, column 3). However, some categories had very low "reversal rates," between 1 and 2 percent (e.g., categories 7, 9, and 14), while several others had very high reversal rates, between 40 and 50 percent (categories 1 and 10).

According to SSA statistics on *all* title SSI disability determination decisions in CY 2004 (including concurrent SSI-DI and both presumptive disability and nonpresumptive disability cases), seven impairment codes had allowance rates of 95 percent or higher (Annex Table 7). Of these, three correspond to current presumptive categories (ALS, birth weight under 1,200 grams, and Down syndrome). The other four were cancers with high fatality rates (e.g., pancreatic and liver cancer). Another five codes had allowance rates of 90 to 94.9 percent. These included one code that corresponds to a presumptive disability category (developmental disabilities including autism). The others were cancers (e.g., lung cancer). Setting the

TABLE 1 Field Office Presumptive Disability Decisions, by Presumptive Disability Category, CY 2004

	(1) Number of FO PD Decisions	(2) Percentage of All FO PD Decisions	(3) Reversal Rate	(4) Percentage of All FO PD Reversals
1. Amputation of a leg at the hip	342	2.0%	48.5%	9.4%
2. Allegation of total deafness	479	2.8%	12.1%	3.3%
3. Allegation of total blindness	320	1.9%	9.1%	2.6%
4. Allegation of bed confinement or immobility without aid	674	3.9%	9.1%	3.5%
5. Allegation of stroke more than 3 months in the past & continued marked difficulty. . .	230	1.3%	16.5%	2.2%
6. Allegation of cerebral palsy, muscular dystrophy or muscular atrophy & marked difficulty in. . .	1,342	7.8%	12.1%	9.2%
7. Allegation of Down syndrome	1,863	10.8%	1.3%	1.4%
8. Allegation of severe mental deficiency. . .	717	4.2%	7.1%	2.9%
9. Birth weight less than 1200 grams. . .	5,691	33.1%	1.9%	6.2%
10. HIV infection confirmed. . .	1,235	7.2%	42.1%	29.4%
11. Low birth weight for gestational age. . .	3,092	18.0%	14.8%	26.0%
12. Hospice services for a terminal illness confirmed. . .	433	2.5%	6.7%	1.6%
13. Allegation of spinal cord injury causing inability to ambulate without. . .	266	1.5%	9.4%	1.4%
14. ESRD with ongoing dialysis and Medicare Form. . .	441	2.6%	1.8%	0.5%
15. Allegation of ALS. . .	19	0.1%	5.3%	0.1%
Total	17,191	100.0%	10.3%	100.0

SOURCE: Unpublished tables provided by the Office of Disability and Income Support Programs, SSA.

cutoff at 85 percent would yield six more codes, all malignancies except chronic renal failure and childhood origin psychosis (adult).

Almost 90 percent of DDS cases granted presumptive disability status were eventually allowed after going through the regular disability determination process, but they did not achieve this rate in every type of case. The DDSs experienced allowance rates of 95 percent or more in 47 impairment codes, accounting for 38 percent of the presumptive disability cases initiated by them (Table 2). These cases included organic mental disorders, cerebral palsy, schizophrenia, leukemia, mental retardation, chronic renal

TABLE 2 DDS Presumptive Disability Decisions, by Impairment Code, CY 2004

				Cumulative			
Allowance Rate	Number of Codes	Number of Decisions	Percentage of Decisions	Allowance Rate	Number of Codes	Number of Decisions	Percentage of Decisions
95-100%	47	44,951	38.0%	95-100%	47	44,951	38.0%
90-94.9%	42	39,373	33.3%	90-100%	89	84,324	71.2%
85-89.9%	35	13,729	11.6%	85-100%	124	98,053	82.8%
80-84.9%	29	10,294	8.7%	80-100%	153	108,347	91.5%
70-79.9%	33	7,023	5.9%	70-100%	186	115,370	97.4%
60-69.9%	10	856	0.7%	60-100%	196	116,226	98.2%
50-59.9%	6	206	0.2%	50-100%	202	116,432	98.3%
0-49.9%	8	340	0.3%	0-100%	210	116,772	98.6%
Unknown		1,643	1.4%			118,415	100.0%

SOURCE: Unpublished tables provided by the Office of Disability and Income Support Programs, SSA.

failure, birth weight under 1,200 grams, lung, liver, and pancreatic cancers, cancer, and developmental disabilities including autism.[40] Reversal rates were higher than 50 percent for some impairments, but they only involved a third of one percent of the cases. There were reversal rates of between 10 percent and 50 percent in 27 percent of DDS presumptive disability cases.

The annual number of presumptive disability decisions has increased greatly since 2001, when there were 60,543. The increase was entirely due to DDSs; field offices granted presumptive disability in slightly fewer cases in 2004 than in 2001, 17,191 compared with 18,862. Although the number of presumptive disability decisions more than doubled, the overall rate of reversals fell from 13 percent to 9 percent. DDSs lowered their reversal rate from 12 percent to 9 percent and the field offices from 17 percent to 10 percent. These differences seem to be due to management practices more than to medical policies.

Revising the Presumptive Disability Categories with Explicit Criteria

Presumptive disability is primarily a social policy. Congress included it in the 1972 act establishing the SSI program because it recognized that applicants for SSI have little or no income or assets and probably need immediate assistance with the costs of living. Claimants must meet the low income and assets criteria for SSI even to be considered for presumptive

[40]Annex Table 6 lists all 47 impairment codes for presumptive disability decisions that had reversal rates less than 5 percent in CY 2004.

disability. Therefore, the committee is unable to recommend specific categories to include or delete because the selection criteria are not solely medical. We can, however, analyze the impacts of setting different levels of potential reversal rates (i.e., presumptive disability cases that turn out not to meet the criteria for allowances) and suggest that SSA adopt explicit criteria and use them to revise the presumptive disability categories.

Recommendation 3-1. SSA should consider dropping some current presumptive disability categories, and perhaps adding some, after deciding on explicit criteria for including categories.

The current presumptive disability categories were created for use by nonmedical personnel in SSA field offices, which means they must have two characteristics. They must be capable of being applied by a layperson, and they must have a high probability of meeting SSA's definition of disability. To be applied by an interviewer in a field office, the categorical condition must be either directly observable during the claims interview or quickly confirmable by contacting the treating physician or other appropriate authority. To have a high probability of meeting SSA's definition of disability, a categorical condition must be one in which the diagnosis alone correlates highly either with inability to work for a year or more or the presence of a terminal illness.

The nonmedical criterion in selecting presumptive disability categories is the degree of risk, i.e., the reversal rate, that SSA is willing to pay for in order to increase the number of true positives. Early in the SSI program, an SSA ruling suggested that a reversal rate of more than 10 percent a month over several months made a category a candidate for deletion.[41] Perhaps this is too stringent. Only nine of the 15 current categories would meet this criterion (Table 3). A reversal rate of 15 percent or less would include 12 of the current categories, and a rate of 20 percent or less would add one more, bringing the total to 13. A reversal rate of 20 percent or less would reach more needy claimants than one of 10 percent or less, but the costs of cases ultimately found to be ineligible would be higher.

At the end of 2003, the average SSI benefit for the blind and disabled under age 65 was $446.97. Taking this as the average cost of a presumptive disability decision and assuming that reversed presumptive disability cases were paid for the full six months, or $2,681.80 each, moving the reversal bar from 10 percent to 15 percent (thus adding 679 presumptive disability cases) would have cost approximately $1.8 million in 2004 (Table 3). Moving it to 20 percent (adding another 38 cases) would have cost another

[41] In Social Security Ruling 80-36 (1980). The ruling was rescinded later when new presumptive disability categories made it obsolete.

TABLE 3 Approximate Costs of Presumptive Disability Cases Ultimately Disallowed, CY 2004 Data

PD Category Allowance Rate	Number of PD Categories	Number of Disallowances	Cost of Disallowances	Cumulative Cost of Lower Allowance Rates
90% or more	9	338	$906,447.75	$906,447.75
85-89.9%	3	679	$1,820,940.90	$2,727,388.65
80-84.9%	1	38	$101,908.33	$2,829,296.98
50-79.9%	2	686	$1,839,713.49	$4,669,010.47

SOURCE: Unpublished tables provided by the Office of Disability and Income Support Programs, SSA.

$102,000. Note also that removing the two presumptive disability categories with reversal rates between 40 percent and 50 percent would have reduced costs by approximately $1.8 million.

The committee also notes that the presumptive disability categories do not include conditions that consistently have high allowance rates, which therefore on equity grounds could be considered as candidates for inclusion as presumptive disability categories. As noted in the findings section, above, title SSI claims having one of 12 primary impairment codes had a 90 percent chance of approval in CY 2004. Of the 12, four correspond closely to existing presumptive disability categories.

The other eight were types of malignancies. Currently, a claim presenting with one of the malignancy codes could only be granted presumptive disability status by a field office if the claimant were in hospice care and had less than six months to live. SSA could consider granting presumptive disability to claimants who know they have one of these cancers, and the diagnosis can be confirmed by contacting their treating physician.

Dropping the bar to impairments with 85 percent approval rates would add four more cancers, chronic renal failure and childhood-origin psychosis in adults. An 80 percent allowance rate adds nine more categories—six cancers, mental retardation, other disorders of the spinal cord, and multiple body dysfunction.

In 2004, the 12 impairment codes with 90 percent allowances rates accounted for 50,171 cases, 2.9 percent of all SSI claims made. Of these, less than 17,000 were actually granted presumptive disability. If the allowance rate cutoff were 85 percent, it would have been 18 codes and 70,486 cases, 4.0 percent of all SSI claims. Of these, 19,434 were presumptive disability cases. If the cutoff were 80 percent, the number of codes would have increased to 31 and the number of cases to 139,072, or 7.9 percent of all SSI claims. Of these, 31,045 were presumptive disability cases.

If SSA decides to adopt a uniform approval rate for presumptive disability cases, Table 3 needs to be expanded to include the costs of adding the cases with impairment codes that meet the established approval rate standard that are not now included. For example, if SSA decided to include conditions in which the approval rate averages 90 percent, the costs of presumptive disability cases in categories with lower approval rates would be eliminated, but the costs of new conditions meeting the 90 percent allowance rate criterion would be added (Table 4).

These calculations indicate that there are a number of conditions in which the probability is high that a claimant who alleges he or she has one will be allowed. The question the committee cannot answer is whether that probability should be 90, 85, 80 percent, or some other number. The answer depends on the trade-off society wishes to make between helping groups of low-income persons with given probability of being determined disabled by SSA and the cost of paying for cases that end up being disallowed.

The preceding discussion assumes that the goal of the presumptive disability policy is to identify early those who are likely to be determined disabled after the regular evaluation process and start paying them. This is consistent with congressional intent, namely, to enable claimants who have a high likelihood of being awarded benefits eventually to begin receiving benefits immediately. However, the result of the current system is that claimants with the same condition may be treated differently, depending on if they do or do not have sufficient medical evidence or an established diagnosis. And as we have discussed above, it will result in claimants with an equally severe but not explicitly categorized presumptive disability impairment being ineligible for presumptive disability status, if their impairment cannot be easily observed or verified.

TABLE 4 Approximate Costs of Adopting Different Allowance Rates to Determine Presumptive Disability Cases, CY 2004 Data

PD Category Allowance Rate	Number of PD Categories	Number of Disallowances	Cost of Paying Disallowed Cases	Number of Impairment Codes	Number of Disallowances	Cost of Paying Disallowed Cases
90% or more	9	338	$906,447	12	1,182	$3,169,083
85-89.9%	3	679	$1,820,940	6	2,324	$6,232,503
80-84.9%	1	38	$101,908	9*	11,293	$30,285,567
50-79.9%	2	686	$1,839,713	48	96,929	$259,944,192

*Includes mental retardation, with an allowance rate of 80.1 percent in 2004.
SOURCE: Unpublished tables provided by the Office of Disability and Income Support Programs, SSA.

Other approaches are possible. SSA could decide to grant presumptive disability in cases where the claimant's condition is worsening and he or she has little or no funds or insurance to pay for medical treatment that might reduce the level of impairment or prevent it from worsening further. Another approach would be to stipulate that certain conditions are potentially so serious that presumptive disability is warranted, even if the award rates for those conditions are far less than 100 percent.

Increasing Consistency in the Use of Presumptive Disability

The percentage of SSI claims that are granted presumptive disability varies widely across SSA field offices and DDSs, a situation that SSA could improve. The percentage of field office presumptive disability cases ranges from 0.1 to 3.5 percent. The range for DDSs is from 0.6 to 34.6 percent.

Field offices had presumptive disability cases in all 15 categories in 11 states. In two states, however, field offices used only one of the 15 categories, accounting for two cases each. Some categories with high allowance rates overall (i.e., highly likely to be allowed) were not used at all in some states, such as Down syndrome, birth weight less than 1,200 grams, ESRD, and ALS (Table 5).

Recommendation 3-2. SSA should mandate use of the presumptive disability procedure by, and take other administrative steps to achieve more consistency among, the field offices and DDSs in the implementation of the presumptive disability policy.

Currently, the use of the presumptive disability procedure is voluntary, which leads to large differences in practice from office to office that are not the result of inherent difficulties in assessing cases. If SSA has a presump-

TABLE 5 Field Office Use of Presumptive Disability Categories for High-Allowance-Rate Impairments, CY 2004

Impairment	Overall Allowance Rate*	Number of States without PD Cases in the Category
Down syndrome	97.6%	3
Birth weight less than 1,200 grams	98.0%	5
Chronic renal failure (ESRD)	88.8%	13
ALS	98.3%	40

*Overall means decisions on all title SSI disability applications, PD and non-PD.
SOURCE: Unpublished tables provided by the Office of Disability and Income Support Programs, SSA.

tive disability process, and it is part of national social policy, it should be applied uniformly from place to place. This is primarily a matter for administrative policy to achieve.

Learning from Terminal Illness (TERI) Procedures

PD is a policy to expedite *payments*. TERI (**TER**minal **I**llness) cases involve expedited *decisions*. According to the SSA program operations manual, "Cases where there is an indication of a terminal illness (TERI) are to be handled in an expeditious manner because of the sensitivity involved." Teleservice and field office interviewers are supposed to be on the alert for potential TERI cases in certain situations, for example, when the claimant or other person—friend, family member, or medical provider—says the illness is terminal, the claimant is receiving hospice care, the claimant has AIDS, or any other situation in which the medical condition is untreatable and expected to end in death. According to SSA's program operations manual, examples of potential TERI conditions include claimants:

- with a chronic dependence on a cardiopulmonary life-sustaining device;
- awaiting a heart, heart/lung, liver or bone marrow transplant (excluding kidney and corneal transplants);
- with chronic pulmonary or heart failure requiring continuous home oxygen and who is unable to care for personal needs;
- with a malignant disease (e.g., cancer) who is home confined or institutionalized, unable to care for personal needs and unresponsive to therapy;
- with diabetes and one or more of the following: multiple amputations due to diabetic gangrene; recurrent cardiovascular events (e.g., infarction or failure); or recurrent cerebrovascular events with neurological deficit;
- with chronic liver disease (e.g., cirrhosis or hepatitis) and a history of massive gastrointestinal hemorrhage;
- who is comatose for 30 days or more; or who is a newborn with a lethal or severe genetic or congenital defect.

Recommendation 3-3. SSA should look at TERI procedures for lessons in making expedited decisions on cases that must meet specific medical criteria. These include uniform special procedures throughout the decision process that promote consistency as well as speed.

TERI cases are subject to special procedures through which the case is expedited through every step of the disability determination process, including the appeals process and the payment process. They are also sent immediately from the field office to the DDS for development and quick decision.

The issue is whether field office interviewers are able to identify TERI cases with some accuracy. This would involve determining the percentage of cases flagged as TERI cases that turn out to meet the criteria and, taking a sample of all cases, the percentage of cases that were not flagged that should have been. Differences between types of cases and from field office to field could be analyzed for better understanding of TERI decision making and ways to improve it, and also of ways to improve presumptive disability procedures.

AFTERWORD

This interim report has addressed 3 of the 10 tasks that the committee is charged with addressing. It focuses on one important part of improving SSA's disability decision process: the qualifications of medical personnel participating in the decision process. It also makes recommendations for improving the implementation of the presumptive disability policy. The committee is addressing the other seven tasks in its next, and final, report, which is due in 2006. These are tasks 1 through 7 in the Annex, which focus on ways to improve other important parts of the process: the medical criteria and procedures that are used to screen applicants for eligibility.

REFERENCES

ABMS (American Board of Medical Specialties). 2005. *2005 Annual Report and Reference Handbook*. Available: www.abms.org/Downloads/Publications/AnnualReport2005.pdf (accessed September 30, 2005).

ABPP (American Board of Professional Psychology). 2005. *Specialty Board Certification in Professional Psychology*. Available: www.abpp.org/brochures/genbrochure2005.pdf (accessed October 7, 2005).

ACUS (Administrative Conference of the United States). 1989. *Improved Use of Medical Personnel in Social Security Disability Determinations*. Recommendation 89-10 of the Administrative Conference of the United States. Available: www.law.fsu.edu/library/admin/acus/3058910.html (accessed October 7, 2005).

AMA (American Medical Association). 2004. *CPT 2005*, Standard Edition. Chicago, IL: American Medical Association.

Anfield R. 2002. Statement of Robert Anfield, M.D., Vice President and Chief Medical Officer, Customer Care Centers, UnumProvident Corporation, before the Subcommittee on Social Security, House Committee on Ways and Means, July 11. Available: waysandmeans.house.gov/legacy.asp?file=legacy/socsec/107cong/7-11-02/107-92final.htm (accessed September 16, 2005).

Barnhart JA. 2003. *Statement of The Honorable Jo Anne B. Barnhart, Commissioner, Social Security Administration*. Testimony before the Subcommittee on Social Security of the House Committee on Ways and Means, September 25, 2003. Available: waysandmeans.house.gov/hearings.asp?formmode=view&id=761 (accessed September 23, 2005).

Barnhart JA. 2005. *Social Security's Proposed Improvements to the Disability Determination Process.* Statement of Jo Anne B. Barnhart, Commissioner of Social Security before the Subcommittee on Social Security of the House Committee on Ways and Means, September 27, 2005. Available: waysandmeans.house.gov/hearings.asp?formmode=view&id=3802 (accessed September 29, 2005).

Barzansky B. 2005. Personal communication by electronic mail on November 14. Barbara Barzansky is Associate Director, Division of Undergraduate Medical Education Policy and Standards, and Secretary, Council on Medical Education, American Medical Association, Chicago, IL.

Bloch F. 1992. *Disability Determination: The Administrative Process and the Role of Medical Personnel.* Westport, CT: Greenwood Press.

Bloch F, Lubbers J, Verkuil P. 2003. *Introducing Nonadversarial Government Representatives to Improve the Record for Decision in Social Security Disability Decisions.* Report to the Social Security Advisory Board. Available: www.ssab.gov/documents/Bloch-Lubbers-Verkuil.pdf (accessed October 7, 2005).

Brennan TA, Horwitz RI, Duffy, FD, Cassel CK, Goode LD, Lipner RS. 2004. The Role of Physician Specialty Board Certification Status in the Quality Movement. *Journal of the American Medical Association*, 292(9):1038-1043.

Canadian Parliament. 2003. *Listening to Canadians: A First View of the Future of the Canada Pension Plan Disability Program.* Fifth Report of the Standing Committee on Human Resources Development and the Status of Persons with Disabilities, June. Available: www.parl.gc.ca/infocomdoc/37/2/HUMA/Studies/Reports/humarp05/humarp05-e.pdf (accessed April 12, 2005).

Choudhry NK, Fletcher RH, Soumerai SB. 2005. Systematic Review: The Relationship between Clinical Experience and Quality of Health Care. *Annals of Internal Medicine*, 142(4):260-273.

CPP/OAS (Canada Pension Plan/Old Age Security). 2004. *Review Tribunals Biennial Report: 2002-2004.* Ottawa, Ontario: Office of the Commissioner of Review Tribunals, Canada Pension Plan/Old Age Security. Available: www.reviewtribunals.gc.ca/pubs/bi_rpt2004/toc_e.html (accessed April 12, 2005).

Demeter SL. 2003. Contrasting the Standard, Impairment, and Disability Examination and Report. Pp. 101-107 in Demeter SL, Andersson GBJ, eds. *Disability Evaluation*, 2nd Ed. St. Louis, MO: Mosby.

Demeter SL, Washington RJ. 2003. The Disability Evaluation and Report. Pp. 625-639 in Demeter SL, Andersson GBJ, eds. *Disability Evaluation*, 2nd Ed. St. Louis, MO: Mosby.

DHHS (Department of Health and Human Services). 2002. *Projected Supply, Demand, and Shortages of Registered Nurses: 2000-2020.* National Center for Health Workforce Analysis, Bureau of Health Professions, Health Resources and Services Administration, U.S. Department of Health and Human Services. Available: bhpr.hrsa.gov/healthworkforce/reports/rnproject/report.htm#chart2 (accessed November 10, 2005).

GAO (General Accountability Office). 2003. *SSA Disability Decision Making: Additional Steps Needed to Ensure Accuracy and Fairness of Decisions at the Hearing Level.* GAO-04-14. November 12. Available: www.gao.gov/new.items/d0414.pdf (accessed July 25, 2005).

GAO. 2004. *Social Security Administration: More Effort Needed to Assess Consistency of Disability Decisions.* GAO-04-656. July 2. Available: www.gao.gov/new.items/d04656.pdf (accessed July 25, 2005).

Geiringer SR. 2000. Independent Medical Evaluation. Pp. 241-256 in Rondinelli RD, Katz RT, eds. *Impairment Rating and Disability Evaluation.* Philadelphia: W. B. Saunders.

Himmelstein JS, Pransky GS, Sweet CP. 2000. Ability to Work and the Evaluation of Disability. Pp. 257-274 in Levy BS, Wegman DH, eds. *Occupational Health: Recognizing and Preventing Work-Related Disease and Injury*, 4th Ed. Philadelphia, PA: Lippincott Williams & Wilkins.

IOM (Institute of Medicine). 2002. *The Dynamics of Disability: Measuring and Monitoring Disability for Social Security Programs.* Washington, DC: National Academies Press.

IOM. 2004. *NIH Extramural Center Programs: Criteria for Initiation and Evaluation.* Washington, DC: National Academies Press.

Leo RJ, Del Regno P. 2001. Social Security Claims of Psychiatric Disability: Elements of Case Adjudication and the Role of Primary Care Physicians. *Primary Care Companion Journal of Clinical Psychiatry*, 3(6):255-262.

Lewin. 2005. *A Study of the Practice Expenses Associated with the Provision of Evaluation and Management Services.* May 13. Falls Church, VA: The Lewin Group.

Lewin (Lewin Group), and Pugh Ettinger McCarthy Associations. 2001. *Evaluation of SSA's Disability Quality Assurance (QA) Processes and Development of QA Options that Will Support the Ling-Term Management of the Disability Program.* Prepared for the Social Security Administration. Report available: www.quintiles.com/NR/rdonlyres/ekhzi4f6bl2iwvway5ibsoerh7acjf6lpnwh3etwt6jd246bw5cdaymmastvdiojiljc7jt3cozp3nosoj56dr2k2zf/1325.pdf (accessed September 15, 2005). Appendixes available: www.quintiles.com/NR/rdonlyres/ekhzi4f6bl2iwvway5ibsoerh7acjf6lpnwh3etwt6jd246bw5cdaymmastvdiojiljc7jt3cozp3nosoj56dr2k2zf/1325.pdf (accessed September 15, 2005).

Mischoulon D. 2002. Potential Pitfalls to the Therapeutic Relationship Arising from Disability Claims. *Psychiatric Annals*, 32(5):299-302.

Nibali K. 2003. Social Security Disability Programs. Pp. 44-61 in Demeter SL, Andersson GBJ, eds. *Disability Evaluation*, 2nd Ed. St. Louis, MO: Mosby.

Pincus HA, Kennedy C, Simmens SJ, Goldman HH, Sirovatka P, Sharfstein SS. 1991. Determining Disability Due to Mental Impairment: APA's Evaluation of Social Security Administration Guidelines. *American Journal of Psychiatry*, 148(8):1037-1043.

Pransky G, Katz JN, Benjamin KL, Himmelstein J. 2002. Improving the Physician's Role in Evaluating Work Ability and Managing Disability: A Survey of Primary Care Practitioners. *Disability and Rehabilitation*, 24(16):867-874.

Robinson JP, Wolfe CV. 2000. Social Security Disability Insurance and Supplemental Security Income. Pp. 159-186 in Rondinelli RD, Katz RT, eds. *Impairment Rating and Disability Evaluation.* Philadelphia: W. B. Saunders.

Scheer SJ. 2000. Physician Assessment of Working Capacity. Pp. 121-138 in Rondinelli RD, Katz RT, eds. *Impairment Rating and Disability Evaluation.* Philadelphia: W. B. Saunders.

Schmidt S. 2005. Personal communication by telephone with Michael McGeary, July 19, 2005. Stephen Schmidt is in the Medical Standards and Rehabilitation Branch, Office Workers' Compensation Programs, U.S. Department of Labor.

SSA (Social Security Administration). 1999. *Consultative Examinations: A Guide for Health Professionals.* SSA Pub. No. 64-025. Baltimore, MD: Office of Disability Programs, Social Security Administration. Available: www.ssa.gov/disability/professionals/greenbook/index.htm (accessed September 30, 2005).

SSA. 2003. *Findings of the Disability Hearings Quality Review Process: ALJ Peer Report V.* December. SSA Pub. No. 30-013. Office of Quality Assurance and Performance Assessment, Social Security Administration.

SSA. 2004a. *Fiscal Year 2005 Annual Performance Plan and Revised FY 04 APP.* Available: www.ssa.gov/performance/2005/ (accessed July 25, 2005).

SSA. 2004b. National Medical Expert Survey of OHA Regional Offices: Compiled Responses. Unpublished internal document furnished by SSA.

SSA. 2005a. *Fiscal Year 2004 Social Security Administration Performance and Accountability Report.* Washington, DC: SSA. Available: www.ssa.gov/finance/ (accessed September 28, 2005).

SSA. 2005b. *2005 Annual Report of the Supplemental Security Income Program.* Updated July 8. Available: www.ssa.gov/OACT/SSIR/SSI05/ssiTOC.html (accessed September 28, 2005).

SSA. 2005c. *Fast Facts and Figures about Social Security, 2005*. Available: www.ssa.gov/policy/docs/chartbooks/fast_facts/2005/ff2005.pdf (accessed September 28, 2005).

SSA. 2005d. Disability Determinations and Appeals, Fiscal Year 2004. Unpublished chart prepared by the Office of Disability Programs, January.

SSA. 2005e. Notice of Proposed Rulemaking: Administrative Review Process for Adjudicating Initial Disability Claims. *Federal Register*, 70(143):43590-43624. Available: a257.g.akamaitech.net/7/257/2422/01jan20051800/edocket.access.gpo.gov/2005/pdf/05-14845.pdf (accessed September 28, 2005).

SSAB (Social Security Advisory Board). 1998. *How SSA's Disability Programs Can Be Improved*. Washington, DC: SSAB. Available: www.ssab.gov/NEW/Publications/Disability/report6.pdf (accessed July 25, 2005).

SSAB. 2001a. *Charting the Future of Social Security's Disability Programs: The Need for Fundamental Change*. Washington, DC: SSAB. Available: www.ssab.gov/Publications/Disability/disabilitywhitepap.pdf (accessed July 25, 2005).

SSAB. 2001b. *Disability Decision Making: Data and Materials*. Washington, DC: SSAB. Available: www.ssab.gov/NEW/Publications/Disability/chartbookA.pdf (accessed July 25, 2005).

SSAB. 2003. *The Social Security Definition of Disability*. Washington, DC: SSAB. Available: www.ssab.gov/documents/SocialSecurityDefinitionOfDisability_000.pdf (accessed July 25, 2005).

Steinbrook R. 2005. Renewing Board Certification. *New England Journal of Medicine*, 353(19):1994-1997.

Strand A. 2002. *Social Security Disability Programs: Assessing the Variation in Allowance Rates*. ORES Working Paper No. 98. Office of Research, Evaluation, and Statistics, Social Security Administration, Washington, DC, SSA.

Talmadge JB. 2003. Resource Personnel Used in a Disability Evaluation. Pp. 640-643 in Demeter SL, Andersson GBJ, eds. *Disability Evaluation*, 2nd Ed. St. Louis, MO: Mosby.

Zayatz T. 2005. *Social Security Disability Insurance Program Worker Experience*. Actuarial Study No. 118. Social Security Administration, Office of the Chief Actuary. Available: www.socialsecurity.gov/OACT/NOTES/as118/DI-WrkerExper_Body.html#wp1057748 (accessed November 11, 2005).

Zinn W, Furutani N. 1996. Physician Perspectives on the Ethical Aspects of Disability Determination. *Journal of General Internal Medicine*, 11(9):525-532.

ANNEX: LIST OF STUDY TASKS

In addressing the Listings, the committee will consider:

1. The value and utility of the current Listings for all users (claimants, SSA, health care professionals, state offices, and officials involved in the adjudication process)
2. Conceptual models for organizing the Listings, beyond the current "body systems" model at 20 C.F.R. Part 404, Subpart P, Appendix I
3. Processes for determining when the Listings require revision and criteria upon which to add new listings or remove old ones

4. Feedback mechanisms to continuously assess and evaluate the Listings for the purpose of improving consistency in application by all adjudicators throughout the country
5. Adaptability of the Listings, including methods to account for variable access to health care services (including diagnostics and pharmaceuticals) in determining whether an individual's condition meets or equals the Listings
6. Methods to assess and quantify the effects of multiple impairments that may not individually cross the eligibility threshold (e.g., SSA's "equivalence" concept)
7. Advisability of and methods for integrating functional assessment into the Listings

In addressing the organization of medical expertise, the committee will:

8. Review SSA's list of presumptive disability conditions and suggest revisions, additions, and/or deletions. The committee will recommend essential criteria for establishing candidate conditions for presumptive disability and recommend the level of professional expertise needed to certify that a presumptive diagnosis is adequately established.
9. Advise on how best to provide medical expertise needed to support the entire disability adjudication process. This will involve describing the type of experts needed (academic specialists, practicing specialists, practicing generalists or nonphysicians), necessary credentials, and where best to locate them (from university medical centers, centers of excellence for specialized care, or community practice settings).
10. Recommend needs for standardized training and certification for consultative examiners who assess claimant's level of function based on integrated evaluation of medical impairment and functional capacity. Advise on content of a training curriculum, appropriate personnel to train, and mechanisms for the certification process.

ANNEX TABLE 1 DDS Medical Consultants by Specialty, June 2004

Specialty	Number	Percentage
Psychology	707	33.1
Internal medicine	341	16.0
Psychiatry	233	10.9
Pediatrics	209	9.8
Family practice	141	6.6
Speech-language pathology	59	2.8
General medicine	42	2.0
Neurology	38	1.8
Cardiology	36	1.7
Orthopedic specialist	35	1.6
Surgery	35	1.6
Ophthalmology	25	1.2
Gynecology/obstetrics	21	1.0
Anesthesiology	21	1.0
Emergency medicine	20	0.9
Physical medicine and rehabilitation	19	0.9
Orthopedic surgery	18	0.8
Osteopathy	14	0.7
Occupational medicine	13	0.6
All others	122	5.7
Total	2,136	100.0

NOTE: The percentage of specialists in each category that are board certified or board eligible is not known.

SOURCE: Unpublished tables provided by the Office of Disability and Income Support Programs, SSA.

ANNEX TABLE 2 Number of DDS Medical Consultants by Specialty and State, June 2004

State DDS	Family Practice	Internal Medicine	Pediatrics	Psychology	Psychiatry	Cardiology	Neurology	Orthopedics	Other	Total
Connecticut	0	9	1	15	4	0	2	0	4	35
Maine	0	0	1	7	0	1	0	1	4	14
Massachusetts	3	24	2	28	6	0	1	0	2	66
New Hampshire	3	1	1	4	0	0	0	0	1	10
Rhode Island	0	8	1	6	2	0	0	0	1	18
Vermont	0	4	2	5	1	1	1	0	0	14
Region I Total	6	46	8	65	13	2	4	1	12	157
New Jersey	0	23	5	22	3	3	0	8	3	67
New York	3	23	16	18	33	0	0	1	15	109
Puerto Rico	0	8	0	8	3	1	1	0	3	24
Delaware	1	3	1	4	1	0	0	0	1	11
District of Columbia	0	3	3	2	0	0	0	0	0	8
Region II Total	4	60	25	56	40	4	1	9	22	219
Maryland	1	4	4	11	5	1	0	0	4	30
Pennsylvania	5	7	4	45	2	0	1	3	12	79
Virginia	6	6	8	20	2	2	0	2	9	55
West Virginia	2	7	2	9	2	0	0	0	1	23
Region III Total	14	24	18	85	11	3	1	5	26	187
Alabama	1	4	6	14	4	3	1	2	7	42
Florida	20	11	33	76	9	2	0	1	28	180
Georgia	1	18	5	24	1	1	2	4	7	63
Kentucky	0	5	4	15	1	0	0	1	14	40
Mississippi	0	3	2	11	1	0	0	2	8	27
North Carolina	9	5	4	19	4	0	1	1	6	49

ANNEX TABLE 2 continued

State DDS	Family Practice	Internal Medicine	Pediatrics	Psychology	Psychiatry	Cardiology	Neurology	Orthopedics	Other	Total
South Carolina	2	4	4	21	1	0	1	1	11	45
Tennessee	2	5	8	20	3	1	1	1	15	56
Region IV Total	35	55	66	200	24	7	6	13	96	502
Illinois	6	11	10	22	4	3	0	0	22	78
Indiana	0	5	1	8	0	1	2	0	10	27
Michigan	8	17	5	15	21	0	2	0	14	82
Minnesota	0	6	2	12	1	0	0	5	2	28
Ohio	12	11	5	41	1	0	0	2	16	88
Wisconsin	0	5	3	9	0	0	1	0	2	20
Region V Total	26	55	26	107	26	4	5	7	66	323
Arkansas	0	1	5	3	2	1	1	3	2	18
Louisiana	2	5	5	19	2	2	1	2	12	50
New Mexico	5	5	2	2	2	0	0	0	1	17
Oklahoma	2	5	1	10	1	0	0	0	1	20
Texas	6	6	2	10	9	1	3	2	6	45
Region VI Total	15	22	15	44	16	4	5	7	22	150
Iowa	7	0	3	17	1	2	0	0	4	34
Kansas	9	4	1	11	3	1	0	0	2	31
Missouri	2	9	9	31	5	2	1	2	20	81
Nebraska	6	1	2	8	0	0	0	0	2	19
Region VII Total	24	14	15	67	9	5	1	2	28	165
Colorado	0	5	2	3	5	2	2	2	4	25
Montana	1	1	1	4	0	0	0	1	2	10
North Dakota	0	3	0	4	1	1	0	1	1	11

South Dakota	1	1	1	4	1	0	0	0	5	13
Utah	0	1	1	6	5	0	1	0	4	18
Wyoming	1	2	0	6	0	0	0	1	6	16
Region VIII Total	3	13	5	27	12	3	3	5	22	93
Arizona	1	6	2	7	9	1	4	1	13	44
California	7	28	19	1	62	2	4	2	49	174
Hawaii	1	3	1	4	2	0	0	0	4	15
Nevada	0	3	3	5	0	0	1	0	2	14
Region IX Total	9	40	25	17	73	3	9	3	68	247
Alaska	0	1	1	0	2	0	2	0	2	8
Idaho	0	1	1	2	0	0	0	1	1	6
Oregon	1	3	1	7	0	0	0	0	4	16
Washington	4	7	3	31	6	1	1	1	9	63
Region X Total	5	12	6	40	8	1	3	2	16	93
All DDSs	141	341	209	706	233	36	38	54	378	2136

NOTE: Psychiatry includes 12 child psychiatrists. Orthopedics includes 18 orthopedic surgeons, 35 orthopedic specialists, and 1 orthopedic-neurologist.
SOURCE: Unpublished tables provided by the Office of Disability and Income Support Programs, SSA.

ANNEX TABLE 3 Case Mix Compared with Mix of Medical Consultant Specialties

Clinical Field	Percentage of MCs in the Clinical Specialty	Percentage of Initial Decisions Involving the Clinical Field
Cardiology	1.7%	6.7%
Child psychiatry	0.6%	0.5%
Child psychology	*	3.7%
Endocrinology	0.2%	3.8%
Family practice	6.8%	0.0%
Gastroenterology	0.3%	2.4%
Internal medicine	16.3%	6.3%
Neurology	1.9%	6.8%
Oncology	0.3%	4.7%
Orthopedics	2.5%	19.9%
Pediatrics	9.8%	0.9%
Psychiatry	10.7%	19.6%
Psychology	31.2%	7.5%
Pulmonology	0.3%	4.7%
Rheumatology	0.3%	6.7%

*Less than 0.1 percent.

NOTE: Part-time medical consultants are assumed to work 20 hours a week.

SOURCE: Unpublished table provided by the Office of Disability and Income Support Programs, SSA

ANNEX TABLE 4 Number of Medical Experts by Specialty, June 2005

Specialty	Number	Percentage
Clinical psychology	415	22.3
Internal medicine	371	19.9
Psychiatry	235	12.6
Orthopedic surgery	121	6.5
Pediatrics	115	6.2
Neurology	102	5.5
Cardiovascular diseases	71	3.8
Ophthalmology	57	3.1
Family practice	31	1.7
Pulmonary diseases	22	1.2
Child psychiatry	21	1.1
Physical medicine and rehabilitation	20	1.0
Rheumatology	19	1.0
General surgery	18	1.0
Occupational medicine	18	0.8
Gastroenterology	15	0.8
General preventive medicine	15	0.8
Urological surgery	14	0.7
Endocrinology	13	0.6
Child psychology	12	0.6
Neurological surgery	12	0.6
Emergency medicine	11	0.6
Medical oncology	11	0.6
All others	122	6.6
Total	1,861	100.0

NOTE: The number of specialties is more than the number of MEs (1,575), because some practice in more than one specialty.
SOURCE: Unpublished table provided by the Office of Hearings and Appeals, SSA.

ANNEX TABLE 5 Number of Medical Experts by Specialty and Federal Region, June 2005

Federal Region	Clinical Psychology	Internal Medicine	Psychiatry	Orthopedic Surgery	Pediatrics	Neurology	Cardiovascular Diseases	Ophthalmology	Other	Total
Region I	18	23	16	10	6	9	4	5	18	109
Region II	13	25	20	7	9	7	5	5	29	120
Region III	31	35	28	3	7	13	5	5	45	172
Region IV	110	85	78	42	39	25	20	12	93	504
Region V	73	56	30	20	23	17	7	8	52	286
Region VI	47	46	22	16	6	14	6	6	48	211
Region VII	12	14	3	1	3	1	3	1	16	54
Region VIII	37	7	0	0	2	4	0	1	10	61
Region IX	43	53	32	16	12	8	19	14	47	244
Region X	31	27	6	6	8	4	2	0	16	100
All regions	415	371	235	121	115	102	71	57	374	1,861

SOURCE: Unpublished table provided by the Office of Hearings and Appeals, SSA.

ANNEX TABLE 6 Impairment Codes of DDS Presumptive Disability Decisions with a Reversal Rate of Less Than 5 percent, CY 2004

SSA Impairment Code	Number of DDS PD Decisions	Number Reversed	Reversal Rate (percent)
4160-Chronic pulmonary heart disease	163	8	4.9
2940-Organic mental disorders	4,505	215	4.8
3060-Somatoform disorders	42	2	4.8
3370-Disorders of the autonomic nervous system	64	3	4.7
4920-Emphysema	193	9	4.7
1830-Malignant neoplasm/ovary and other uterine adnexa	314	14	4.5
1640-Malignant neoplasm/thymus, heart, mediastinum	23	1	4.3
3430-Cerebral palsy	1,835	78	4.3
4430-Peripheral vascular disease	516	21	4.1
2950-Schizophrenic/paranoid functional disorders	4,944	198	4.0
1920-Malignant neoplasm/other parts of the nervous system	76	3	3.9
1900-Malignant neoplasm/eye	31	1	3.2
1710-Malignant neoplasm/connective and other soft tissue	99	3	3.0
1910-Malignant neoplasm/brain	830	23	2.8
3360-Other disorders of the spinal cord	517	14	2.7
1410-Malignant neoplasm/tongue	192	5	2.6
7600-Multiple body dysfunction	714	18	2.5
1510-Malignant neoplasm/stomach	249	6	2.4
1990-Malignant neoplasm/unspecified sites	131	3	2.3
2070-Leukemias	1,058	24	2.3
8060-Vertebral fracture/cord lesion	766	18	2.3
2630-Malnutrition/weight loss	139	3	2.2
7840-Loss of voice	983	20	2.0
2990-Childhood origin psychosis (adult)	637	12	1.9
3180-Mental retardation	9,643	185	1.9
1720-Malignant melanoma of skin	179	3	1.7
5850-Chronic renal failure	4,173	62	1.5
2990-Developmental disabilities including autism (children)	2,558	36	1.4
1620-Malignant neoplasm/trachea, bronchus, lung	2,606	35	1.3
1980-Malignant neoplasm/distant sites	78	1	1.3
3320-Parkinson's disease	154	2	1.3
1500-Malignant neoplasm/esophagus	367	4	1.1
1630-Malignant neoplasm/pleura	98	1	1.0
3350-Anterior horn cell disorder (ALS)	113	1	0.9
7580-Chromosome anomaly/Down syndrome	1,443	8	0.6
7650-Birth weight under 1200 grams	3,291	12	0.4
1550-Malignant neoplasm of liver and intrahepatic bile ducts	710	2	0.3
0940-Neurosyphilis	3	0	0.0
1560-Malignant neoplasm/gallbladder	56	0	0.0

ANNEX TABLE 6 continued

SSA Impairment Code	Number of DDS PD Decisions	Number Reversed	Reversal Rate (percent)
1570-Malignant neoplasm/pancreas	400	0	0.0
1760-Malignant Kaposi's sarcoma	8	0	0.0
1780-Malignant neoplasm/skeletal system	4	0	0.0
2730-Disorders of plasma protein metabolism	3	0	0.0
3210-Arachnoiditis	10	0	0.0
5010-Asbestosis	6	0	0.0
7050-Hidradenitis suppurativa	16	0	0.0
9330-Chronic fatigue syndrome	11	0	0.0

SOURCE: Unpublished table provided by the Office of Disability and Income Support Programs, SSA.

ANNEX TABLE 7 SSA Impairment Codes by Allowance Rate, from Highest to Lowest, CY 2004

SSA Impairment Code	Number of Decisions	Number of Allowances	Allowance Rate (percent)
All codes	2,532,798	947,266	37.4
1550-Malignant neoplasm of liver and intrahepatic bile ducts	4,653	4,616	99.2
1570-Malignant neoplasm/pancreas	3,304	3,258	98.6
3350-Anterior horn cell disorder (ALS)	1,534	1,506	98.2
7650-Birth weight under 1200 grams	17,235	16,890	98.0
7580-Chromosome anomaly/Down syndrome	5,242	5,111	97.5
1980-Malignant neoplasm/distant sites	619	599	96.8
1630-Malignant neoplasm/pleura	806	776	96.3
1560-Malignant neoplasm/gallbladder	450	432	96.0
1620-Malignant neoplasm/trachea, bronchus, lung	19,291	18,307	94.9
1500-Malignant neoplasm/esophagus	2,916	2,744	94.1
2990-Developmental disabilities including autism (children)	10,759	9,920	92.2
1910-Malignant neoplasm/brain	6,302	5,754	91.3
1510-Malignant neoplasm/stomach	1,966	1,779	90.5
5850-Chronic renal failure	22,195	19,998	90.1
1780-Malignant neoplasm/skeletal system	20	18	90.0
1720-Malignant melanoma of skin	1,832	1,618	88.3
2070-Leukemias	6,166	5,408	87.7
1760-Malignant Kaposi's sarcoma	40	35	87.5
1410-Malignant neoplasm/tongue	1,392	1,197	86.0
2990-Childhood origin psychosis (adult)	3,898	3,352	86.0
2030-Multiple myeloma	2,164	1,859	85.9
1590-Malignant neoplasm/other digestive organs, peritoneum	741	636	85.8
1990-Malignant neoplasm/unspecified sites	552	471	85.3
1830-Malignant neoplasm/ovary and other uterine adnexa	3,394	2,882	84.9
3180-Mental retardation	77,102	65,460	84.9
3360-Other disorders of the spinal cord	3,428	2,856	83.3
7600-Multiple body dysfunction	2,555	2,128	83.3
1920-Malignant neoplasm/other parts of the nervous system	280	230	82.1
1520-Malignant neoplasm/small intestine	552	449	81.3
1890-Malignant neoplasm/kidney, other urinary organs	2,740	2,206	80.5
0420-Malignant neoplasm/bone marrow or stem cell transplantation	5	4	80.0
7400-Anencephalus/catastrophic anomaly	569	453	79.6
2630-Malnutrition/weight loss	1,112	876	78.8
1640-Malignant neoplasm/thymus, heart, mediastinum	173	136	78.6
1700-Malignant neoplasm/bone and articular cartilage	1,550	1,207	77.9

ANNEX TABLE 7 continued

SSA Impairment Code	Number of Decisions	Number of Allowances	Allowance Rate (percent)
3430-Cerebral palsy	9,864	7,546	76.5
3320-Parkinson's disease	3,853	2,894	75.1
1950-Malignant neoplasm/other sites	5,399	4,049	75.0
8060-Vertebral fracture/cord lesion	4,699	3,449	73.4
1880-Malignant neoplasm/bladder	1,535	1,122	73.1
7840-Loss of voice	5,162	3,742	72.5
1380-Late effects of acute poliomyelitis	1,859	1,346	72.4
1710-Malignant neoplasm/connective and other soft tissue	902	650	72.1
7410-Spina bifida	1,867	1,344	72.0
1530-Malignant neoplasm/colon, rectum, anus	11,184	8,019	71.7
2950-Schizophrenic/paranoid functional disorders	56,218	40,308	71.7
3300-Cerebral degeneration/childhood	616	439	71.3
3750-Cardiac transplantation	319	226	70.8
1420-Malignant neoplasm/salivary glands	234	165	70.5
4380-Late effects of cerebrovascular disease	32,139	22,529	70.1
1790-Malignant neoplasm/uterus	2,566	1,783	69.5
4430-Peripheral vascular disease	8,979	6,240	69.5
4160-Chronic pulmonary heart disease	2,137	1,481	69.3
2840-Aplastic anemia	738	505	68.4
7830-Malnutrition, marasmus/growth impairment	2,388	1,631	68.3
3590-Muscular dystrophies	3,188	2,155	67.6
3150-Developmental/emotional disorders—infant	4,521	3,034	67.1
0300-Leprosy	3	2	66.7
4960-Cronic pulmonary insufficiency/COPD	40,287	26,348	65.4
1940-Malignant neoplasm/other endocrine glands and related	242	158	65.3
3310-Other cerebral degenerations	3,901	2,536	65.0
2940-Organic mental disorders	57,567	36,958	64.2
3210-Arachnoiditis	231	145	62.8
9070-Late effects/nervous system injuries	6,740	4,125	61.2
3690-Blindness/low vision	24,669	14,752	59.8
4280-Heart failure	15,865	9,440	59.5
1740-Malignant neoplasm/breast	17,865	10,558	59.1
3620-Other retinal disorders	3,455	2,038	59.0
3153-Speech and language delays	32,332	18,914	58.5
4460-Periarteritis nodosa/allied condition	296	171	57.8
1870-Malignant neoplasm/penis, male genital organs	158	91	57.6
7500-Congenital anomalies/upper alimentary tract	372	212	57.0
1850-Malignant neoplasm/prostate	3,233	1,827	56.5
4920-Emphysema	4,382	2,471	56.4
2760-Diabetic acidosis	222	123	55.4
4540-Varicose veins/low extremities	2,374	1,294	54.5
3570-Diabetic/peripheral neuropathy	13,714	7,460	54.4
2020-Lymphoma	7,075	3,799	53.7
3890-Deafness	15,352	8,183	53.3

ANNEX TABLE 7 continued

SSA Impairment Code	Number of Decisions	Number of Allowances	Allowance Rate (percent)
7460-Congenital heart anomalies	5,542	2,910	52.5
0940-Neurosyphilis	25	13	52.0
0430-Symptomatic HIV positive	18,168	9,429	51.9
8540-Intracranial injury	5,785	2,968	51.3
1900-Malignant neoplasm/eye	194	99	51.0
2770-Disorders of metabolism/cystic fibrosis	1,426	719	50.4
3400-Multiple sclerosis	14,183	7,148	50.4
4250-Cardiomyopathy	15,472	7,581	49.0
1170-Skin/mucus membrane infections	720	351	48.7
7140-Rheumatoid & other inflammatory arthritis	19,437	9,330	48.0
3060-Somatoform disorders	1,425	681	47.8
1860-Malignant neoplasm/testis	791	375	47.4
2960-Mood disorders (children)	21,121	9,927	47.0
2390-Neoplasm/unspecified/unknown behavior	308	144	46.8
7050-Hidradenitis suppurativa	295	135	45.8
4410-Aortic aneurysm	1,341	607	45.3
1730-Other malignant neoplasm of skin	463	209	45.1
3610-Retinal detachment with retinal defects	1,592	716	45.0
2250-Benign neoplasm/brain, nervous system	3,049	1,332	43.7
4590-Other diseases of the circulatory system	7,004	3,061	43.7
3370-Disorders of the autonomic nervous system	1,408	614	43.6
1840-Malignant neoplasm/other female genital organs	1,141	496	43.5
4140-Chronic ischemic heart disease	44,127	19,195	43.5
4030-Hypertensive vascular/renal disease	376	162	43.1
7200-Ankylosing/inflamnatory spondylopathies	1,007	430	42.7
2820-Hereditary hemolytic anemias including sickle cell	4,167	1,771	42.5
5010-Asbestosis	289	122	42.2
7300-Osteomyelitis/other infections involving bone	1,837	775	42.2
1930-Malignant neoplasm/thyroid gland	782	327	41.8
5710-Chronic liver disease/cirrhosis	30,970	12,853	41.5
7150-Osteoarthritis/allied disorders	113,194	45,730	40.4
4480-Diseases of capillaries	145	57	39.3
0930-Cardiovascular syphilis	36	14	38.9
2730-Disorders of plasma protein metabolism	93	36	38.7
3490-Other nervous system disorders	15,534	5,996	38.6
3000-Anxiety-related disorders	46,037	17,724	38.5
3138-Oppositional/defiant disorder	7,776	2,955	38.0
3650-Glaucoma	2,958	1,121	37.9
3580-Myoneural disorders	3,118	1,160	37.2
5810-Nephrotic syndrome	2,447	903	36.9
3120-Conduct disorder	5,856	2,102	35.9
2960-Affective disorders (adult)	277,560	99,089	35.7
7590-Other congenital anomalies	3,324	1,160	34.9
2850-Other anemias	1,864	641	34.4

ANNEX TABLE 7 continued

SSA Impairment Code	Number of Decisions	Number of Allowances	Allowance Rate (percent)
3660-Cataract	2,400	826	34.4
2790-Disorders immune mechanism (except HIV)	1,009	345	34.2
3010-Personality disorders	14,295	4,860	34.0
1360-Other infectious/parasitic diseases	1,488	487	32.7
5780-Gastrointestinal hemorrhage	979	311	31.8
9050-Late effects/musculoskeletal and connective tissue injuries	14,412	4,525	31.4
7100-Diffuse diseases of connective tissue	9,056	2,835	31.3
2880-Diseases of white blood cells	145	45	31.0
3140-Attention deficit hyperactivity disorder	94,862	29,312	30.9
3950-Diseases of aortic valve	3,889	1,190	30.6
4100-Acute myocardial infarction	5,254	1,608	30.6
3070-Eating and tic disorders	349	106	30.4
2870-Purpura/other hemorrhagic conditions	499	151	30.3
2380-Neoplasm/uncertain behavior	204	60	29.4
5190-Other diseases of respiratory system	8,111	2,385	29.4
1350-Sarcoidosis	1,904	554	29.1
5300-Diseases of esophagus	984	286	29.1
3860-Vertiginous syndromes	2,155	625	29.0
7330-Other bone/cartilage disorders	16,067	4,659	29.0
4940-Bronchiectasis	674	193	28.6
7649-Birth weight between 1,200 and 2,000 grams	6,951	1,981	28.5
2810-Deficiency anemias	1,365	388	28.4
4020-Hypertensive vascular disease	7,426	2,109	28.4
3980-Other rheumatic heart disease	629	177	28.1
9490-Burns	1,925	537	27.9
4510-Phlebitis/thrombophlebitis	1,012	280	27.7
4240-Valvular heart diseases/other stenotic defects	3,923	1,067	27.2
3910-Rheumatic fever/heart involvement	169	45	26.6
4270-Cardiac dysrhythmias	4,966	1,311	26.4
2890-Other diseases blood/blood forming organs	1,313	339	25.8
5050-Pneumoconiosis	240	61	25.4
5560-Idiopathic proctocolitis	1,369	344	25.1
6940-Bullous disease	517	128	24.8
4130-Angina pectoris	1,761	426	24.2
2860-Coagulation defects	826	199	24.1
2720-Hyperlipidemia	175	42	24.0
7160-Other and unspecified arthropathies	27,885	6,469	23.2
6960-Dermatitis	1,951	451	23.1
2780-Obesity	20,758	4,754	22.9
5550-Regional enteritis/granulomatous colitis	4,723	1,053	22.3
3680-Visual disturbances	6,158	1,324	21.5
8690-Internal injury	506	108	21.3
8940-Lower limb open wounds	3,117	664	21.3
3152-Learning disorder	36,123	7,622	21.1
8270-Lower limb fractures	34,015	7,075	20.8

ANNEX TABLE 7 continued

SSA Impairment Code	Number of Decisions	Number of Allowances	Allowance Rate (percent)
2740-Gout	1,511	308	20.4
3195-Borderline intellectual functioning	31,621	6,356	20.1
7240-Back disorders	311,813	62,674	20.1
0110-Pulmonary tuberculosis	472	90	19.1
6950-Ichthyosis	567	103	18.2
7280-Muscle, ligament, fascia disorders	58,995	10,619	18.0
2550-Disorders of adrenal glands	386	69	17.9
2500-Diabetes mellitus	67,988	11,966	17.6
5690-Other disorders gastrointestinal system	13,943	2,440	17.5
9330-Chronic fatigue syndrome	1,974	342	17.3
2530-Disorders of pituitary gland	441	75	17.0
7800-Sleep-related disorder	2,371	403	17.0
7090-Other disorders skin/subcutaneous tissue	3,399	557	16.4
5330-Peptic ulcer	1,022	165	16.1
8390-Dislocations	2,435	392	16.1
3460-Migraine	8,011	1,282	16.0
3540-Carpal tunnel syndrome	5,627	889	15.8
8840-Upper limb open wounds	3,676	573	15.6
5530-Hernias	3,048	451	14.8
8180-Upper limb fractures	12,756	1,862	14.6
8290-Other fractures	8,432	1,214	14.4
4910-Chronic bronchitis	1,653	230	13.9
2510-Hypoglycemia	123	17	13.8
3780-Strabismus/disorders eye movements	557	76	13.6
3450-Epilepsy	37,165	4,980	13.4
7370-Curvature of spine	4,530	607	13.4
4010-Essential hypertension	32,188	3,863	12.0
6080-Disorders of male genital organs	434	49	11.3
5990-Other disorders of urinary tract	3,823	413	10.8
2520-Disorders of parathyroid	265	28	10.6
4930-Asthma	60,855	6,086	10.0
5350-Gastritis/Duodenitis	1,480	144	9.7
8790-Other open wounds	432	42	9.7
3880-Other ear disorders	3,019	281	9.3
8030-Skull fracture without intracranial injury	460	35	7.6
8480-Sprains & strains	19,846	1,111	5.6
2460-Disorders of thyroid	3,592	198	5.5
6290-Disorders of female genital organs	1,582	63	4.0
0440-Asymptomatic HIV positive	8,438	262	3.1
3040-Substance dependence/drugs (child)	100	1	1.0
3030-Addiction disorder/alcohol (adult)	8,069	0	0.0
3030-Substance dependence/alcohol (child)	39	0	0.0
3040-Addiction disorders/drugs (adult)	7,167	0	0.0
Unknown, missing, invalid codes	145,328	8,284	5.7

SOURCE: Unpublished table provided by the Office of Disability and Income Support Programs, SSA.

D

Appendix Tables

APPENDIX TABLE 3-1 Applicants for Social Security Disability Benefits by Program and Selected Diagnostic Group, CY 2004

Diagnostic Group	SSDI Only	SSDI/SSI	SSI Only Adult	SSI Child	All
Number					
Retardation	14,353	12,445	23,314	26,416	76,528
Other mental	112,880	183,957	147,480	218,781	663,098
Cardiovascular	62,123	54,874	32,163	7,065	156,225
Musculoskeletal	266,977	218,923	112,062	6,478	604,440
Neoplasms	65,274	31,987	14,971	3,411	115,643
Nervous/sensory	88,265	70,589	47,261	32,538	238,653
Endocrine	26,934	31,120	19,060	3,584	80,698
Respiratory	30,371	29,762	19,351	37,822	117,306
All	741,385	724,693	466,183	395,775	2,328,036
Percentage					
Retardation	1.9	1.7	5.0	6.7	3.3
Other mental	15.2	25.4	31.6	55.3	28.5
Cardiovascular	8.4	7.6	6.9	1.8	6.7
Musculoskeletal	36.0	30.2	24.0	1.6	26.0
Neoplasms	8.8	4.4	3.2	0.9	5.0
Nervous/sensory	11.9	9.7	10.1	8.2	10.3
Endocrine	3.6	4.3	4.1	0.9	3.5
Respiratory	4.1	4.1	4.2	9.6	5.0
All	100.0	100.0	100.0	100.0	100.0

SOURCE: Calculated from tables provided by SSA.

APPENDIX TABLE 3-2 Awardees of Social Security Disability Benefits by Program and Selected Diagnostic Group, CY 2004

Diagnostic Group	SSDI Only	SSDI/SSI	SSI Only Adult	SSI Child	All
Number					
Retardation	12,977	8,930	19,436	24,262	65,605
Other mental	62,801	68,815	65,257	93,703	290,576
Cardiovascular	30,454	17,584	12,686	3,427	64,151
Musculoskeletal	86,407	34,184	27,746	1,129	149,466
Neoplasms	54,158	22,772	10,871	3,305	91,106
Nervous/sensory	53,160	27,684	23,365	16,153	120,362
Endocrine	9,383	5,282	4,754	304	19,723
Respiratory	18,827	11,295	7,149	3,886	41,157
All	356,696	219,198	187,603	180,303	943,800
Percentage					
Retardation	3.6	4.1	10.4	13.5	7.0
Other mental	17.6	31.4	34.8	52.0	30.8
Cardiovascular	8.5	8.0	6.8	1.9	6.8
Musculoskeletal	24.2	15.6	14.8	0.6	15.8
Neoplasms	15.2	10.4	5.8	1.8	9.7
Nervous/sensory	14.9	12.6	12.5	9.0	12.8
Endocrine	2.6	2.4	2.5	0.2	2.1
Respiratory	5.3	5.2	3.8	2.2	4.4
All	100.0	100.0	100.0	100.0	100.0

SOURCE: Calculated from tables provided by SSA.

APPENDIX TABLE 3-3 Distribution of Annual Disability Insurance Awards Among Disabled Workers by Diagnostic Group, FY 1961 - FY 2003

Number of Awards	1961	1963	1967	1969
Total	279,758	224,229	310,947	344,741
Congenital anomalies	1,637	1,646	na	3,004
Endocrine, nutritional, and metabolic diseases	7,070	7,563	10,743	12,169
Infectious/parasitic diseases	15,153	10,859	10,945	9,828
Injuries	na	6,496	19,815	28,473
Mental disorders—Total	26,864	24,526	35,344	43,225
Retardation	na	na	na	na
Other	na	na	na	na
Neoplasms	23,103	25,042	33,358	35,740
Diseases of the—				
Blood/blood-forming organs	566	597	na	na
Circulatory system	71,860	66,468	81,507	105,760
Digestive system	4,300	4,437	7,627	8,719
Genitourinary system	1,608	1,725	na	2,717
Musculoskeletal system/ connective tissue	23,241	21,744	41,090	47,357
Nervous system/sense organs	44,709	32,712	38,278	21,967
Respiratory system	20,030	19,107	24,646	23,265
Skin/subcutaneous tissue	794	719	na	na
Other	125	588	7,594	2,517
Unknown	38,698	na	na	na

NOTE: na = not available.
SOURCE: 2003 Annual Statistical Report on the Social Security Disability Insurance Program, Table 36.

1971	1973	1975	1977	1978	1981
415,897	491,776	592,049	568,874	464,415	351,847
4,365	5,276	6,576	6,681	5,850	3,118
15,823	18,131	23,176	21,725	16,855	14,768
8,524	7,957	7,579	5,807	4,512	2,596
31,810	30,418	32,341	31,942	27,490	20,868
42,687	47,014	67,213	70,825	54,329	36,318
na	na	na	na	na	na
na	na	na	na	na	na
39,629	50,644	59,852	59,833	54,878	56,410
1,043	1,347	1,491	1,516	1,236	942
131,854	158,202	177,311	167,801	134,634	85,994
11,629	14,614	17,474	15,342	12,407	7,363
3,501	4,810	5,719	5,271	4,719	6,230
66,558	85,431	110,637	107,840	86,921	58,639
26,442	31,139	39,960	36,751	29,314	28,516
30,103	34,656	39,485	35,002	28,005	21,520
1,667	1,854	2,306	1,766	2,017	1,345
262	283	929	772	1,248	616
na	na	na	na	na	6,604

APPENDIX TABLE 3-3 (continued)

Number of Awards	1983	1985	1987	1989
Total	311,490	377,371	415,848	425,582
Congenital anomalies	2,827	2,480	787	534
Endocrine, nutritional, and metabolic diseases	14,904	16,976	21,114	14,279
Infectious/parasitic diseases	6,730	2,985	4,676	3,773
Injuries	15,646	16,558	20,889	21,531
Mental disorders—Total	50,633	68,610	81,241	88,500
Retardation	na	na	na	na
Other	na	na	na	na
Neoplasms	52,379	55,120	55,339	60,352
Diseases of the—				
Blood/blood-forming organs	958	890	1,205	1,524
Circulatory system	68,352	72,764	76,758	70,235
Digestive system	5,272	5,626	6,122	6,803
Genitourinary system	6,489	3,348	5,801	9,010
Musculoskeletal system/ connective tissue	41,872	49,214	63,807	71,419
Nervous system/sense organs	26,203	28,733	35,206	34,756
Respiratory system	17,978	20,213	22,978	21,400
Skin/subcutaneous tissue	848	1,110	1,173	828
Other	a	992	na	20,638
Unknown	na	31,752	18,752	na

NOTE: na = not available.
a Data not shown to prevent disclosure of information about particular individuals.

1991	1993	1995	1997	1999	2001	2003
536,434	635,238	645,645	587,700	620,559	661,900	755,706
575	543	722	654	645	a	1,152
19,931	30,862	33,370	33,807	36,975	19,500	23,407
28,245	37,450	27,993	15,327	11,743	11,200	10,879
24,129	23,206	27,566	25,930	25,925	25,400	28,612
126,184	166,045	147,900	122,901	138,980	168,600	191,679
na	na	16,681	12,888	16,608	22,500	19,338
na	na	131,219	110,113	122,372	146,100	172,341
69,244	80,266	64,401	62,279	65,681	62,000	70,942
1,904	2,075	2,006	1,815	1,911	2,200	2,408
78,339	88,623	83,065	76,531	74,755	82,500	85,896
8,648	10,026	11,167	11,310	13,389	15,600	17,084
10,874	13,390	11,956	12,151	13,842	16,300	16,968
92,469	94,255	141,306	135,430	146,754	162,100	199,014
41,551	45,742	46,477	45,496	49,869	54,600	64,369
23,798	27,494	28,831	26,483	26,981	28,300	32,007
1,021	1,118	1,643	1,473	1,416	a	1,622
9,522	14,143	14,746	14,436	10,252	10,000	1,871
na	na	2,496	1,677	1,441	1,800	7,796

APPENDIX TABLE 3-3 (continued)

Percentage of Awards	1961	1963	1967	1969
Total	100.0	100.0	100.0	100.0
Congenital anomalies	0.6	0.7	0.0	0.9
Endocrine, nutritional, and metabolic diseases	2.5	3.4	3.5	3.5
Infectious/parasitic diseases	5.4	4.8	3.5	2.9
Injuries	0.0	2.9	6.4	8.3
Mental disorders—Total	9.6	10.9	11.4	12.5
Retardation	na	na	na	na
Other	na	na	na	na
Neoplasms	8.3	11.2	10.7	10.4
Diseases of the—				
Blood/blood-forming organs	0.2	0.3	0.0	0.0
Circulatory system	25.7	29.6	26.2	30.7
Digestive system	1.5	2.0	2.5	2.5
Genitourinary system	0.6	0.8	0.0	0.8
Musculoskeletal system/ connective tissue	8.3	9.7	13.2	13.7
Nervous system/sense organs	16.0	14.6	12.3	6.4
Respiratory system	7.2	8.5	7.9	6.7
Skin/subcutaneous tissue	0.3	0.3	0.0	0.0
Other	0.0	0.3	2.4	0.7
Unknown	13.8	0.0	0.0	0.0

NOTE: na = not available.

1971	1973	1975	1977	1978	1981
100.0	100.0	100.0	100.0	100.0	100.0
1.0	1.1	1.1	1.2	1.3	0.9
3.8	3.7	3.9	3.8	3.6	4.2
2.0	1.6	1.3	1.0	1.0	0.7
7.6	6.2	5.5	5.6	5.9	5.9
10.3	9.6	11.4	12.5	11.7	10.3
na	na	na	na	na	na
na	na	na	na	na	na
9.5	10.3	10.1	10.5	11.8	16.0
0.3	0.3	0.3	0.3	0.3	0.3
31.7	32.2	29.9	29.5	29.0	24.4
2.8	3.0	3.0	2.7	2.7	2.1
0.8	1.0	1.0	0.9	1.0	1.8
16.0	17.4	18.7	19.0	18.7	16.7
6.4	6.3	6.7	6.5	6.3	8.1
7.2	7.0	6.7	6.2	6.0	6.1
0.4	0.4	0.4	0.3	0.4	0.4
0.1	0.1	0.2	0.1	0.3	0.2
0.0	0.0	0.0	0.0	0.0	1.9

APPENDIX TABLE 3-3 (continued)

Percentage of Awards	1983	1985	1987	1989
Total	100.0	100.0	100.0	100.0
Congenital anomalies	0.9	0.7	0.2	0.1
Endocrine, nutritional, and metabolic diseases	4.8	4.5	5.1	3.4
Infectious/parasitic diseases	2.2	0.8	1.1	0.9
Injuries	5.0	4.4	5.0	5.1
Mental disorders—Total	16.3	18.2	19.5	20.8
Retardation	na	na	na	na
Other	na	na	na	na
Neoplasms	16.8	14.6	13.3	14.2
Diseases of the—				
Blood/blood-forming organs	0.3	0.2	0.3	0.4
Circulatory system	21.9	19.3	18.5	16.5
Digestive system	1.7	1.5	1.5	1.6
Genitourinary system	2.1	0.9	1.4	2.1
Musculoskeletal system/ connective tissue	13.4	13.0	15.3	16.8
Nervous system/sense organs	8.4	7.6	8.5	8.2
Respiratory system	5.8	5.4	5.5	5.0
Skin/subcutaneous tissue	0.3	0.3	0.3	0.2
Other	a	0.3	0.0	4.8
Unknown	0.0	8.4	4.5	0.0

NOTE: na = not available.

a Data not shown to prevent disclosure of information about particular individuals.

1991	1993	1995	1997	1999	2001	2003
100.0	100.0	100.0	100.0	100.0	100.0	100.0
0.1	0.1	0.1	0.1	0.1	a	0.2
3.7	4.9	5.2	5.8	6.0	2.9	3.1
5.3	5.9	4.3	2.6	1.9	1.7	1.4
4.5	3.7	4.3	4.4	4.2	3.8	3.8
23.5	26.1	22.9	20.9	22.4	25.5	25.4
na	na	2.6	2.2	2.7	3.4	2.6
na	na	20.3	18.7	19.7	22.1	22.8
12.9	12.6	10.0	10.6	10.6	9.4	9.4
0.4	0.3	0.3	0.0	0.3	0.3	0.3
14.6	14.0	12.9	13.0	12.0	12.5	11.4
1.6	1.6	1.7	1.9	2.2	2.4	2.3
2.0	2.1	1.9	2.1	2.2	2.5	2.2
17.2	14.8	21.9	23.0	23.6	24.5	26.3
7.7	7.2	7.2	7.7	8.0	8.2	8.5
4.4	4.3	4.5	4.5	4.3	4.3	4.2
0.2	0.2	0.3	0.3	0.2	a	0.2
1.8	2.2	2.3	2.5	1.7	1.5	0.2
0.0	0.0	0.4	0.3	0.2	0.3	1.0

APPENDIX TABLE 3-4 SSI Annual Awards for Adults Ages 18-64 by Diagnostic Group, FY 1974 - FY 2003

Number of Awards	1974	1975	1976	1977
Total	1,796,230	508,950	403,350	375,950
Congenital anomalies	310	220	100	180
Endocrine, nutritional, and metabolic diseases	1,270	600	640	710
Infectious/parasitic diseases	940	430	320	340
Injuries	1,760	760	720	690
Mental disorders				
Retardation	18,350	9,330	7,180	7,640
Other	11,010	6,600	6,380	7,030
Neoplasms	300	180	100	150
Diseases of the—				
Blood/blood-forming organs	270	180	100	50
Circulatory system	2,470	1,270	1,430	1,490
Digestive system	290	140	140	150
Genitourinary system	290	160	180	230
Musculoskeletal system/ connective tissue	3,440	1,760	1,480	1,950
Nervous system/sense organs	7,310	3,350	2,920	3,080
Respiratory system	840	490	600	560
Skin/subcutaneous tissue	70	30	30	20
Other	110	40	10	50
Unknown	1,747,200	483,410	381,020	351,630

NOTE: Data are from Supplemental Security Record (Characteristic Extract Record Format), 10 percent sample, and are consistent with those in the 2003 SSI Annual Statistical Report, Table 49.

SOURCE: Unpublished table provided by Clark Pickett, Office of Research, Evaluation, and Statistics, Social Security Administration, February 11, 2005.

1978	1979	1980	1981	1982	1983
323,170	292,380	293,740	248,340	202,590	262,660
120	120	240	270	500	2,220
640	890	1,220	1,350	2,090	8,620
290	290	330	370	750	2,180
750	870	970	1,410	2,730	9,130
7,920	7,590	8,840	9,940	10,970	31,210
6,730	7,980	9,600	8,890	13,300	42,180
200	260	330	380	2,060	14,320
120	160	160	120	190	700
1,440	1,480	2,190	1,760	5,520	25,670
180	150	220	200	660	2,710
240	180	330	280	710	3,030
1,830	1,810	2,750	2,780	5,110	16,380
3,150	3,590	4,130	4,810	7,040	21,870
430	560	670	700	2,190	10,080
30	60	40	40	180	360
20	10	60	80	150	660
299,080	266,380	261,660	214,960	148,440	71,340

APPENDIX TABLE 3-4 (continued)

Number of Awards	1984	1985	1986	1987
Total	322,390	324,070	391,600	373,320
Congenital anomalies	2,470	1,980	830	530
Endocrine, nutritional, and metabolic diseases	11,730	14,240	16,360	18,410
Infectious/parasitic diseases	3,020	2,420	2,470	3,690
Injuries	10,280	9,470	10,860	11,710
Mental disorders				
Retardation	41,270	42,600	55,550	44,730
Other	65,890	70,670	119,480	99,580
Neoplasms	17,850	18,250	18,500	19,070
Diseases of the—				
Blood/blood-forming organs	860	730	1,040	990
Circulatory system	33,430	33,880	36,520	36,110
Digestive system	2,790	3,580	3,480	3,310
Genitourinary system	3,510	3,630	5,220	5,600
Musculoskeletal system/ connective tissue	22,230	23,860	24,640	28,150
Nervous system/sense organs	25,520	23,880	25,130	25,910
Respiratory system	11,730	12,680	13,740	13,140
Skin/subcutaneous tissue	580	680	450	670
Other	770	640	430	290
Unknown	68,460	60,880	56,900	61,430

1988	1989	1990	1991	1992	1993
361,070	388,120	446,940	504,860	636,300	630,030
450	730	830	750	910	960
14,580	16,100	19,880	23,030	34,190	33,030
11,070	14,270	20,030	24,310	35,330	32,030
12,130	12,990	14,390	15,570	18,250	16,430
39,990	39,880	45,060	53,270	74,280	72,280
86,870	93,560	112,420	131,160	171,090	178,130
18,830	20,020	21,880	24,050	25,840	25,330
1,110	1,020	1,290	1,650	2,020	1,640
35,700	36,290	41,530	45,820	54,470	49,650
4,120	4,430	5,110	6,200	6,890	6,780
5,980	7,150	7,990	8,550	8,940	9,150
29,790	35,630	43,720	52,510	64,910	63,050
25,050	26,430	29,280	31,380	35,330	34,810
13,260	13,390	15,270	16,800	19,880	18,700
490	450	560	770	970	940
250	250	310	260	490	510
61,400	65,530	67,390	68,780	82,510	86,610

APPENDIX TABLE 3-4 (continued)

Number of Awards	1994	1995	1996	1997
Total	580,640	571,080	526,690	461,260
Congenital anomalies	990	850	940	880
Endocrine, nutritional, and metabolic diseases	30,220	29,950	28,650	26,460
Infectious/parasitic diseases	26,900	25,740	23,210	16,630
Injuries	16,260	15,760	15,850	13,470
Mental disorders				
Retardation	57,710	47,790	40,630	34,840
Other	160,940	158,510	136,480	115,400
Neoplasms	26,180	27,220	26,490	25,230
Diseases of the—				
Blood/blood-forming organs	1,440	1,070	1,330	1,140
Circulatory system	47,660	47,260	44,320	39,980
Digestive system	7,340	7,590	7,300	7,030
Genitourinary system	8,840	9,140	8,640	9,050
Musculoskeletal system/ connective tissue	59,990	63,670	61,160	53,640
Nervous system/sense organs	32,480	32,070	30,620	25,780
Respiratory system	18,940	18,650	18,760	15,530
Skin/subcutaneous tissue	790	1,040	910	970
Other	470	490	420	460
Unknown	83,490	84,280	80,980	74,770

1998	1999	2000	2001	2002	2003
489,240	493,960	483,020	502,590	533,470	537,420
640	900	1,160	1,700	1,790	2,060
27,040	28,070	14,000	15,030	15,320	15,700
14,790	14,000	13,440	12,560	11,950	11,360
14,780	15,390	16,030	16,680	18,930	17,120
34,320	34,820	35,030	35,530	35,290	34,250
127,700	138,020	146,930	157,590	168,970	171,650
25,370	25,820	26,500	26,950	27,660	28,520
1,240	1,430	1,310	1,670	1,590	1,570
40,200	40,090	42,110	45,110	47,240	46,440
7,610	9,020	9,180	10,140	11,080	11,720
8,970	8,970	9,650	9,490	9,820	10,480
58,530	63,370	69,980	75,190	84,140	86,570
29,100	29,990	30,000	32,510	34,530	35,120
16,540	16,580	17,080	17,450	18,520	18,710
820	860	840	1,090	1,000	940
430	590	530	740	1,010	990
81,160	66,040	49,250	43,160	44,630	44,220

APPENDIX TABLE 3-4 (continued)

Percentage of Awards	1974	1975	1976	1977	1978	1979
Congenital anomalies	0.0	0.0	0.0	0.1	0.0	0.0
Endocrine, nutritional, and metabolic diseases	0.1	0.1	0.2	0.2	0.2	0.3
Infectious/parasitic diseases	0.1	0.1	0.1	0.1	0.1	0.1
Injuries	0.1	0.1	0.2	0.2	0.2	0.3
Mental disorders						
Retardation	1.0	1.8	1.8	2.0	2.5	2.6
Other	0.6	1.3	1.6	1.9	2.1	2.7
Neoplasms	0.0	0.0	0.0	0.0	0.1	0.1
Diseases of the—						
Blood/blood-forming organs	0.0	0.0	0.0	0.0	0.0	0.1
Circulatory system	0.1	0.2	0.4	0.4	0.4	0.5
Digestive system	0.0	0.0	0.0	0.0	0.1	0.1
Genitourinary system	0.0	0.0	0.0	0.1	0.1	0.1
Musculoskeletal system/ connective tissue	0.2	0.3	0.4	0.5	0.6	0.6
Nervous system/sense organs	0.4	0.7	0.7	0.8	1.0	1.2
Respiratory system	0.1	0.1	0.1	0.1	0.1	0.2
Skin/subcutaneous tissue	0.0	0.0	0.0	0.0	0.0	0.0
Other	0.0	0.0	0.0	0.0	0.0	0.0
Unknown	97.3	95.0	94.5	93.5	92.5	91.1

1980	1981	1982	1983	1984	1985	1986	1987	1988
0.1	0.1	0.2	0.8	0.8	0.6	0.2	0.1	0.1
0.4	0.5	1.0	3.3	3.6	4.4	4.2	4.9	4.0
0.1	0.1	0.4	0.8	0.9	0.7	0.6	1.0	3.1
0.3	0.6	1.3	3.5	3.2	2.9	2.8	3.1	3.4
3.0	4.0	5.4	11.9	12.8	13.1	14.2	12.0	11.1
3.3	3.6	6.6	16.1	20.4	21.8	30.5	26.7	24.1
0.1	0.2	1.0	5.5	5.5	5.6	4.7	5.1	5.2
0.1	0.1	0.1	0.3	0.3	0.2	0.3	0.3	0.3
0.7	0.7	2.7	9.8	10.4	10.5	9.3	9.7	9.9
0.1	0.1	0.3	1.0	0.9	1.1	0.9	0.9	1.1
0.1	0.1	0.4	1.2	1.1	1.1	1.3	1.5	1.7
0.9	1.1	2.5	6.2	6.9	7.4	6.3	7.5	8.3
1.4	1.9	3.5	8.3	7.9	7.4	6.4	6.9	6.9
0.2	0.3	1.1	3.8	3.6	3.9	3.5	3.5	3.7
0.0	0.0	0.1	0.1	0.2	0.2	0.1	0.2	0.1
0.0	0.0	0.1	0.3	0.2	0.2	0.1	0.1	0.1
89.1	86.6	73.3	27.2	21.2	18.8	14.5	16.5	17.0

APPENDIX TABLE 3-4 (continued)

Percentage of Awards	1989	1990	1991	1992	1993	1994
Congenital anomalies	0.2	0.2	0.1	0.1	0.2	0.2
Endocrine, nutritional, and metabolic diseases	4.1	4.4	4.6	5.4	5.2	5.2
Infectious/parasitic diseases	3.7	4.5	4.8	5.6	5.1	4.6
Injuries	3.3	3.2	3.1	2.9	2.6	2.8
Mental disorders						
Retardation	10.3	10.1	10.6	11.7	11.5	9.9
Other	24.1	25.2	26.0	26.9	28.3	27.7
Neoplasms	5.2	4.9	4.8	4.1	4.0	4.5
Diseases of the—						
Blood/blood-forming organs	0.3	0.3	0.3	0.3	0.3	0.2
Circulatory system	9.4	9.3	9.1	8.6	7.9	8.2
Digestive system	1.1	1.1	1.2	1.1	1.1	1.3
Genitourinary system	1.8	1.8	1.7	1.4	1.5	1.5
Musculoskeletal system/ connective tissue	9.2	9.8	10.4	10.2	10.0	10.3
Nervous system/sense organs	6.8	6.6	6.2	5.6	5.5	5.6
Respiratory system	3.4	3.4	3.3	3.1	3.0	3.3
Skin/subcutaneous tissue	0.1	0.1	0.2	0.2	0.1	0.1
Other	0.1	0.1	0.1	0.1	0.1	0.1
Unknown	16.9	15.1	13.6	13.0	13.7	14.4

1995	1996	1997	1998	1999	2000	2001	2002	2003
0.1	0.2	0.2	0.1	0.2	0.2	0.3	0.3	0.4
5.2	5.4	5.7	5.5	5.7	2.9	3.0	2.9	2.9
4.5	4.4	3.6	3.0	2.8	2.8	2.5	2.2	2.1
2.8	3.0	2.9	3.0	3.1	3.3	3.3	3.5	3.2
8.4	7.7	7.6	7.0	7.1	7.3	7.1	6.6	6.4
27.8	25.9	25.0	26.1	27.9	30.4	31.4	31.7	31.9
4.8	5.0	5.5	5.2	5.2	5.5	5.4	5.2	5.3
0.2	0.3	0.2	0.3	0.3	0.3	0.3	0.3	0.3
8.3	8.4	8.7	8.2	8.1	8.7	9.0	8.9	8.6
1.3	1.4	1.5	1.6	1.8	1.9	2.0	2.1	2.2
1.6	1.6	2.0	1.8	1.8	2.0	1.9	1.8	2.0
11.1	11.6	11.6	12.0	12.8	14.5	15.0	15.8	16.1
5.6	5.8	5.6	5.9	6.1	6.2	6.5	6.5	6.5
3.3	3.6	3.4	3.4	3.4	3.5	3.5	3.5	3.5
0.2	0.2	0.2	0.2	0.2	0.2	0.2	0.2	0.2
0.1	0.1	0.1	0.1	0.1	0.1	0.1	0.2	0.2
14.8	15.4	16.2	16.6	13.4	10.2	8.6	8.4	8.2

APPENDIX TABLE 3-5 Distribution of Annual SSI Awards for Children Under Age 18 Among Diagnostic Groups, FY 1974-2003

Number of Awards	1974	1975	1976	1977	1978
Total	69,500	62,880	45,030	50,970	47,050
Congenital anomalies	360	420	270	240	390
Endocrine, nutritional, and metabolic diseases	40	60	40	60	60
Infectious/parasitic diseases	90	140	90	100	60
Injuries	190	130	150	230	140
Mental disorders					
Retardation	9,360	9,870	7,500	7,880	8,010
Other	750	870	510	670	890
Neoplasms	40	30	10	30	30
Diseases of the—					
Blood/blood-forming organs	150	210	190	210	220
Circulatory system	60	90	140	80	80
Digestive system	20	10	0	20	0
Genitourinary system	60	60	30	40	90
Musculoskeletal system/ connective tissue	110	180	120	190	100
Nervous system/sense organs	3,260	3,320	2,360	2,600	2,930
Respiratory system	50	40	60	70	80
Skin/subcutaneous tissue	0	40	0	30	0
Other	20	30	10	60	60
Unknown	54,940	47,380	33,550	38,460	33,910

NOTE: Data are from Supplemental Security Record (Characteristic Extract Record Format), 10 percent sample, and are consistent with those in the 2003 SSI Annual Statistical Report, Table 49.

SOURCE: Unpublished table provided by Clark Pickett, Office of Research, Evaluation, and Statististics, Social Security Administration, February 11, 2005.

1979	1980	1981	1982	1983	1984	1985
45,810	46,260	39,050	35,670	42,110	45,740	46,590
420	650	900	1,150	3,850	4,360	4,180
70	70	130	320	580	900	780
50	70	140	100	180	200	230
160	240	190	200	550	630	610
8,830	9,830	8,990	8,220	15,470	17,840	19,090
970	980	910	770	2,210	2,650	3,140
80	90	200	340	1,550	1,780	1,780
180	190	230	230	580	960	850
70	140	110	180	510	420	500
50	20	50	40	110	140	120
80	130	80	130	320	370	420
350	150	150	180	600	580	540
3,060	3,500	3,990	4,150	9,360	9,630	9,670
70	190	170	220	450	680	810
0	10	0	0	40	20	10
110	210	280	500	1,650	2,280	2,140
31,260	29,790	22,530	18,940	4,100	2,300	1,720

APPENDIX TABLE 3-5 (continued)

Number of Awards	1986	1987	1988	1989	1990
Total	51,020	48,480	47,560	51,520	76,070
Congenital anomalies	2,790	2,600	2,260	2,710	3,300
Endocrine, nutritional, and metabolic diseases	630	820	540	810	1,280
Infectious/parasitic diseases	80	120	130	320	490
Injuries	430	530	470	610	640
Mental disorders					
Retardation	22,870	20,910	20,300	21,430	31,430
Other	3,850	3,830	3,860	4,670	10,580
Neoplasms	1,960	2,000	1,770	2,060	1,990
Diseases of the—					
Blood/blood-forming organs	1,150	860	880	1,020	1,330
Circulatory system	460	390	370	520	670
Digestive system	240	270	220	250	360
Genitourinary system	320	350	280	280	430
Musculoskeletal system/ connective tissue	900	1,010	830	900	1,470
Nervous system/sense organs	11,120	10,400	10,590	10,910	14,090
Respiratory system	990	720	980	880	1,800
Skin/subcutaneous tissue	40	30	30	40	50
Other	1,720	1,700	1,890	1,760	2,890
Unknown	1,470	1,940	2,160	2,350	3,270

1991	1992	1993	1994	1995	1996	1997
126,190	221,080	236,220	203,190	177,550	144,270	116,280
6,690	8,040	7,320	6,780	7,320	6,970	5,970
1,520	2,370	1,670	1,320	1,310	990	830
500	920	810	640	670	470	380
1,210	1,620	1,320	1,170	960	1,050	1,100
			135,480	112,620	84,880	62,480
49,080	88,720	92,340	70,440	54,570	42,260	29,680
27,470	55,660	67,570	65,040	58,050	42,620	32,800
2,620	2,850	3,130	3,390	3,100	2,900	2,500
1,960						
1,150	2,520	2,530	1,830	1,650	1,520	1,220
550	1,400	1,290	910	1,070	940	830
750	820	650	610	600	500	680
	870	640	730	620	490	480
2,080	2,800	2,080	1,430	1,510	1,310	1,250
16,180	21,800	19,610	15,620	14,070	12,250	10,370
3,070	5,430	4,710	5,010	4,830	4,460	4,170
100	120	160	120	190	50	130
4,560	8,940	11,620	15,270	16,930	17,420	16,590
6,700	16,200	18,770	12,880	10,100	8,070	7,300

APPENDIX TABLE 3-5 (continued)

Number of Awards	1998	1999	2000
Total	135,600	139,400	144,540
Congenital anomalies	6,580	6,230	7,050
Endocrine, nutritional, and metabolic diseases	980	940	1,070
Infectious/parasitic diseases	280	360	250
Injuries	1,000	1,080	980
Mental disorders	75,760	81,900	84,580
Retardation	31,280	29,110	26,940
Other	44,480	52,790	57,640
Neoplasms	2,720	2,650	2,610
Diseases of the—			
Blood/blood-forming organs	1,590	1,340	1,290
Circulatory system	800	840	950
Digestive system	810	720	960
Genitourinary system	510	520	530
Musculoskeletal system/ connective tissue	1,390	1,200	1,430
Nervous system/sense organs	11,210	10,820	10,940
Respiratory system	4,050	4,140	4,520
Skin/subcutaneous tissue	110	100	170
Other	18,860	20,640	22,250
Unknown	8,950	5,920	4,960

2001	2002	2003
156,900	169,130	179,590
7,010	7,400	8,220
910	900	1,070
280	340	170
1,090	1,010	990
95,410	107,430	
26,470	27,150	26,110
68,940	80,280	91,160
3,000	2,850	2,830
1,470	1,260	1,320
770	960	1,010
1,340	1,090	1,420
550	510	580
1,650	1,470	1,180
10,800	11,740	11,000
4,550	4,470	4,300
140	160	170
23,120	23,330	24,470
4,810	4,210	3,590

APPENDIX TABLE 3-5 (continued)

Percentage of Awards	1974	1975	1976	1977	1978	1979
Congenital anomalies	0.5	0.7	0.6	0.5	0.8	0.9
Endocrine, nutritional, and metabolic diseases	0.1	0.1	0.1	0.1	0.1	0.2
Infectious/parasitic diseases	0.1	0.2	0.2	0.2	0.1	0.1
Injuries	0.3	0.2	0.3	0.5	0.3	0.3
Mental disorders						
Retardation	13.5	15.7	16.7	15.5	17.0	19.3
Other	1.1	1.4	1.1	1.3	1.9	2.1
Neoplasms	0.1	0	0	0.1	0.1	0.2
Diseases of the—						
Blood/blood-forming organs	0.2	0.3	0.4	0.4	0.5	0.4
Circulatory system	0.1	0.1	0.3	0.2	0.2	0.2
Digestive system	0	0	0	0	0	0.1
Genitourinary system	0.1	0.1	0.1	0.1	0.2	0.2
Musculoskeletal system/ connective tissue	0.2	0.3	0.3	0.4	0.2	0.8
Nervous system/sense organs	4.7	5.3	5.2	5.1	6.2	6.7
Respiratory system	0.1	0.1	0.1	0.1	0.2	0.2
Skin/ubcutaneous tissue	0	0.1	0	0.1	0	0
Other	0	0	0	0.1	0.1	0.2
Unknown	79.1	75.3	74.5	75.5	72.1	68.2

1980	1981	1982	1983	1984	1985	1986	1987	1988
1.4	2.3	3.2	9.1	9.5	9.0	5.5	5.4	4.8
0.2	0.3	0.9	1.4	2.0	1.7	1.2	1.7	1.1
0.2	0.4	0.3	0.4	0.4	0.5	0.2	0.2	0.3
0.5	0.5	0.6	1.3	1.4	1.3	0.8	1.1	1.0
21.2	23.0	23.0	36.7	39.0	41.0	44.8	43.1	42.7
2.1	2.3	2.2	5.2	5.8	6.7	7.5	7.9	8.1
0.2	0.5	1.0	3.7	3.9	3.8	3.8	4.1	3.7
0.4	0.6	0.6	1.4	2.1	1.8	2.3	1.8	1.9
0.3	0.3	0.5	1.2	0.9	1.1	0.9	0.8	0.8
0	0.1	0.1	0.3	0.3	0.3	0.5	0.6	0.5
0.3	0.2	0.4	0.8	0.8	0.9	0.6	0.7	0.6
0.3	0.4	0.5	1.4	1.3	1.2	1.8	2.1	1.7
7.6	10.2	11.6	22.2	21.1	20.8	21.8	21.5	22.3
0.4	0.4	0.6	1.1	1.5	1.7	1.9	1.5	2.1
0.0	0.0	0.0	0.1	0.0	0.0	0.1	0.1	0.1
0.5	0.7	1.4	3.9	5.0	4.6	3.4	3.5	4.0
64.4	57.7	53.1	9.7	5.0	3.7	2.9	4.0	4.5

APPENDIX TABLE 3-5 (continued)

Percentage of Awards	1989	1990	1991	1992	1993	1994
Congenital anomalies	5.3	4.3	5.3	3.6	3.1	3.3
Endocrine, nutritional, and metabolic diseases	1.6	1.7	1.2	1.1	0.7	0.6
Infectious/parasitic diseases	0.6	0.6	0.4	0.4	0.3	0.3
Injuries	1.2	0.8	1.0	0.7	0.6	0.6
Mental disorders						
Retardation	41.6	41.3	38.9	40.1	39.1	34.7
Other	9.1	13.9	21.8	25.2	28.6	32.0
Neoplasms	4.0	2.6	2.1	1.3	1.3	1.7
Diseases of the—						
Blood/blood-forming organs	2.0	1.7	1.6	1.1	1.1	0.9
Circulatory system	1.0	0.9	0.9	0.6	0.5	0.4
Digestive system	0.5	0.5	0.4	0.4	0.3	0.3
Genitourinary system	0.5	0.6	0.6	0.4	0.3	0.4
Musculoskeletal system/ connective tissue	1.7	1.9	1.6	1.3	0.9	0.7
Nervous system/sense organs	21.2	18.5	12.8	9.9	8.3	7.7
Respiratory system	1.7	2.4	2.4	2.5	2.0	2.5
Skin/subcutaneous tissue	0.1	0.1	0.1	0.1	0.1	0.1
Other	3.4	3.8	3.6	4.0	4.9	7.5
Unknown	4.6	4.3	5.3	7.3	7.9	6.3

1995	1996	1997	1998	1999	2000	2001	2002	2003
4.1	4.8	5.1	4.9	4.5	4.9	4.5	4.4	4.6
0.7	0.7	0.7	0.7	0.7	0.7	0.6	0.5	0.6
0.4	0.3	0.3	0.2	0.3	0.2	0.2	0.2	0.1
0.5	0.7	0.9	0.7	0.8	0.7	0.7	0.6	0.6
30.7	29.3	25.5	23.1	20.9	18.6	16.9	16.1	14.5
32.7	29.5	28.2	32.8	37.9	39.9	43.9	47.5	50.8
1.7	2.0	2.1	2.0	1.9	1.8	1.9	1.7	1.6
0.9	1.1	1.0	1.2	1.0	0.9	0.9	0.7	0.7
0.6	0.7	0.7	0.6	0.6	0.7	0.5	0.6	0.6
0.3	0.3	0.6	0.6	0.5	0.7	0.9	0.6	0.8
0.3	0.3	0.4	0.4	0.4	0.4	0.4	0.3	0.3
0.9	0.9	1.1	1.0	0.9	1.0	1.1	0.9	0.7
7.9	8.5	8.9	8.3	7.8	7.6	6.9	6.9	6.1
2.7	3.1	3.6	3.0	3.0	3.1	2.9	2.6	2.4
0.1	0.0	0.1	0.1	0.1	0.1	0.1	0.1	0.1
9.5	12.1	14.3	13.9	14.8	15.4	14.7	13.8	13.6
5.7	5.6	6.3	6.6	4.2	3.4	3.1	2.5	2.0